To Leslie,
From Us To You
Mike Byrne + Bernice Byrne

THE BIRTH OF THE BEATLES STORY

OUR TIME WITH THE BEATLES
AND HOW WE BECAME THE FOUNDERS OF THE MOST
SUCCESSFUL BEATLES EXHIBITION IN THE WORLD

By MIKE & BERNADETTE BYRNE
with ALISON RODD

Published 2022

NEW HAVEN PUBLISHING LTD

www.newhavenpublishingltd.com

newhavenpublishing@gmail.com

ISBN: 978-1-912587-66-7

This book is dedicated to Phil Birtwistle.
Without your friendship, encouragement and financial help,
The Beatles Story might never have become a reality.

IMAGE CREDITS

Every effort has been made to contact and credit all those whose images have been used in this book.

We apologise if there have been any omissions of the appropriate accreditation, and will of course remedy this in future editions.

We would like to thank the following for their kind permission to reproduce their photographs/images:

Trinity Mirror / Mirrorpix / Alamy – 1

Pictorial Press / Alamy – 8a

Bill Harry – 8c, 10b, 11c, 12a/b, 20, 21a/b/c/d/e, 42a, 47a

Margaret Roberts / Peter Kaye Photography – Front and back covers, 11c, 28b, 30a/b,31, 32b, 37c, 44

Lee & Geoff Waymont – 15

Spud Murphy – 16b

Graham Spencer - 19a

Wikimedia Commons ABC Television Public Domain – 26

Liverpool Record Office, Liverpool Libraries – 28, 38, 41b, 58d, 63c

Liverpool Echo / Trinity Mirror – 9c, 50, 101, 102, 103, 104a, 105, 136

Mike McCartney – 37a

Wikimedia – Sefton Park Walk 67 – 51a

Ron Jones – 51b, 53a/b/c, 61

Trisch Jones / Jamie Hughes – 54a

Charles Rosenay – 54b

Colin Tittle 55, 67a

Mark Naboshek – 71b, 72a/b, 73a/b/c/d/e, 74b/e, 76e, 77a/b

The Beatles Story – 97a/b, 110a/b, 111 a/b/c/d, 112a, 113c, 114c, 115a, 116a, 118 a/b/d/e, 119b, 121a/c, 123b/c/d, 125a/b/c, 126, 127a, 128a/b, 129b, 130d/e, 131a, 132a, 133e, 134a, 135a

Other images are credited to Mike and Bernadette Byrne.

INDEX

IN THE BEGINNING

THE AUTHORS - AN INTRODUCTION

Michael Byrne and Bernadette Farrell, the founders of The Beatles Story exhibition, and authors of this book, grew up in separate suburbs of 1940s post-war Liverpool. The time and place of their births allowed them to witness and be part of one of the most important and special times in popular music history. Living their teenage years in Liverpool in the 1960s inspired their ultimate business ambition: to build the world's biggest permanent tribute to The Beatles.

LIVERPOOL WATERFRONT IN 1959

Not far away, four young lads were also growing up, making instruments and learning how to play them. They were unaware that they would go on to become the most famous and successful pop group of all time.

1960s Liverpool was such an exhilarating time and place to be a teenager and the authors' memories, feelings and emotions were woven into every component of the building of The Beatles Story. Their influences and experiences as teenagers would go on to form the beating heart of the exhibition. It's an important, historical and exciting story to tell... a story of pride in the city of Liverpool as well as its most famous sons.

MIKE'S CHILDHOOD AND EARLY YEARS IN GROUPS

Mike: My parents were quite traditional in their musical tastes, which was normal at the time. In the early 1950s, we had a small wireless and they would listen to Mantovani's orchestra music and musicals such as *The Sound of Music* and *South Pacific*. They even listened to a ventriloquist called Archie Andrews, which we found hilarious - a ventriloquist - on the radio!

Later on, of an evening, I was allowed to commandeer the radio and would tune in to Radio Luxembourg to hear the latest popular music coming out at the time. I will never forget the moment I first heard Elvis Presley's 'Heartbreak Hotel' blaring out one Sunday evening. I was thirteen and hadn't heard anything like it before. It was so fresh and exciting, and my only thought was "That's what I want to do - I want to be Elvis!"

A few years before this, when I was nine, I had a major accident that would shape the rest of my life. I was walking home from school after missing the bus. It began to snow, and I was having a great time, sliding down the hill and skidding into people's driveways. At the bottom of one driveway, I tripped and fell head-first into the road. My timing could not have been worse, as when I tried to save myself, a coal lorry went over both of my hands. I was knocked unconscious, and when I came round, I was sitting on the steps of a double-decker bus (which had been driving behind the lorry), surrounded by some very worried-looking adults. I couldn't feel any pain as I was in shock, and although my right hand looked ok, my left hand was wrapped in bloody bandages as it had been completely crushed. Doctors at Alder Hey Children's Hospital tried to rebuild a new thumb from the mangled remains, but despite seven operations, 132 stitches, and two years of hospital visits, I lost my left thumb.

ELVIS - HEARTBREAK HOTEL
– SHEET MUSIC

> *"That's what I want to do - I want to be Elvis!"*
> *-Mike*

As a result of this, I missed a lot of schooling. It became impossible for me to keep up with my class and I fell out of the habit of learning. To keep me occupied during the long days in hospital, my grandad (who was a member of an amateur musical group at Horne Brothers Department Store) gave me a mouth organ, which I soon got the hang of, once I started playing it. I think I was probably quite annoying to the other patients, but I enjoyed learning to play, and this ignited my passion for performing music. It might have had a less positive effect on the kids in the beds next to me!

After the accident, my scoutmaster presented me with a bravery award. There was no such thing as compensation in those days (and in truth, the lorry driver had done nothing wrong!) but the local council, whose lorry had done the damage, decided an encyclopaedia would be ample reparation for my lost thumb! Nowadays, this seems like a small gesture on their part.

Although I enjoyed reading the wealth of fascinating facts on offer in the book, there was something else inside which had a profound effect on me, and on the rest of

The
PICTORIAL
Encyclopædia

SOMEONE SAID IT COULDN'T BE DONE
AS HE WITH A CHUCKLE REPLIED,
MAYBE IT COULDN'T, BUT HE WOULD BE ONE
WHO WOULD NOT SAY SO TILL HE TRIED.
SO HE STARTED RIGHT IN, WITH A TRACE OF A GRIN
ON HIS FACE. IF HE WORRIED HE HID IT,
AND STARTED TO SING, AS HE TACKLED THE THING
THAT COULDN'T BE DONE, AND HE DID IT.

SAMPSON LOW. MARSTON & Co.Ltd
25 GILBERT STREET. W.1.

MIKE, HIS YOUNGER BROTHER CHRIS,
AND PARENTS, EDITH & BERNARD

MIKE - RECEIVING BRAVERY AWARD
FROM HIS SCOUT LEADER

ENCYCLOPAEDIA PRESENTED TO MIKE, AGED 10,
TO COMMEND HIS 'FORTITUDE & COURAGE'

INSET: 'SOMEONE SAID IT COULDN'T BE DONE'
POEM

my life. A poem had been pasted inside the front cover. It was written in 1919 by Edgar Albert Guest and was called 'Someone Said It Couldn't Be Done'.

This poem became the guiding inspiration for some of the biggest decisions in my life, including creating The Beatles Story. If I ever had a doubt, I would recite this poem in my head, and press on.

After my accident, my parents were keen for me to resume my education and sent me to St. Edwards College in West Derby. There should have been an entrance exam, but as I had missed so much school, my dad persuaded them to let me in without taking it. He had been a pupil there himself, and as a tailor, provided their school uniforms. The school was very academic but had an excellent orchestra and choir, and they recognised my singing ability and recruited me straight away for the choir. My Auntie Francis's house was only a ten-minute bike ride away, so she'd invite me there for lunch sometimes. I used to jump at the opportunity because her husband, Uncle Bill, was a pianist and he taught me the rudiments of playing the piano. Soon after this, I asked my parents if I could start piano lessons. When I was thirteen, my dad bought me an upright Blüthner piano, and a teacher would come over once a week to give me lessons. It must have been a challenge for him because of my missing thumb, especially doing scales!

Giving me piano lessons must have been a challenge for him because of my missing thumb...

I soon became bored of playing classical pieces in my lessons, as my friends and I were becoming heavily influenced by Lonnie Donegan - 'The King of Skiffle'. Skiffle was a style of music that came over from America, which was a mix of blues, jazz, and folk music, and was often performed on improvised instruments. This made it easy for kids to start their own skiffle groups without having to buy instruments! There was always a guitar, but to complete the group, we improvised with washboards, comb and paper kazoos, spoons, pots, and pans. We made tea chest basses from old tea chests which the local greengrocer would kindly pass on to us.

Not far from my house was an empty concrete air-raid shelter, a leftover relic from World War Two, which became the venue for our very own Skiffle Club, every Friday night. We would spread the word that there would be a skiffle session that Friday and local teenagers from the neighbourhood would come down to watch our loud and echoey versions of 'Rock Island Line', 'Cumberland Gap', and 'Puttin' on The Style'.

Our early foray into the world of showbusiness culminated when we were sixteen, on the last day of school. Ronnie McLoughlin, Pete Dunne and I decided to form a group to play some rock 'n' roll at the end of term school concert. I was on piano, Pete on guitar, and Ronnie was our singer. It was a strict, Catholic school, and traditionally, school concerts featured violinists, choirs, and classical music.

Our raucous performance of 'Blue Suede Shoes', 'Peggy Sue', and 'It's Only Make Believe' came as a bit of a shock, to say the least, and met with a mixed reception. Our school friends were cheering and clapping, but the Christian Brothers were horrified by the racket we were making, and we probably would have been expelled if we hadn't been leaving at the end of that term.

My school days had ended, but when it came to choosing a career, I didn't have a clue what I wanted to do. Becoming a musician wasn't seen by my parents as a sensible career plan and wasn't given as an option.

Luckily for me, my dad, Bernard, had opened his own business on North John Street in central Liverpool - a high-class tailor and outfitters. It was a natural step for me to go into the family business and I quickly learned how to measure customers for suits, and most importantly, remember that the customer was always right (!) Coincidentally, the Hard Day's Night Hotel, Liverpool's Beatle-themed hotel, is now in that same building.

One big plus about working there was that The Cavern Club, a little-known, damp basement venue in Mathew Street, was just 150 yards away. Originally a jazz venue, it had started to feature skiffle and beat groups towards the end of the 50s and I could watch lunchtime sessions and pay the one shilling entrance fee; just 5 pence in today's money. I saw groups such as Rory Storm & The Hurricanes, Gerry and the Pacemakers, The Remo 4, The Searchers, The Big 3, and The Beatles.

Working in a quiet menswear shop, with its formal clientele, wasn't my idea of fun at the time, and my ambition to perform was burning inside me. I was desperate to be in a group, so I started one with a lad who lived opposite my house and two of his friends. We called ourselves The Thunderbirds, a name our guitarist, Rod McDonald, came up with. He was into motorbikes, and this was a model of Norton, a brand of motorcycles popular at the time. We also had Clive Smith on drums and Dennis Aspinall on rhythm guitar. I was the lead singer.

We would rehearse every week in Clive's house while his mum made us tea and jam butties, and after a couple of months we got our first paid gig. It was at the Catholic Institute Coffee bar (The C.I.) in Sandfield Park, across from my old school. We didn't have a particular style. I liked Elvis, Rod was a big Buddy Holly fan, and we all liked the Shadows, so we played a mix of covers of popular songs of the time.

We couldn't afford more than one amplifier so both guitars and my vocal had to go through the same one, which must have sounded terrible. The audience was local kids and teenagers who could walk there. Not only did we get paid, but we were offered a fortnightly residency, and thought we were on our way to the big time!

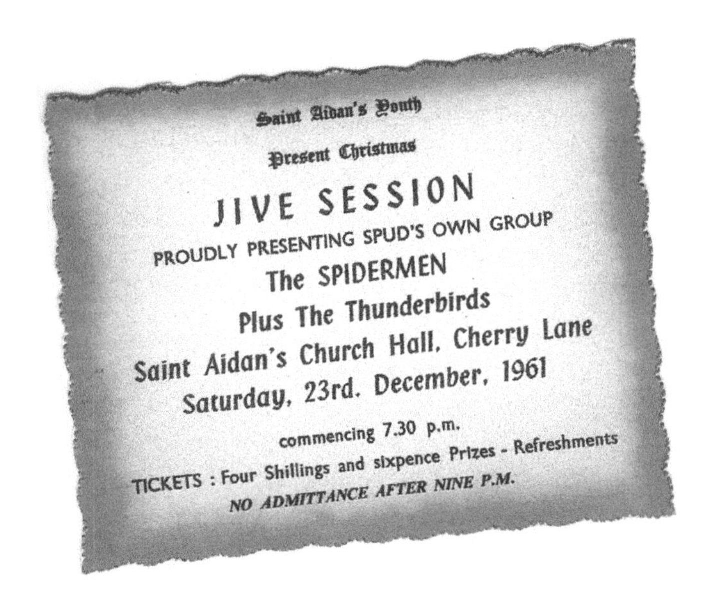

Saint Aidan's Youth
Present Christmas
JIVE SESSION
PROUDLY PRESENTING SPUD'S OWN GROUP
The SPIDERMEN
Plus The Thunderbirds
Saint Aidan's Church Hall, Cherry Lane
Saturday, 23rd. December, 1961
commencing 7.30 p.m.
TICKETS : Four Shillings and sixpence Prizes - Refreshments
NO ADMITTANCE AFTER NINE P.M.

THUNDERBIRDS CALLING CARD

THE THUNDERBIRDS AT THE C.I. COFFEE BAR

RORY STORM

The biggest group in Liverpool at this time was Rory Storm and The Hurricanes.

They played more than any other group and were booked at all the top venues, mainly because of their flamboyant showmanship and professionalism. They were very well-rehearsed and choreographed. Johnny Guitar (so named, not surprisingly, as he was a guitarist) and Ringo (named after his fondness for wearing lots of rings... real name Richard Starkey) had their own featured sets in the show. Rory would shout, "And now it's Ringo Starr time..." and leave the stage, so the spotlight would fall on Ringo, who would sing 'Matchbox' and 'Boys'. Ringo was a great drummer even before he joined The Beatles.

I would go to watch them whenever I could, as Rory was an inspiration - the most amazing showman I'd ever seen. A tall, blonde god, wearing head to toe pink or gold lame suits. When he played at the huge outdoor swimming pool in New Brighton, the band would play the solo on Ray Charles' 'What'd I Say', and Rory would run up to the top diving board, strip off, dive in and then come out singing! He was wild and the audience loved him.

In 1960, they were booked as the resident band at Butlin's Holiday Camp in Pwllheli, North Wales, and my friend Ronnie and I convinced our parents to let us have a holiday there without them for a week. We packed our bags and took the two-hour journey by coach from town.

Every week there was a talent contest in the main ballroom, and I decided to enter and sing Jerry Lee Lewis's 'Whole Lotta Shakin' Goin On'. The most remarkable thing about this was that the backing band was The Hurricanes, so I found myself backed by both Rory and Ringo! I think it went ok, but I came second to an eight-year-old girl who sang a song from a musical. I didn't mind, as I'd had the chance to sing with my hero, and with Ringo Starr on the drums behind me.

Not only did I get to play with the best group in Liverpool, but when they had finished playing for the night we would head to the beach for a party. We would light a fire and have a few drinks; the guitars would come out and there would be an impromptu jam session. Sometimes we were joined by Rory's sister Iris, who worked there as a Redcoat (the name given to holiday hosts who worked at Butlin's). She later married 70s star Alvin Stardust.

The band played a mixture of skiffle songs with some rock 'n' roll thrown in for good measure. In fact, Rory had started out as Al Caldwell's Texans, and they had appeared at The Cavern in May 1957. He had also started his own club called the Morgue Skiffle Cellar, and on the opening night, March 1958, he booked John Lennon's Quarrymen to appear!

After this, when we got back to Liverpool, I became quite friendly with Rory. In fact, one night, during the break of one of his shows, he suggested we rename my group Mike and the Thunderbirds. He had a prominent stutter when he spoke, but onstage there was no sign of it at all.

I'd had the chance to sing with my hero, and with Ringo Starr on the drums behind me.

He lived in Broadgreen with his mum, dad, and sister Iris, in a large house that he had christened "Stormsville" (Rory had changed his name by deed poll to Rory Storm; his real name was Alan Caldwell). Stormsville became a social hub where bands liked to meet up. His mum, Vi, was very hospitable and loved feeding the musicians who would turn up at all hours, in varying degrees of sobriety. We would go there after our shows for chip butties, tea and whisky. It could sometimes get rowdy, which drove his dad, Ernie, mad and he would retreat into the back room. It was an open house and I felt welcome there any time, day or night, even when Rory wasn't there!

He loved American style, flashy cars and he once bought a pink Vauxhall Cresta in cash for £800. It was a British-made car designed to look like an American model, and compared to the other cars of the time, it really stood out with its sleek, modern design. It impressed the fans and I used to love getting a lift in it with him; it felt so exciting and adventurous as I didn't have a car, let alone a pink Cresta!

NEW BRIGHTON 'BEAT & BATHE' POSTER

NEW BRIGHTON OUTDOOR POOL

MIKE, AGED 17 AT BUTLIN'S WITH RORY STORM

JOHNNY GUITAR, MIKE, RORY, RORY'S MUM, VI, SISTER IRIS (WHO WAS A REDCOAT), ANOTHER REDCOAT, & RORY'S DAD, ERNIE.

We became good friends and would sometimes play on the same bill. I'd still go to watch him, even after Ringo left the band and he had a succession of drummers in his place. He made a record under the management of Brian Epstein, but it didn't have much success.

When The Beatles started overtaking The Hurricanes as Liverpool's favourite band, Rory began to look at other opportunities, playing in France at US airbases and eventually becoming a DJ in Holland. I think Rory deserved to have achieved more success than he did, he was such a trailblazing showman on the Merseybeat scene who influenced so many of us at the time.

IRON DOOR CLUB MEMBERSHIP CARD

RORY AND HIS MUM, VI, IN THEIR HOME – AKA STORMSVILLE

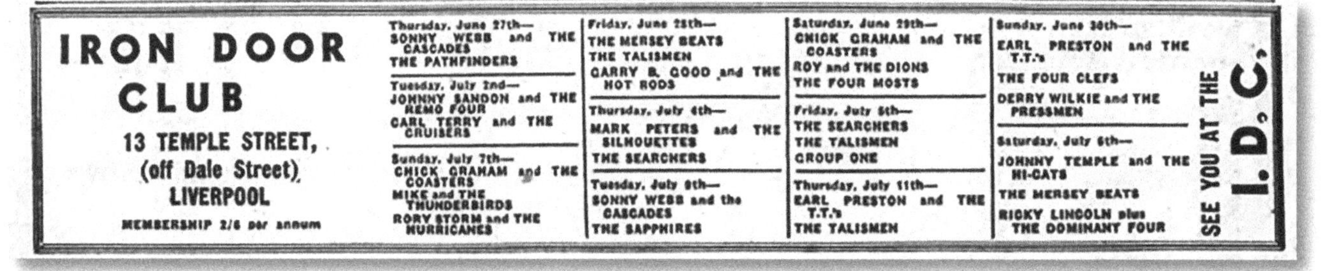

IRON DOOR CLUB

13 TEMPLE STREET, (off Dale Street), LIVERPOOL

MEMBERSHIP 2/6 per annum

Thursday, June 27th—
SONNY WEBB and THE CASCADES
THE PATHFINDERS

Tuesday, July 2nd—
JOHNNY SANDON and THE REMO FOUR
CARL TERRY and THE CRUISERS

Sunday, July 7th—
CHICK GRAHAM and THE COASTERS
MIKE and THE THUNDERBIRDS
RORY STORM and THE HURRICANES

Friday, June 28th—
THE MERSEY BEATS
THE TALISMEN
GARRY B. GOOD and THE HOT RODS

Thursday, July 4th—
MARK PETERS and THE SILHOUETTES
THE SEARCHERS

Tuesday, July 9th—
SONNY WEBB and the CASCADES
THE SAPPHIRES

Saturday, June 29th—
CHICK GRAHAM and THE COASTERS
ROY and THE DIONS
THE FOUR MOSTS

Friday, July 5th—
THE SEARCHERS
THE TALISMEN
GROUP ONE

Thursday, July 11th—
EARL PRESTON and THE T.T.'s
THE TALISMEN

Sunday, June 30th—
EARL PRESTON and THE T.T.'s
THE FOUR CLEFS
DERRY WILKIE and THE PRESSMEN

Saturday, July 6th—
JOHNNY TEMPLE and THE HI-CATS
THE MERSEY BEATS
RICKY LINCOLN plus THE DOMINANT FOUR

SEE YOU AT THE I.D.C.

IRON DOOR CLUB ADVERT – FROM MERSEY BEAT

RECORDING OUR FIRST RECORD
FOLLOWING IN THE FOOTSTEPS OF THE BEATLES

After playing coffee bars and youth clubs for a while, The Thunderbirds decided to make a record. We'd heard about Phillips Sound Recording Services (operated by Percy Phillips) in Kensington, Liverpool. This was the same studio where The Quarrymen (soon to become The Beatles with John, Paul, and George) had recorded their first two songs: Buddy Holly's 'That'll be the Day' and a McCartney/Harrison original, 'In Spite of All the Danger'.

A-SIDE - WEB OF LOVE

B-SIDE - GUITAR ESPANIOLA

We recorded two songs that Rod and I had co-written, 'Web of Love' and a Shadows-style instrumental called 'Guitar Espaniola'. We made four copies, one for each member of the group, and we took them home to play to our friends and family, but that was as far as it went.

We progressed from playing coffee bars to bigger and better venues, one of which was the Aintree Institute, a beat venue in the north end of the city promoted by Brian Kelly, a well-known promoter who ran BeeKay Promotions. I think Rory had introduced us. Brian had heard The Thunderbirds play and booked us for a number of shows that year.

One weekend, we were booked on consecutive nights to The Beatles. The night after our show, I went to see them play at the Aintree Institute, and this was the first time I'd seen them with their new image. They were dressed all in black with leather jackets. They had spent three months in Hamburg this year and were influenced by Astrid Kirchherr's existentialist or 'exis' look.

She and her friends, like Klaus Voorman and Jürgen Vollmer, copied the style of Parisian university students, favouring lots of black clothing such as capes, scarves, and leather. She was the Hamburg photographer who would later become Stuart Sutcliffe's fiancé. Seeing their newly polished yet raw performance after months of playing long hours was an awesome experience. For some reason, I remember Paul singing Elvis's 'I Feel So Bad' that night.

"That's the last you'll effin' see of that"

Perhaps that was how he felt!

A few days later, after another Cavern lunchtime session, I was in The Grapes pub on Mathew Street, during an extended lunch hour (!) from my day job. The Beatles were there, and I was telling Paul what a great show they did at the Aintree Institute the previous Saturday.

I told him that I'd forgotten to collect my fee from the promoter. John Lennon, sitting at the next table, overheard us talking and said, "That's the last you'll effin see of that!"

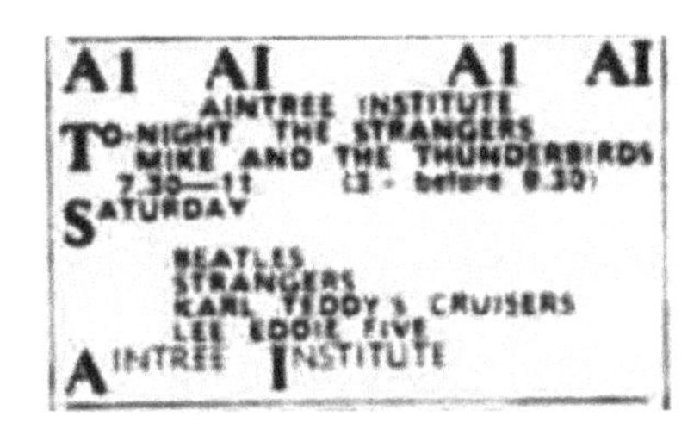
AI AI AI AI
AINTREE INSTITUTE
TO-NIGHT THE STRANGERS
MIKE AND THE THUNDERBIRDS
7.30—11 (3/- before 8.30)
SATURDAY
BEATLES
STRANGERS
KARL TEDDY'S CRUISERS
LEE EDDIE FIVE
AINTREE INSTITUTE

AINTREE INSTITUTE ADVERT - 22ND SEPTEMBER 1961

12, Oakbank Road,
Greenbank Park,
Liverpool, 18.
27th, September 1962.

Mike Byrne Esq.,
169, Whitehedge Road,
LIVERPOOL.19.

The Thunderbirds.

Dear Mike,

I recently gave you three bookings namely

Sunday 14th, October 62.
" 11th, November 62.
" 9th, December 62.

at a fee of £7.0.0. each booking for the Black Cat Club.

Sundays at the Black Cat Club have been falling off recently and a good publicity boost is needed. We are at present plugging "Sunny Webb and the Cascades' at the Iron Door Club and may reap the benefit of this publicity by switching them to the Black Cat Club on Sundays as a resident group. With this in miew would you mind if I transferred your bookings on the above dates from the Black Cat Club to the Iron Door Club . Playing times will be less, but the

Contd/;

DON'T BE LATE
MAKE A DATE
WITH
EIGHT OF THE FABULOUS
BEAT GROUPS
STARRING IN A
GRAND MARATHON
WHERE ?
AT THE
IRON DOOR CLUB
OF COURSE
FANTASTIC LINE UP
ROY AND THE DIONS
JOHNNY TEMPLER & THE HI-CATS
By Popular Demand The Return Of
THE METEORS
FROM MANCHESTER
ALSO
IAN AND THE ZODIACS
VIC AND THE SPIDERMEN
MIKE AND THE THUNDERBIRDS
THE PROFILES
THE EXCHECKERS
SEVEN HOURS OF NON-STOP
BEAT
STARTS 4 P.M. TO 11 P.M.
SUNDAY NEXT NOVEMBER 17
IRON DOOR CLUB 13 Temple St. off Dale St.
Members 7/- Non-Members 9/-

IRON DOOR CLUB 'GRAND MARATHON' ADVERT

- 2 -

fee will remain the same.

A contract for the Iron Door Club is attached . Please sign and return this at your convenience.

Yours sincerely,

L. Ackerley
(L.Ackerley)

THE THUNDERBIRDS CONTRACT – BLACK CAT CLUB

THE BLACK CAT CLUB

As our Club now enters its 5th glorious year, we continue to be one of Liverpool's "top-spots" for entertainment, and that friendly atmosphere, which is so hard to find in the multitude of clubs and dance halls that spring up so suddenly to-day.

We welcome you to our most respected membership, and ask you to uphold the proud tradition that makes this club great.

For the Committee,
Fred O'Sullivan,
Secretary.

BLACK CAT CLUB MEMBERSHIP CARD

SAMPSON & BARLOW, LONDON ROAD

The Thunderbirds also had a short residency at the Black Cat Club, which was on the top floor of a three-storey building on London Road (above Sampson & Barlow's, a catering and events company).

It was essentially a country music club but with the advent of Merseybeat they were trying beat groups on a Sunday night. It was a good gig for us, except for having to lug our gear up to the top floor. On the floor below us was The Cassanova Club, which was run by another Liverpool promoter, Sam Leach.

He booked The Beatles to play there several times in 1961. They must have continued to use the room for rehearsals, as one day, while we were carrying our gear to the top floor Black Cat Club, I could hear another band rehearsing. I stuck my head through the door and to my surprise found The Beatles mid-practice with Pete on drums. They were playing a George and John instrumental original called 'Cry for A Shadow' which they used to play at The Cavern. I listened for a while then closed the door and carried on to the top floor. It was never released by The Beatles but was included on the Anthology in 1995. It stuck in my mind because it's the only instrumental that I remember them doing.

This was such an exciting time in Liverpool - you could sense the opportunity for groups and musicians, and that a movement was happening. I knew that someone was going to make it big and get a record contract, and out of all the bands in Liverpool, I was sure that it would be The Beatles.

I stuck my head through the door and to my surprise found The Beatles mid-practice with Pete on drums

The Mersey Beat newspaper had been launched in the July of 1961, when Bill Harry, a fellow student of John's from art school, spotted an opportunity to promote the thriving and ever-changing music scene in Liverpool. He approached several daily newspapers suggesting they cover it, but they weren't interested, so he decided to do it himself. There were so many bands competing with each other to be the best and win recording contracts, but it was The Beatles who got the most publicity in the paper thanks to John's friendship with Bill.

This card is to be shown at all meetings attended

Cards and Passes are not transferable.

This card does not guarantee admission if the management deems the premises full.

A member is entitled to sign in two guests on each night except Saturday.

Membership fees for 1965/6 are due on or before 30th June, 1965.

Peppermint Lounge

SAMPSON & BARLOW'S
FABULOUS NEW
BALLROOM
LONDON ROAD
(Entrance in Fraser Street)
LIVERPOOL 3.
Tel: NOR. 0018

MEMBERSHIP CARD
1964/65

PEPPERMINT LOUNGE MEMBERSHIP CARD

BLACK CAT CLUB
- MERSEY BEAT ADVERT

In January 1962, a vote was held to decide who the most popular group of the time was. The Beatles were declared the winners, but only after Rory Storm was demoted when it was discovered that forty votes had come in with the same handwriting, in the same green ink, from one postal area, and they had all been a vote for Rory Storm! It later turned out that The Beatles had done something similar!

On the 22nd of August 1962, three days after Ringo Starr had joined The Beatles, after the controversial and hugely unpopular decision to sack Pete Best, Granada TV came to The Cavern to film The Beatles at a lunchtime session. I was working as usual that day in my dad's shop when Paul McCartney dashed in, in a panic, saying "Mike, we need something to wear for the 'telly' and it has to be black!" The only four matching tops that we had were some short-sleeved sweaters. Paul said they would do. So he took them for their TV debut, and they featured in a few of their Cavern appearances following that. I don't remember if we ever got paid for them, but you can see The Beatles wearing them on the Granada film footage.

This is testament to the influence Brian Epstein had on their image and professionalism. I doubt very much that they wanted to wear such smart tops as by the time it got to the evening show at The Cavern, John and George had changed out of them. Brian Epstein changed their stage appearance overnight.

PAUL IN THE SWEATER MIKE SOLD TO HIM

Paul McCartney dashed in, in a panic, saying "Mike, we need something to wear for the 'telly', and it has to be black!"

PAGE 4 — MERSEY BEAT — JAN. 4-18

MERSEY BEAT POPULARITY POLL

RESULTS

1. The Beatles
2. Gerry and the Pacemakers
3. The Remo Four
4. Rory Storm and the Hurricanes
5. Johnny Sandon and the Searchers
6. Kingsize Taylor and the Dominoes
7. The Big Three
8. The Strangers
9. Faron and the Flamingos
10. The Four Jays
11. Ian and the Zodiacs
12. The Undertakers
13. Earl Preston and the T.T's.
14. Mark Peters and the Cyclones
15. Karl Terry and the Cruisers
16. Derry and the Seniors
17. Steve and the Syndicate
18. Dee Fenton and the Silhouettes
19. Billy Kramer and the Coasters
20. Dale Roberts and the Jaywalkers

SURVEY

There has been tremendous interest in the "Mersey Beat Popularity Poll" and we were pleased at the response we recieved in voting forms. Fortunately only one or two forms were disqualified as they did not conform to the rules.

That the first four groups were most popular was a foregone conclusion all signs have indicated their popularity; the crowds that flock to their performances, the regularity of their bookings, the letters and requests for photographs and news concerning them. Of the four the Remo Four are acknowledged to be the best instrumental group on Merseyside, and the Beatles have been regarded as a top group throughout 1961.

No one could predict the next three positions, and they came as a pleasant surprise. A comparatively new group, the Searchers, have a big advantage in the remarkable vocalist Johnny Sandon. The Dominoes, the Kingsize group, changed personnel during the year, and for a short time broke up. That they should be placed so high in the results after such a set back is indeed a credit to their showmanship, and one can imagine they would have been placed even higher had the break-up not occurred. The Big Three, too, deserve credit for being so high up, being a trio in a competitive field where so many other groups have larger line-ups places them at a disadvantage. They have come through with flying colours.

The Flamingos are another group to be congratulated, having only appeared during the last quarter of the year. Of course, Faron was popular earlier in the year with his former group, the Tempest Tornadoes, and Raven fans, no doubt, follow the Flamingos.

Standing at number ten are the four young men with the goonish sense of humour—The Four Jays. There is no doubt at all that there will be some startling changes in next year's results. Had the poll been held a few weeks later Billy Kramer and the Coasters would probably have been higher, for their appearance at halls and clubs recently have gained them many new fans.

The Seniors, holding a valuable record contract, will certainly find success in 1962. The Bluegenes, placed at No. 23, will also be recording in the New Year. Many readers stated that they withheld voting for the Bluegenes, which explains their low placing. Obviously Bob Wooler's statement that they stand alone influenced many voters. Altogether 34 groups received places, but at present we are only concerned with the top twenty. We look forward to next year's poll, and to the new groups appearing during 1962.

GERRY AND THE PACEMAKERS who come Second

THE FOUR JAYS who come Tenth

JAZZ at the Glenpark Club
273 LORD STREET
SOUTHPORT
Every SUNDAY 1 p.m.—5 p.m.
Every MONDAY 7 p.m.—11 p.m.

ARE YOU A MEMBER OF THE
STORYVILLE JAZZ CLUB
13 TEMPLE STREET (off Dale Street)
TRADITIONAL JAZZ EVERY WEEKEND
STRICTLY MEMBERS' ONLY
Membership forms available at "Mersey Beat" Office or Club

FOR A SPEEDY AND EFFICIENT SERVICE FOR ALL PUBLICITY PHOTOGRAPHS Consult
PETER KAYE PHOTOGRAPHY
174 PARK ROAD
ROYal 1316

Why not visit
JOE'S RESTAURANT
139 DUKE ST.
OPEN UNTIL 4 A.M.
CURRIES, GRILLS ETC.

MERSEY BEAT POPULARITY POLL

WORKING ABROAD IN THE 1960s

The Thunderbirds continued to play around Liverpool, getting better gigs and increasing fees, eventually playing at The Cavern on Friday 20th September 1963. Coincidentally the other two groups on at The Cavern that night were The Mark 4, who I worked with briefly, and The Roadrunners, who I joined permanently in 1965.

By this time, The Beatles were touring the world, and although many fans felt bereft and disappointed that 'their' Beatles, who they had loyally supported and loved, had left them behind, the Liverpool music scene was still buzzing. Record labels wanted to sign more groups from Liverpool in the hope of emulating The Beatles' success. We were just one of more than 350 groups on Merseyside trying to make it big and hoping for a record contract.

A group called The Merseybeats was one such group and they had a record deal and several records in the charts. In February 1964, one of their singles, 'I Think of You', peaked at number five and they were due to appear on Top of The Pops. However, their bass player, Billy Kinsley, had quit the band following a dispute, and they needed a stand-in for the performance. I knew their lead singer, Tony Crane, quite well at the time, and one dreary Monday, he came into my dad's shop and asked me what I was doing on Thursday. I explained I'd be working here in the shop, and he asked if I'd like to be on Top of The Pops instead! Of course, I jumped at the chance and asked my dad for the day off.

Luckily, he agreed, and I found myself miming along to the song at the BBC studio in Manchester, which was in a converted Wesleyan church. Sadly, I can't find footage of this anywhere and I sometimes wonder if I dreamt the whole thing up, it was such an unlikely thing to happen.

By the end of 1963, I was beginning to grow out of The Thunderbirds. I'd been with them for two and half years, but we weren't progressing as quickly as I'd hoped so I decided to look for a band with ambitions to make it really big.

THEM GRIMBLES

We broke up, but I was only without a group for a few weeks because Rod phoned to say he had joined a group called Them Grimbles, and they were looking for a singer. I auditioned and got the job. Them Grimbles had a completely different sound which included a Hammond organ, saxophone, and six members, who were influenced by rhythm and blues, soul and jazz, which really appealed to me. I had to learn a whole new set of music by the likes of Ray Charles, who I was a big fan of, as well as Mose Alison and Jon Hendricks.

bers to know well in advance.
Remember the idea behind a Folk column in a Beat paper is to bring Folk song to an even bigger audience.

AS READERS of Folksound were told some time ago a tour of Britain by the Clancy Brothers and Tommy Makem was in process of being arranged.
Folk lovers and Club secretaries in particular will be pleased to know that this visit is now definitely on.

The famous Irish group start their tour of the island on September 18 at Fairfield Halls, Croydon. Then follow up with appearances all over the country.
More news of their tour together with a feature on The Clancys will appear in Folksound in the near future.

THEM GRIMBLES
For Bookings Ring:
Liverpool NOR 0471
Liverpool GAT 2404
ORMSKIRK 2200
(Evenings)

AMERICAN RECORD IMPORTER
J.A.K. ROBERTS
13 KENT ROAD,
WALLASEY
CHESHIRE
WAL 5114
WAL 5114
TRADE & INDIVIDUAL ENQUIRIES INVITED

THEM GRIMBLES
FOLK SOUND ADVERT

Them Grimbles had an agent, Jim Turner, who found work for us, both at home and abroad, and I soon found myself playing bigger and better venues such as The Iron Door and The Cavern.

In the winter of 1964, I told my dad that I was leaving my job in his shop to play abroad with Them Grimbles. It was one of the hardest things I had to do. For some unknown reason, thankfully he didn't object too much. Although he was a strict parent with traditional values, I think he could understand that I loved music more than anything and working in a menswear shop wasn't going to make me happy.

Overnight, I became a professional musician (even if it did mean occasionally having no work and signing on the dole!). No nine to five job for me anymore, no worries, and an exciting future to look forward to! For years after this, my mum, Edith, would regularly ask: "Michael, when are you going to get a proper job?"

I was 21 and it was the first time any of us had been abroad. We had no idea what was waiting for us in Germany. We needed a road manager and a van that would carry seven people and all our equipment. We found a guy called Tony, who had a van that had been converted from an old ambulance. It had the figure of a Michelin Man on the roof as a mascot.

On the night we were leaving for Germany, we did a local gig, then set off right after the show. Full of nerves and excitement, we were raring to get on the road and start our big adventure.

But our journey didn't exactly go to plan. Firstly, we only made it two miles down the road before running out of petrol! We sat on Queens Drive, having not even made it out of Liverpool, and waited for Tony to bring some petrol back. After an hour, we got back on the road again, only to have one of the wheels fall off somewhere near Birmingham, about a hundred miles into the journey. Apparently, we had overloaded the van and the axle had snapped. We probably should have turned back then (and sacked the road manager) but we were determined to make our international debut and somehow made it to our ferry on time. We crossed the English Channel and made it to Brussels in time for breakfast.

Them Grimbles would go on to spend four weeks working at the Star Palast Club in Kiel, followed by two weeks at the Star Palast Club in Luneburg. The clubs were owned by Manfred Woittalla and often featured big names such as Bill Haley, Jerry Lee Lewis, and Ray Charles as their headline artists. They filled the other nights with unknown and cheap groups from the UK like us, who were known for being able to play American music better than bands

ROB 'MCGRIMBLE' AND MIKE

THEM GRIMBLES AT THE IRON DOOR IN 1964

THEM GRIMBLES AMBULANCE/TOUR BUS - PICTURED OUTSIDE THE CAVERN
– THIS PICTURE ONLY SURFACED RECENTLY TO MIKE'S SURPRISE!

BUSINESS CARD WITH HAND-DRAWN 'GRIMBLE' WHICH WE WOULD SIGN ON AUTOGRAPHS

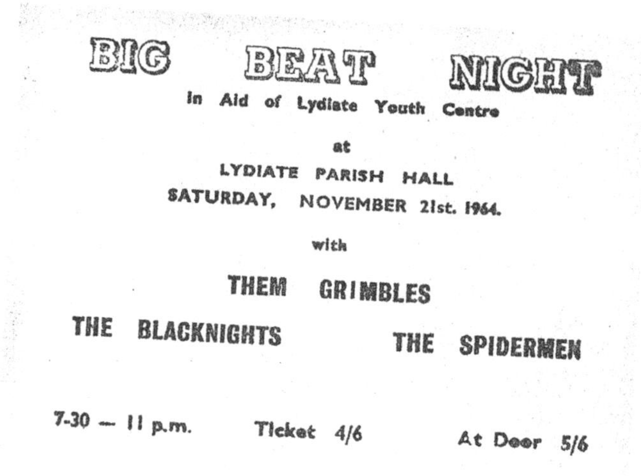

BIG BEAT NIGHT

In Aid of Lydiate Youth Centre

at

LYDIATE PARISH HALL

SATURDAY, NOVEMBER 21st. 1964.

with

THEM GRIMBLES

THE BLACKNIGHTS THE SPIDERMEN

7-30 — 11 p.m. Ticket 4/6 At Door 5/6

from Germany. It was also relatively easy for us to jump into a van, drive to Dover, hop onto the Calais ferry, and cross through France overnight towards the northern coast of Germany; fuelled by musical ambition and dreams of international fame and a recording contract.

The reality was a lot less glamorous than we had anticipated. Six exhausted individuals arrived in freezing temperatures in the middle of winter, wearing inadequate clothing and lugging a van full of equipment. When we arrived at the club, the doormen told us to go in and get a drink. Although we desperately needed some rest, we couldn't get into our sleeping quarters as we would be moving into the room occupied by the band who were currently on stage, blasting out the latest American rock 'n' roll hits. I think it was another Liverpool band, possibly The Gonks. We had to wait for them to finish, sometime in the early hours of the morning, then clear their gear out, before loading straight into the van to start their long journey back to England.

It certainly wasn't worth the wait when we did get in there. I don't know what we were expecting… a hotel? A hostel? That would have been luxury compared to what we were faced with. A hellhole underneath the club in the basement, with three bunk beds and a single filthy sink to share between seven of us. We had to use the customers' toilet in the club and were expected to live like this for four weeks!

We didn't have access to a kitchen, so most days we would find a cheap cafe and have toast and coffee which would have to last us until our evening meal, usually something like Erbsensuppe, a thick soup made of peas and other vegetables. If money allowed, once a week we would treat ourselves to halbes hähnche (half a roasted chicken), but money was tight, so some days we lived on bread and jam (known as 'jam butties' if you were from Liverpool!)

On weeknights, we would play six-hour shifts starting at 8pm and playing hour on, hour off, alternating with another group who I think were German, until 2am. At weekends, we started at 4pm and played ten-hour shifts, which were gruelling for us all, and I'd try not to speak on the alternate hours off, to try to maintain my voice. This is why The Beatles said that their time in Hamburg made their playing so tight - playing the same songs, night after night, really helped us hone our craft and return to England a better band.

STAR PALAST POSTCARD

In the beginning, the audience reaction was nothing like we were used to in Liverpool, where we had a loyal following. They seemed quite indifferent to us and didn't pay a lot of attention. They weren't familiar with the songs we were playing - a semi-jazz set of covers such as 'Get on The Right Track' by Ray Charles, and 'Gimme That Wine' by Lambert, Hendricks and Ross.

At the end of that week, Chris Hadfield, the organist, and I went to the boss's office to get paid. The owner, Herr Woittalla, was quite aggressive and said we were a

'scheisser grup' which translates to 'shit group'. He said his customers didn't like our style of music and we would only get paid when we started playing rock 'n' roll such as Chuck Berry and 'Pretty Woman'. We had a choice to make - go back home or learn a new set pretty quickly. We chose the latter as we had only just arrived!

Somehow, we survived the full four weeks and won the audience over, despite me losing my voice (at one time for three days) through singing so many hours a night. On the last night of our residency, we went to collect our money, and although we did get paid, Herr Woittalla pulled a gun out of his desk drawer and waved it at us. It was his way of showing us he was in charge and that we should be grateful for anything he gave us!

We got out of there as quickly as possible, though we were actually heading towards Luneberg to play at his other Star Palast Club! We had another two-week contract to play there, and this time, we went down well, with a polished set of rock 'n' roll and jazz in our repertoire, and the luxury of an old school dormitory to sleep in, plus use of a bathroom. Things were looking up!

At the end of our German adventure, we returned to Liverpool feeling like a much-improved group musically, and we continued to perform on the Northwest music circuit including bigger venues such as The Tower Ballroom in New Brighton.

In the August of 1965, we inadvertently found ourselves at the centre of a controversial story that was featured in The Sunday People newspaper. We were playing a show in Carlisle which had been booked in for a while, but unbeknown to us, a venue in Yorkshire had also booked us on the same night, having heard that we were a great 'crowd puller'. At least they thought they had booked us, but another group from Jim Turner's agency turned up and pretended to be us! The promoter sensed that something wasn't right when they arrived in a van with 'The Tabs' written on the side, and he questioned things further when their equipment had the same name written on it.

The group continued to insist that they were Them Grimbles and even introduced themselves on stage as such.

The promoter didn't believe them and after examining the photo he had been sent more closely, he knew he'd been sent a different group. Eventually, the truth came out and they admitted that they were in fact The Tabs! Our agent had obviously thought he'd get away with it, and the newspaper article alluded to the fact that Merseybeat groups tended to look the same, hence the headline "You Can't Tell a Tab from a Grimble!"

IT'S COME TO SOMETHING WHEN

You can't tell a Tab from a Grimble

(THEY ALL MAKE THE SAME NOISE, ANY...

HOW do you tell one long-haired beat group from another?

If you know the secret there's a chap up in Yorkshire who would like your help.

He is Keith McGregor, who runs dances at the town hall in Morley, Yorks.

The problem of sorting out the popsters is worse up there. Because it's within easy travelling time of Liverpool, where all the groups try to look and sound like their local heroes, the Beatles.

Keith McGregor's troubles began when he booked a group called "Them Grimbles" for a Saturday night dance.

He agreed on a fee of £25, as he heard that these Liverpool lads were good "crowd pullers."

An agent gave him a picture which he said showed the group. There were six musicians peeping from beneath thick thatches of hair.

BAFFLED HIM

On the night of the dance, 24-year-old Mr. McGregor saw a van draw up at the town hall with six pop players who looked similar to the ones in the photograph.

They had Liverpool accents, too.

But on the side of the van were the words "The Tabs."

Mr. McGregor rubbed his eyes and had another look at the contract. It definitely said "Them Grimbles" would appear.

So he tackled the boys about it and they insisted they were "Them Grimbles," Mr. McGregor told me at his home in Mary Street, East Ardsley, Yorkshire.

"Things got even more confusing when I tackled the lads themselves about their name," he went on. "They said they were 'Them Grimbles.' But when they unpacked their instruments the name 'The Tabs' was all over them!

"So I showed them the photograph—and eventually the truth came out. They admitted to being 'The Tabs.' They said they didn't know who the lads were on the picture."

Mr. McGregor was furious. He had paid £25 advertising "Them Grimbles" and he had got "The Tabs."

The group had even appeared on stage as "Them Grimbles" and had to go on stage and announce their real name.

But he was in for even one more shock.

When he checked the photograph with the local variety agent he found that it was not "Them Grimbles" or "The Tabs" in the picture. It was a different group altogether.

THAT DID IT!

"That just about did it," said Mr. McGregor. "Long hair, Liverpool accent—the lot. I was completely fed up."

There is even more muddle than Mr. McGregor realises.

Robert Little, 20-year-old leader of "Them Grimbles," told me that there are FIVE in his group, not six.

And they were definitely not at Morley town hall that night. They were in Carlisle.

Ronald Ellis, acting manager [illegible] to discuss the booking with me.

Mr. Jim Turner, who drew up the contract for "Them Grimbles" to appear at Morley, was equally tight-lipped.

Smartly dressed Mr. Turner, in his late twenties, sat back coolly in his tiny office in Bold Street, Liverpool, and said: "I have no comment to make."

When I produced a copy of the contract, he pointed to a clause and said: "I can't be responsible for any non-fulfilment of contracts by managers or artistes—it says so here."

So the situation is still as clear as the Mersey mud.

I'd advise anyone who books a Liverpool group to insist on seeing their birth certificates before they play! Or their M.B.E.s!

YOU CAN'T TELL A TAB FROM A GRIMBLE - SUNDAY NEWSPAPER ARTICLE

LEAVING HOME

I was spending my nights playing ballrooms, clubs and beat cellars and my mornings lying in bed until midday. Straight after we'd done a show, we would go to Allan Williams' Blue Angel club, 'the Blue' for short, where we would meet up with friends and often not make it home until the early hours of the morning.

After months of me working late, and sleeping in even later, my dad issued an ultimatum: either get a proper job and stop lazing around in bed all day or move out! I didn't want to upset him, but I wasn't going to leave the group. We were on the road to fame and fortune and had a recording contract in our sights! It was clearly time for me to get my own place, and I thought the best place would be in town so I could walk home after a night at the Blue. I discovered that a friend of Brian Epstein's called Yankel Feather owned some flats in Falkner Street, which were reasonably priced (for a fledgling musician); plus, this was a great location for getting in and out of town.

It wasn't long before I was happily residing in a one-bedroom flat on the ground floor of 36 Falkner Street. It comprised of a combined living room and bedroom, with a small kitchen that led onto a back yard. Tenants had to share a bathroom on the first floor. It was pretty basic, with linoleum on the floor and a sheepskin rug and a two-bar electric fire for warmth. But it was my first place and it felt great to have my independence.

I didn't know that this flat had some impressive musical heritage of its own. It was the very same flat that John Lennon and his new wife Cynthia had lived in after they got married in August 1962. They lived there until Julian was born in April 1963, when they must have outgrown the tiny space and moved in with John's Aunt Mimi and Uncle George.

MEETING DETTE

Bernadette and I met in 1965. It was after a Cavern lunchtime session when our drummer, Pete Clark, invited me to meet his girlfriend, Rene, and her friend Bernadette at a popular coffee bar called The Kardomah. I didn't have anything else to do, so decided to tag along, and this is when we first met. We hit it off straight away and stayed for another coffee and cheese toasty after Pete and Rene had left.

After we started dating, Bernadette used to visit me at the flat and we would listen to the latest LPs and make meals for each other. After spotting tiny footprints in some leftover frying pan fat one day, she was less keen to visit.

BERNADETTE AND HER FIRST CAR - A FIAT 500

DETTE WITH HER DANSETTE AUTO CHANGER RECORD PLAYER

THE ROADRUNNERS

In the summer of 1965, after two trips to Germany, playing in Kiel, Hannover, Brunswick, and Luneberg, Them Grimbles returned to Liverpool with just enough work to get by. We had been promised a recording contract by our agent, but it didn't materialise, perhaps because London-based recording companies had started to lose interest in groups from Liverpool. The group lost its momentum, bookings tailed off and we became disillusioned about the future, so after eighteen months, I decided to call it a day.

I was at a bit of a loss as to what to do next, when one night I was in the Blue Angel talking to Bob Adcock, The Roadrunners' road manager; he told me that The Roadrunners' lead singer, Mike Hart, had just left the group. I asked if I could join them, and they said yes! (Bob Adcock went on to become Led Zeppelin's tour manager). They were the best R&B band in Liverpool and the timing was perfect, so I jumped at the chance to join. Not only that, but despite the waning interest in Liverpool bands,

ROADRUNNERS PUBLICITY PICTURE

ACETATES OF ROADRUNNERS' 'MR. PITIFUL' & 'MONKEY TIME'

The Roadrunners had a recording contract with Fontana Records lined up.

We didn't have any material of our own ready, so we recorded two Motown and soul cover versions from our repertoire, Major Lance's 'Monkey Time' and Otis Redding's 'Mr. Pitiful'. We were really happy with the end result, but sadly they decided not to release them, perhaps because they were looking for original songs! The recordings didn't see the light of day until an acetate surfaced in a car boot sale in 2015, found by a Swedish collector Ralf Narvel, in Sweden of all places! We had no idea how it ended up there.

The Roadrunners were getting regular bookings, including two separate residencies in Germany. The first trip was another shambolic adventure. It started well for half of the band, including me, as we made our way to London in an Aston Martin which belonged to a friend of a friend. The others waited behind for a van to bring the equipment.

We arrived at Frankfurt at 5am, via a boat and three trains. We were lucky to make it, as on one leg of the train journey, we had all fallen asleep and I woke up just as the

THE ROADRUNNERS

The boys with The beat

The Roadrunners have been one of the most popular Liverpool groups practically since the day they first formed, way back in 1962, but as they've just recently signed with Four Pennies manager Alan Lewis it looks as though their appearances in their home city will become quite rare. Mr. Lewis is based in Manchester and the agency that will look after the bookings of the Roadrunners is in London, so this is yet another major group to leave the Mersey scene because of better offers.

The group was got together by guitarist Pete Mackay and together with the only other remaining original member of the group, organist John Peacock, he's seen a lot of personnel changes. At one time the front singer was Mike Hart and the group's line-up boasted two saxes, but now the group is fronted by ex-Grimble Mike Byrne and includes Mike Kontzle on guitar and Terry McCluskey on drums.

The group has been over to the Star Club in Hamburg several times, ang made a single and an album "live" from the club, both of which entered the German charts. They were the first group in Liverpool to make a "small band" sound, and in that respect were way ahead of other Merseyside groups.

The music they play is principally R and B., but it's a very progressive sound they make, and the chabnge in line-up since Mike Hart left, ang the loss of two saxes hasn't altered the group's popularity at all.

They plan to go back to the Star Club shortly. They aim to concentrate on Continental work, and to generally build up their reputation over there.

GEOFF LEACK

THE BOYS WITH THE BEAT - ARTICLE IN MUSIC ECHO

train was preparing to depart from our stop, Mainz. We grabbed our belongings, which were strewn around the carriage, and jumped off one by one. I was second to last, and at this point, the train was gathering speed, and Terry, our drummer, shoved me off the train! I went rolling down the platform with my bags on top of me and was lucky not to end up in the hospital. We got a taxi to the club, which was shut, and as we had nowhere else to go, we went to a police station. The rest of the group were hours behind us and made it just in time for the show - ten minutes before we were due to go on stage!

"It was often like a scene from a wild-west movie with tables and chairs being thrown across the dancefloor, while we carried on playing"

The first residency was at The Storyville Club in Frankfurt, remarkable for its Saturday night fights between the servicemen from the nearby US air force base and the locals. It was often like a scene from a wild-west movie with tables and chairs being thrown across the dancefloor, while we carried on playing. The second stint was at The Storyville Club in Cologne in December, and I recall the owner asked if we could learn some Beatles numbers, as by then they were famous across the world. 'I Feel Fine' had come out in the October of 1964 and had reached number three in the West German Singles Chart. So we learned that, and the audience loved it. The previous year, The Beatles had recorded two of their hit singles as a double A-side in German - 'I Wanna Hold Your Hand' and 'She Loves You' - 'Komm, Gib mir Deine Hand' and 'Sie Liebt Dich'. There had been a wave of acts recording their songs in foreign languages to broaden appeal in the 60s, but this was the only time The Beatles did this.

We came back to the UK on 31st December, but again, our transport was far from reliable. When we got to the German border at Aachen, our van broke down and we didn't have any insurance or recovery plan in place. There was, however, a sort of unwritten understanding on the Liverpool group scene that whenever there was van trouble, other groups would help out. This was usually when we were travelling around the UK, so this was really testing the "International Rescue Club" to its limit. We phoned the Blue Angel because we knew someone would be there at that time and luckily, The Escorts' road manager, Bruce McCaskell, agreed to come and rescue us from Ostend. We still had to sleep in the van overnight and it was absolutely freezing - we woke up to frost on the ground and icicles hanging inside the van! I decided there and then that I wasn't spending another night risking hypothermia and told the group I was hitch-hiking to the ferry in Ostend. I preferred to do that than sit still and freeze. The Storyville Club arranged to recover the van and our equipment and have it sent back to Liverpool. We somehow all eventually made it back safely.

We continued working on the Liverpool and Northwest group circuit and we were also offered a tour of Sweden, but it was four months long and we decided against it. However, one day after watching a Cavern session, we were chatting with Bob Wooler, the Cavern DJ. He had been talking to NEMS in London who were looking for a Liverpool band to play in Switzerland. It would be a month-long residency in Gstaad, one of the most exclusive ski resorts in the world at that time. Bob had recommended us and wanted to know if we were interested.

It wasn't great money, but we would get free accommodation, food, and all travel expenses, plus we would have the honour of playing at the 21st birthday party of a London millionaire's son. We had never been to Switzerland and didn't know where it might lead. Gstaad had a reputation for being a playground of the rich, where film stars and royalty would go to ski and be seen. This was an opportunity we didn't want to miss, and Bernadette was happy for me to go as long as I promised to write every day. Which I did!

ECHO Week ending September 4, 1965

● THE ROADRUNNERS recorded for Fontana last Thursday. The group have been offered a tour of Sweden and have been asked to do a musical at St. George's Hall, Liverpool, by an American agent.

● Two weeks ago M.E. published GERRY MARSDEN's wedding date to

● Within five weeks, THE HILLSIDERS will have another single, an E.P. and an L.P. out on the market. Also they have five tracks on a Country and Western album titled "Guest Night With The Hillsiders."

● PATSY NICOLS, lead vocalist with THE BLUE MOUNTAIN BOYS, has been offered an extensive tour of

THE ROADRUNNERS — left to right: PETE MACKY, JOHN PEOCOCK, MIKE BYRNE, MIKE KONTZLE, TERRY McCLUSKER.

ROADRUNNERS IN THE MUSIC ECHO - ANNOUNCING RECORDING CONTRACT AND TOUR OF SWEDEN

ROADRUNNERS NEW DISC

THE next German release from THE ROADRUNNERS, may be "Mr. Pitiful". They were recently appearing at the Storyville Club, Frankfurt. The group will be recording several numbers for

SINK CLUB

— TO-NIGHT —
DIRECT FROM GERMAN TOUR!
(FIRST APPEARANCE IN LIVERPOOL)
THE ROADRUNNERS!
& THE CORDES!
MEMBERS 3/6 VISITORS 4/6.
SUNDAY SESSION
COLTS and ALMOST BLUES!
MEMBERS 3/6 VISITORS 4/6

HOPE HALL TO-NIGHT
THE ROADRUNNERS
Friday: THE SECRETS
Join Hope Hall and Bring Your Friends—It has Atmosphere

FIRST EVER FABULOUSLY EXCITING

ALL NITE BEAT BOAT

Starring these Top Groups

★ THE CLAYTON SQUARES ★ EARL PRESTON'S REALMS
★ THE HIDEAWAYS ★ ST. LOUIS CHECKS
★ THE ROAD RUNNERS ★ AMOS BONNEY & THE TTs

and Special Guest Stars

THE SENSATIONAL MEASLES

MIDNIGHT EASTER SUNDAY, 18th APRIL, 1965
IMPORTANT! SEE OVERLEAF
Nº 1471

AT THE CAVERN
TO-NIGHT—SATURDAY—TO-NIGHT
THE ROADRUNNERS
ALMOST BLUES
KARL TERRY & THE T.T.'s
TO-MORROW—SUNDAY—TO-MORROW
A 9-HOUR MARATHON
9 HOURS — 9 ACTS
LITTLE STEVIE WONDER
THE HIDEAWAYS
EARL PRESTON'S REALMS
THE FIX
THE RICHMOND
THE CRYING SHAMES
THE ALMOST BLUES
THE AZTECS
SIDEWINDERS

● THE ROADRUNNERS are to join Manchester agency ALAN LEWIS ENTERPRISES. Negotiations are currently under way for the group's record to be released on Fontana.

LA LAMPE D'ALLADIN PUBLICITY POSTER

GSTAAD HOTEL POSTCARD FROM 1960s

After making our way from Liverpool to Victoria station in London, we travelled by train to Rougemont in Switzerland, with all our equipment and clothes. It took three days. We changed trains in London and Paris and once when we got to Montreaux, we had to get our gear and ourselves onto the Jungfrau Railway, which was the highest in Europe.

We must have been a sight to behold: four long-haired musicians, surrounded by guitars and amplifiers on the station platform and not one of us able to speak the local lingo, Schweitzer-Deutsch. We didn't have any excess money with us, so couldn't afford to eat in railway restaurants en-route and survived on sandwiches and coffee.

We must have been a sight to behold: four long-haired musicians, surrounded by guitars and amplifiers...

When we finally arrived in Gstaad, we could see that it was not just any ski resort, not that we had been to any others to compare it to! It was posh, on a par with St. Moritz. It was like being in a James Bond film - a picture-postcard village full of luxurious chalets and beautiful people, and we were in awe of the glamour and wealth on show. We were just four lads from Liverpool, amazed to see posters of ourselves all over the town advertising 'Liverpool's Premier Beat Group'.

Our first show was at the extravagant 21st birthday party for Nick Lilley, a descendent of the founders of the Lilley & Skinner shoe company, and it was to be held at an upmarket nightclub and restaurant called La Lampe D'Alladin which was owned by a wealthy Egyptian from Cairo. It was a dimly lit venue consisting of a small dancefloor in front of the low, compact stage, and candle-lit dining tables around that.

There were private booths on one side for the VIPs to enjoy their evenings discreetly. It was a real eye-opener as to how 'the other half' lived and partied! Our show was a great success; we played two 60-minute spots and we were allowed to stay and socialise with the guests. Our new best friend, the millionaire Nick Lilley, had an E-type Jag and his friend had an Aston Martin DB6 which, by the way, they had flown over from England. We found ourselves enjoying the good life even if we were just four poor lads from Liverpool. He arranged for us to have free skiing lessons, and I remember after one session, the instructor took us to an outdoor cafe in the centre of

Gstaad and ordered Martini Rosso for us. We'd never experienced anything like it. Sitting in the sun, surrounded by snow-covered mountains and being stared at by the locals because we looked like The Beatles, and very out of place!

For a short time, Nick generously loaned us his E-type Jag to explore the area. Such was his wealth that he didn't think about the potential implications of such a loan! After a while, he wanted the E-type back and hired a VW Beetle for us instead, which proved to be a wise decision, as not long after, I skidded off the road, caving in the wing, and our driving days in Gstaad were over.

We stayed in Gstaad for a month and became minor celebrities, which secured our invitations to several parties in private luxury chalets. We didn't pay for drinks the whole time we were there! We looked very out of place among all of the well-heeled, wealthy skiers, but it didn't matter, we were an interesting novelty and we played songs that they knew by The Beatles, Motown artists and other popular acts.

The restaurant owner also owned an art gallery just outside of Gstaad and invited us to go there and just be seen - again because we were a novelty with our long hair and English accents.

During our residency, many famous people came to La Lampe D'Alladin including David Niven, Elizabeth Taylor and Richard Burton, the Vanderbilt family plus members of European royalty such as the Crown Prince of Norway. One night after we had finished our second set, we spotted Richard Burton and Elizabeth Taylor sitting in a private booth. To our absolute amazement, they invited us over and told us that they had really enjoyed the gig and would be coming back the week later with their two boys. I can't remember much about it except that she was very beautiful, and he was very drunk.

Another time, Nick told us he'd invited Jackie Kennedy to the show that night. We were really excited and nervous, but unfortunately she didn't come and we didn't get to meet her. However, a few days later, we did see her in the flesh at Charlie's Bar, which was probably the most popular bar in Gstaad. This was a reflection of just how glamorous Gstaad was, that the former First Lady chose to have her holidays there. It was a great trip that exposed us all to a very different way of life. My love of skiing continues to this day!

BACK HOME IN LIVERPOOL

While I was away, Bernadette decided that my flat would benefit from a make-over. This was 1966 and the psychedelic era was well underway so Bernadette, along with two of her friends, embraced the current trends with gusto. They covered one wall with a giant magazine collage featuring headlines and celebrities of the time. The other walls were hand-painted with psychedelic patterns in orange, black and purple gloss paint! I was suitably impressed when I was greeted with this quite striking transformation.

MIKE GETTING READY TO GO SKIING - NOTE THE INAPPROPRIATE SKI WEAR!

MIKE AND BERNIE IN MIKE'S FLAT - IN FRONT OF THE COLLAGE BERNIE SURPRISED HIM WITH!

When we returned to Liverpool, The Roadrunners thought a recording contract was on the cards and that we could look forward to lots of work through our new agent Alan Lewis. But to our surprise, neither of these things happened, and the group's momentum dwindled.

Being away from Liverpool so much I realised how much I'd missed Bernadette, and when I got back, I was happy to have some time off in my newly decorated flat. The Roadrunners wanted to carry on, but I eventually parted ways with them and spent a brief time singing for another Liverpool group called The Cordes, before deciding to get married and settle down. Perhaps if I'd given it longer, a record deal might have materialised, but the attention on Liverpool groups had certainly dwindled in the late 1960s.

Perhaps if I'd given it longer, a record deal might have materialised...

MIKE AND BERNIE LEANING ON THE PSYCHEDELIC WALL

BERNADETTE'S EARLY MEMORIES & MUSICAL INFLUENCES

Bernie: I was born after the war into a music-filled household. It was a time of frivolity as years of hardship and rations had ended and life was for enjoying again. My parents met at a ballroom competition, and although they had different partners, they would regularly go out of an evening to the local dancehall, and bring friends back to our house, to play music on the piano and have singalongs. My dad's partner was Gerry Chang who happened to be Allan Williams's mother-in-law. (Allan was The Beatles' first manager - the man who famously "gave The Beatles away.")

BERNADETTE'S PARENTS, BILL AND PEGGY IN THE 1940S

Glenn Miller, Bert Ambrose and Al Bowlly were firm favourites. My mum, Peggy, was the manageress of the Rivoli cinema, which meant that as kids, we were allowed to go there after school for free and watch the news and films while she was working. We were introduced to American film stars, music and culture from a young age.

My older sister, Maureen, used to go to local dancehalls, where they would dance to the likes of Frankie Vaughan, Victor Silvester and Guy Mitchell, and she would buy their records from the local record shop. They were made of shellac and would break very easily. The radio was always on in our house, so apart from the kids' programmes such as Archie Andrews and Sparky and his magic piano, we had the chance to tune into music that was popular with American servicemen, many of whom were stationed near us at Burtonwood. My aunt eventually married an American serviceman and moved over to the east coast of the USA.

"It was a time of frivolity as years of hardship and rations had ended and life was for enjoying again"

Often in families, younger siblings follow in their older siblings' footsteps. My sister attended Billy Martin's School of Dance and used to take part in formation competitions that were held around the country. I eventually joined the junior classes that took place on a Saturday afternoon. As we learned the steps, we started to take part in various formation classes and performed for an audience, usually our parents! I was in the Charleston group and at the time thought I was 'the bee's knees.'

The trend in music was changing, from the cool, suave, ballad singer such as Dean Martin or Guy Mitchell, to another influence from America, none other than Elvis Presley. My friend Joan and I were initially fans of Eddie

Cochran, but as soon as we saw Britain's answer to Elvis, Cliff Richard, we became ardent fans. We first saw him on one of the earliest popular music shows, called Oh Boy!

We both loved his music and whenever he appeared on our black and white TV, we were glued to it! We both made scrapbooks of Cliff, but unfortunately, when we moved house, some years later, they got lost in the move. I think my mother might have thrown them away.

BERNADETTE AS A TEENAGER

Around this time, lots of kids, mostly boys, started to form their own groups, but as they couldn't afford to buy their own instruments, they often tried to make them using old tea chests and washboards. This, along with a strong Irish population in Liverpool, led to the emergence of skiffle groups - a kind of country music. Lonnie Donegan was spearheading the craze with a recording of an American folk song, 'Rock Island Line'.

I first became aware of the sheer power of music when I heard that teenagers were dancing in the aisles and had even torn up seats in the cinema during a showing of Blackboard Jungle, which featured the Bill Haley song 'Rock Around the Clock'. There was an outcry from older generations who feared that rock 'n' roll music was turning their children into delinquents.

When the new British pop stars such as Cliff, Marty Wilde and Vince Eager appeared on our TVs, their managers realised they had a potential goldmine in their hands, and could make them even more popular if they put their stable of TV stars out on the road at all major theatres, knowing that their fans would pay to see them in person. Cliff made a number of appearances in Liverpool, and my friend Joan and I would make sure we got there early to queue for tickets. We first saw him at the Philharmonic Hall in 1959.

He was wearing a shocking pink jacket, tie and socks and we couldn't believe he was even better looking than on TV. Sometimes we had to queue from early in the morning, but sometimes we would wait all night. We were only thirteen and my friend's dad would come down with a flask and sandwiches to keep us going. Some others even took sleeping bags. We'd always try to get

CLIFF RICHARD – THE UK'S ANSWER TO ELVIS

front-row seats at the Empire or Philharmonic Hall and would scream with excitement throughout the show.

In 1960, as the group scene evolved, Joan and I would look at adverts in the Liverpool Echo to see who was playing where. We started going to Lowlands, which was a club in West Derby village, opposite Pete Best's mum's club, The Casbah. It was a nice little cellar club with a small stage down in the basement and a tiny dancefloor. There was a little coffee bar, which mostly sold soft drinks, tea and biscuits. We saw groups like Faron's Flamingos, Rory Storm and The Hurricanes, Gerry and the Pacemakers and The Hollies there. We occasionally chatted to some of them, but it was more like a social evening with friends. We would go there by bus and home the same way, making sure we were home by a reasonable time.

SEEING THE BEATLES FOR THE FIRST TIME

Our parents were usually ok about us going to the shows. There was never any alcohol - well, certainly not where we were concerned - but there were a few venues we were told we mustn't go to because they were known for being a bit rough. Hambleton Hall was one such place, with a reputation for violent fights breaking out between rival gangs of teddy boys; Joan's father had warned us not to go there as it was in a very rough area. But we wanted to see Faron's Flamingos as we had seen them before and thought they were great. So we pretended we were going to the Aintree Institute then took the number 10 bus to Huyton instead.

The venue was small, with a stage at one end, and it was quite crowded when we got there. We hung our coats in the ladies' cloakroom, which was also the toilet block, then made our way to the front, to get a good view. I remember we were getting into the beatnik look at the time and were wearing long, chunky knitted sweaters which we'd had knitted especially for us.

Our first thought was "they don't look like the usual type"

Faron did a great show and wowed us all in his white suit (heavily influenced by Elvis). Gerry and The Pacemakers were also on the bill and The Beatles were topping it but unbelievably, we weren't that bothered about seeing them as we hadn't really heard much about them.

However, when The Beatles came on stage, they looked a lot different from the other groups of the time, many of whom wore linen suits or waistcoats and ties. We were immediately struck by their extraordinary appearance, dressed in leather jackets, apart from Paul who was wearing a dark-coloured reefer jacket. They looked more

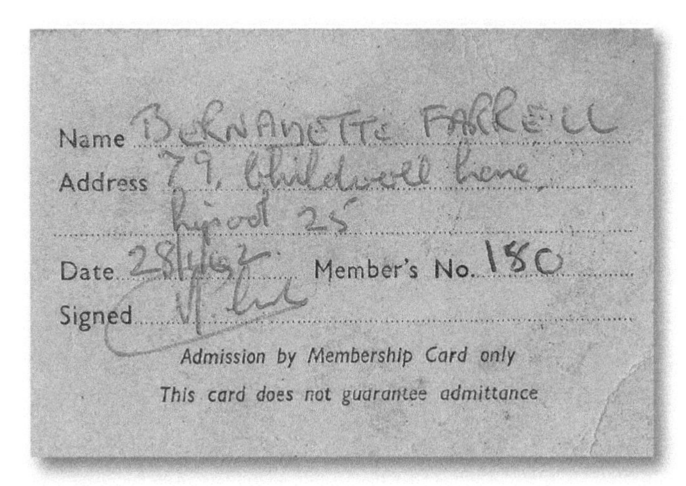
Name BERNADETTE FARRELL
Address 79, Childwall Lane,
Liverpool 25
Date 28/1/62 Member's No. 180
Signed
Admission by Membership Card only
This card does not guarantee admittance

LOWLANDS MEMBERSHIP CARD

LOOK !

THREE TOP GROUPS AGAIN

NEXT WEDNESDAY NIGHT
AT HAMBLETON HALL
Page Moss, Huyton

— What a terrific line up for —
WEDNESDAY, 25th JANUARY 1961

- The Sensational Beatles
- Derry & The Seniors
- Faron & The Tempest Tornadoes

YES! You must come along early and bring your friends !

PAY AT THE DOOR **2/6 before 8 p.m. 3/- afterwards**

NOTE ! No admission after 9-30 p.m.

HAMBLETON HALL FLYER PROMOTING 'THE SENSATIONAL BEATLES'

IRON DOOR CLUB, TEMPLE STREET

NEMS STORE – GREAT CHARLOTTE STREET – THE ENTRANCE TO ELLISON LEA HAIR SALON WAS ON THE RIGHT

Calling all Jive Fans !

HAVE YOU HEARD ABOUT THE

— SENSATIONAL —
JIVE DANCES

every

FRIDAY & SATURDAY

7-45 to 11 p.m. 3/- 7-30 to 11 p.m. 4/-

at AINTREE INSTITUTE

BUSES TO DOOR
20 20e 22 35 61 91 92 92a 93 95 96 500

every Saturday features
THE DYNAMIC BEATLES

★ TELL YOUR FRIENDS THE GREAT NEWS ★

COME ONE, COME ALL
TO AINTREE INSTITUTE !
for the best in Jive on Friday and Saturday nights.

BEEKAY PROMOTIONS.

AINTREE INSTITUTE FLYER ADVERTISING 'THE DYNAMIC BEATLES'

like bikers or teddy boys! They had just returned from their first trip to Hamburg and because the stage was higher than us, we had a great view of their footwear. Two of them had cowboy boots on, but Paul was wearing slip-on leather ankle boots. Stuart Sutcliffe was also onstage playing bass guitar at the back in leather, wearing sunglasses. Our first thought was "they don't look like the usual type", but once they started to play, we were sold on them immediately. John stood out because he was so forceful at the front and reminded us of Eddie Cochran as his hair was brushed back off his face. I remember that we thought Paul was good-looking too. Not only did they look different, but their attitude immediately set them apart from other groups. There was a confidence about them, and Joan and I were transfixed.

It was an unforgettable show. They played a range of rock 'n' roll hits including 'Clarabella', 'Dizzy Miss Lizzy' and 'Long Tall Sally'. But the night stays in my mind for other reasons too. As my parents had warned, Hambleton Hall was a rough venue, and our evening of fun took a disastrous turn when a riot broke out in the ladies' cloakroom. We didn't know what was happening, but there was water everywhere because a sink had been pulled off the wall. To top it off, Joan's coat had been stolen and we didn't know how we were going to explain this to her parents because we'd been forbidden to go there! So, there we were, two fifteen-year-olds, crying in the car park trying to figure out how to get home, and knowing we would be in trouble when we did. Luckily for us, Gerry and the Pacemakers saw us and said that if we waited for them to pack up their gear, they'd give us a lift home.

It was freezing, Joan had no coat, and we were very grateful to get a lift home in their van!

So we'd had our first taste of The Beatles and we were hooked. We agreed that we had to go and see them again as soon as possible, and found out from the Mersey Beat newspaper (the font of all Liverpool music news) where they were playing.

From 1961 to 1962, we saw them play at various venues around Liverpool such as The Iron Door, the Aintree Institute and The Cavern (more on this later). The Aintree Institute was a large venue with a high stage - they would cram people in so there would often be a crush by the stage. We would try to stand as close as possible to the front, to get a view of our favourite Beatle and shout our requests to them.

Such was our commitment, despite not having any transport, we would also venture further afield to see them at The Plaza Ballroom in St Helen's, where one night, we were again at the front, and requested 'Long Tall Sally', and Paul said, "This one kills me throat, but I'll do it for these two flossies here!"

One time I thought I'd come up with a great way to see my favourite band perform. A friend of the family, Brian Collins, managed the Rialto Ballroom in Toxteth (he took over from my mum) and I excitedly told him all about The Beatles and what a great draw they would be. I persuaded him to book them, which he did twice in 1962. Sadly, my cunning plan didn't pay off as my mum wouldn't let me go - she said the Rialto was in a rough area. It also didn't get a great turnout. I was devastated on both counts.

MY FIRST JOB AND GOING TO THE CAVERN

Although I was a keen learner, I absolutely hated school - I attended Everton Valley, which was a convent school run by very strict nuns, and I couldn't wait to leave, so decided it would be a great idea to follow my older sister, Maureen, into hairdressing. She managed to arrange an apprenticeship for me, at the salon where she worked, Ellison Lea on Great Charlotte Street.

It was one of the top salons in Liverpool and I was overjoyed to start earning my own money: £1, 17 shillings and sixpence a week. One of the girls who worked there showed me how to open a bank account, which was uncommon for 15-year-olds at the time! Not only could I buy my own clothes, but I was having my hair styled for free!

The salon was above the first branch of NEMS to be opened in the city centre, long before the larger Whitechapel shop was opened. It was part of the Epstein family business and Brian, the eldest son of Harry and Queenie Epstein, was in charge of the record department. We used to regularly go down to his shop, to look through the albums and listen to them in the listening booths. Brian's office was on the first floor, and he would come out and look down the stairs, to see if we were buying anything, or just standing in the booths enjoying the latest releases for free. We would listen for as long as we could get away with it, before being chased out when they realised we weren't buying that day! Luckily, the staff knew us well, and were quite tolerant until a paying customer would want to use the booth.

Over the road from Ellison Lea was another salon called Andre Bernard, where Paul McCartney's brother Mike worked. Also working in the salon was comedian and future London Palladium host, Jimmy Tarbuck, and Lewis Collins from the TV series The Professionals! We used to wave at them from the second-floor window.

Coincidentally, George Harrison had an apprenticeship across the road at Blacklers Department Store as an electrician, but I didn't know this at the time - I only found out many years later.

A massive plus point of my new job was that it was only a ten-minute walk from The Cavern, which meant I could get to the lunchtime sessions on my break; usually, I would go at least twice a week and only when The Beatles were on. Another friend, Marianne, wasn't working so she used to get down there early and save our seats. I'd try to make sure that our receptionist booked my last appointment no later than 11 o'clock so that I'd be finished in plenty of time to make my way down to Mathew Street; if I ran, I could make it there in less than ten minutes! Mathew Street mostly consisted of the backs of warehouses such as the Fruit Exchange and it was very rundown at the time. It was quite grimy and unkempt. I'd always say a quick hello to Paddy Delaney, the doorman, on the way in. He was a lovely, friendly man and he got to know us all quite well.

PADDY DELANEY CHECKING MEMBERSHIP CARDS

BERNADETTE AND FRIENDS IN THEIR COVETED FAVOURITE SEATS!
- (L-R) SUSAN, MARIANNE, JOAN AND BERNADETTE

When it was busy, entering The Cavern was like opening an oven door. It had its own smell, a mixture of hotdogs, smoke, toilets, sweat, and disinfectant (which was used to try to mask the stench of the night before) - five ingredients that combined to produce the unique Cavern smell. The paint on the walls was peeling and when it was very hot, condensation would drip onto our heads from above. My colleagues at the salon always knew when I'd been down to The Cavern as I'd reek of the place when I went back to work. In fact, one day, my boss, Ted Lea, said I looked like a drowned rat when I got back - that was how humid it was! He told my sister, Maureen, that I had to stop coming back to the salon reeking of disinfectant with flat, wet hair stuck to my head!

There was a sort of unwritten law about who sat where in The Cavern. My two friends and I would sit in the alcove to the left of the stage as you faced it, and I'd push my way through the packed-in crowd to 'our' spot, hoping that Marianne had managed to secure our seats.

It was such an incredible atmosphere. Bob Wooler would be hosting, playing the latest records before the band came on and in between sets. The audience would be chattering loudly so they could hear each other over the records. Lunchtime sessions lasted two hours but we couldn't always stay for all of it. It was pretty dark and very smoky, with a couple of spotlights lighting the stage. There was very little room for dancing so people would just have to stomp their feet on the spot.

As we were sat down at the side of the stage, we had a bird's-eye view of their shoes, and we used to watch Paul and George's feet, working in rhythm to the music. One would bang his toe, the other would bang his heel. The audience shouted requests, which they would happily play. John would often respond with curt, funny, and sometimes insulting comments to try and get a laugh.

It was quite easy to become friendly with The Beatles. Everyone would hang around the little coffee bar at the back after the show. George was friendly but I don't remember talking to him that much in The Cavern. Paul was chattier and definitely the PR man. Pete kept to himself and didn't mix as much as the others. John was known for being sarcastic, with a cruel wit but a great sense of humour.

THE BEATLES HAVING A LAUGH ON STAGE AND GEORGE POSING FOR THE PHOTO

"You could have knitted us something useful like a guitar case!"

One example of this was when I had decided to make a gift for Paul's birthday. One of my clients at the salon made knitted dolls, so I asked her to make a knitted version of Paul, but in the guise of an insect beetle. I got some material from my brother's old clothes to make jeans and a waistcoat, we made a shirt out of Joan's school blouse, and my brother made a metal guitar at school in his metal-work class. It had antennae made from pipe-cleaners too. We dressed the doll and took it to The Cavern. We needed to get to the band room next to the stage and Paddy would often guard the door to stop unwanted intruders, but he liked our knitted gift and let us in, and we presented it to Paul. Paul and the others were very kind and said it was lovely... then John piped up, "You could have knitted us something useful like a guitar case!" That was so typical of John. We were a bit embarrassed but pleased that we managed to deliver our gift to Paul personally.

I remember when Brian Epstein first came down to The Cavern on 9th November 1961. I was stood at the coffee bar at the back, and I remember seeing him come down the stairs. I recognised him from his shop. I remember Bob Wooler announced that he would like to welcome a special guest to the venue, "Mr. Brian Epstein of NEMS." He was with Alistair Taylor, and they stood out because of their smart appearance - they were in suits and overcoats. Not what the rest of the Cave-dwellers wore!

Watching The Beatles at lunchtime sessions around this time was probably when we saw them at their best. The girls didn't scream at them until later, so we could see and hear them properly.

BERNADETTE: I ASKED THEM TO SIGN THE BACK OF A PHOTOGRAPH MOUNT AS IT WAS THE ONLY THING I HAD ON ME AT THE TIME - JOHN'S SIGNATURE IS PARTIALLY RIPPED OFF.

BRIAN EPSTEIN

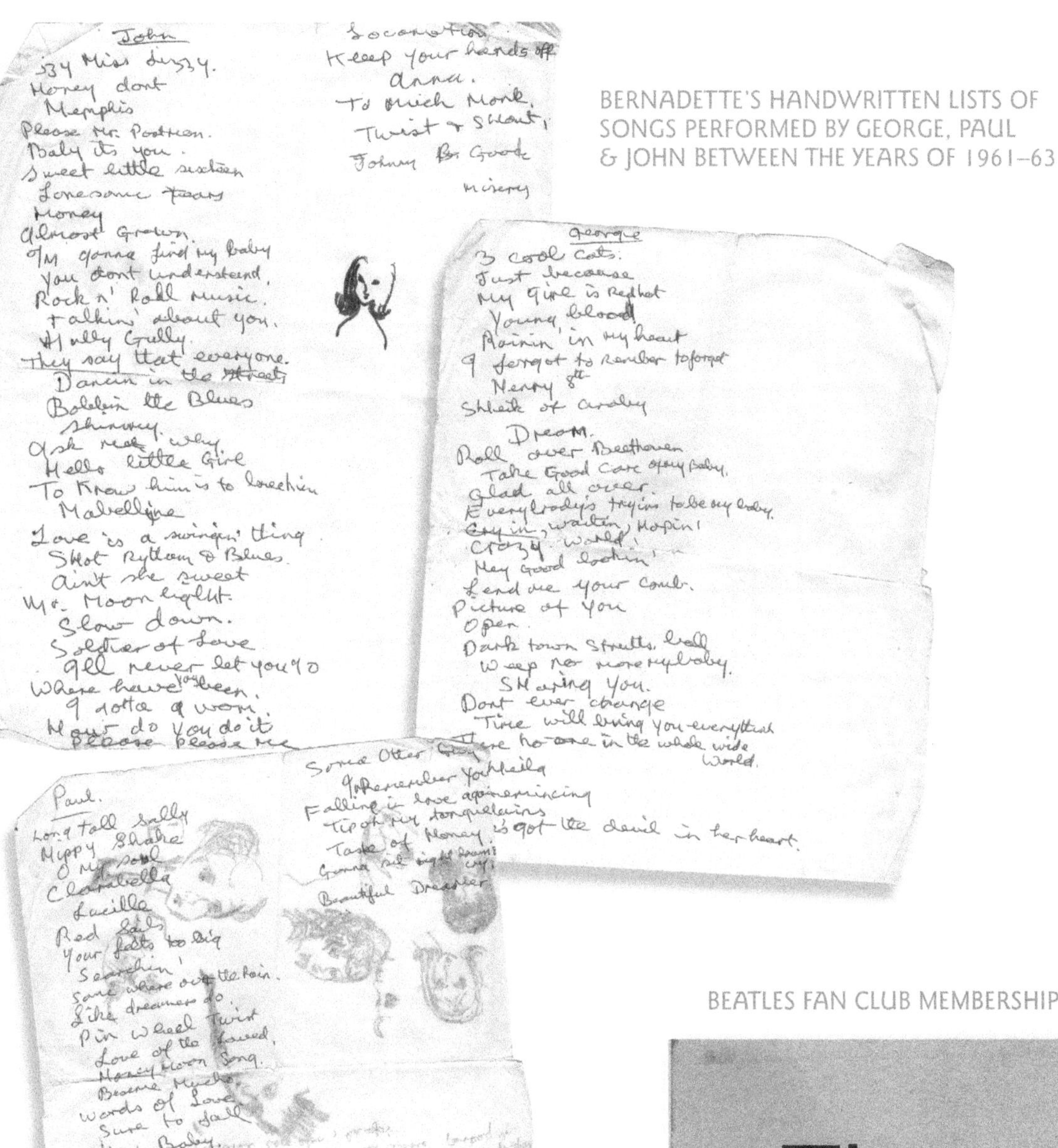

John
34 Miss Lizzy.
Honey dont
Memphis
Please Mr. Postman.
Baby its you.
Sweet little sixteen
Lonesome tears
Money
Almost Grown
I'm gonna find my baby
You dont understand.
Rock n' Roll music.
Talkin' about you.
Hully Gully.
They say that everyone.
Dancin in the street
Shimmy.
Hello little Girl
To Know him is to love him
Love is a swingin' thing
Shot Rythm & Blues.
Aint she sweet
Mr. Moonlight.
Slow down.
Soldier of Love
I'll never let you go
Where have you been.
I gotta a woman
How do you do it
Please please me
Locomotion.
Keep your hands off Anna.
To much monk.
Twist & Shout.
Johnny B. Goode
misery

George
3 cool cats.
Just because
My girl is red hot
Young blood
Rainin' in my heart
I forgot to remember to forget
Henry 8th
Sheik of Araby
Dream.
Roll over Beethoven
Take Good Care of my baby.
Glad all over.
Everybody's tryin to be my baby.
Cryin, waitin, Hopin!
Crazy world!
Hey good lookin'
Lend me your comb.
Picture of you
Open.
Dark town Strutters ball
Weep no more my baby.
Sharing you.
Dont ever change
Time will bring you everything
There's no-one in the whole wide World.

Paul.
Long Tall Sally
Hippy Shake
O My soul
Clarabella
Lucille
Red Sails
Your feets too big
Searchin'!
Somewhere over the rain.
Like dreamers do.
Pin wheel Twist
Love of the loved.
Honeymoon Song.
Besame Mucho.
Words of Love
Sure to fall
Hey Baby.
Dream baby.
If you gotta make a fool
Wedding Bells
Buzz Buzz
That's alright mama
September in the rain.
Till there was you
Everyday.
Love me do
PS I love you
Rip it up
Some Other Guy
Falling in love again
Taste of Honey
She's got the devil in her heart.
Beautiful Dreamer

BERNADETTE'S HANDWRITTEN LISTS OF SONGS PERFORMED BY GEORGE, PAUL & JOHN BETWEEN THE YEARS OF 1961–63

BEATLES FAN CLUB MEMBERSHIP CARD

MEMBERSHIP CARD

Name MISS BERNADETTE FARRELL

No. 212

Next subscription due APRIL 63.

Member's Signature Bernadette Farrell

The Beatles Fan Club

C/o Miss R. BROWN,
90 BUCHANAN ROAD,
WALLASEY,
CHESHIRE.

By 1962, their popularity was soaring; they'd had an official fan club for a while and in April they ran an advert in Mersey Beat to say that they would be playing at The Cavern on April 5th, and anyone who bought a ticket would get a free signed postcard and could apply for a free membership to the fan club. Of course, we couldn't miss out on this and made sure we were there that night!

In 1985, I was chatting to Pete Best at The Beatle Convention, and I showed it to him as a reminder. He signed it again for me which is why I have five signatures on this card!

Sometime in 1962, we were milling around at the back of The Cavern after a Beatles lunchtime session when my friend and I got chatting to Bobbie Brown, who had set up the very first Beatles Fan Club. She was still running it and said she was struggling to cope with the band's growing popularity and the associated fan-mail that came with it. We offered to help out and went over to her house in Wallasey, where she ran the club from. We helped her to sort through the letters so that they could be delivered to the intended Beatle. Not long after this, her friend Freda Kelly took over the running of the fan club, and she would become the longest-serving secretary of the Beatles Fan Club.

In early August 1962, I went down to a lunchtime session and bumped into a group of irate fans outside the club. They asked if I'd heard what had happened and revealed their outrage and upset that Pete Best had been sacked! It was all anyone talked about, and people were in shock that such a thing could happen. For a while afterwards, at shows, you would hear some of Pete's fans shout "Pete forever, Ringo never!" In fact, poor George was on the receiving end of a black eye from one of Pete's fans. I think they held them all responsible and took their rage out on the nearest Beatle!

We were excited when we found out Granada TV was coming down to film their first-ever TV appearance on August 22nd. However, we were not impressed as we couldn't get near our usual seats and had to stand on some chairs at the back to get a glimpse of the show. It was absolutely packed, and you could tell that their appeal was outgrowing The Cavern.

SIGNED POSTCARD
- OBTAINED AT THE CAVERN ON APRIL 5TH

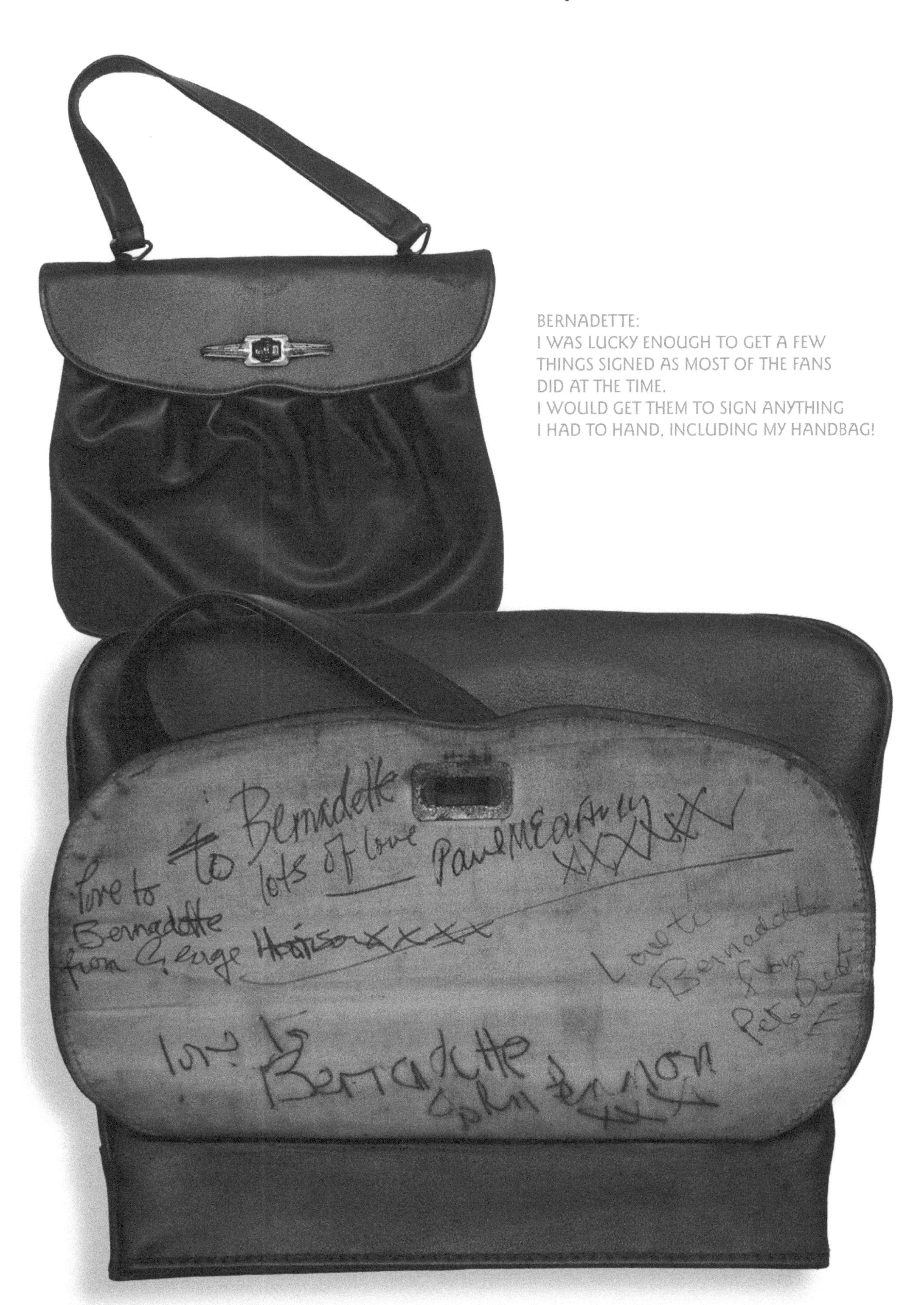

BERNADETTE:
I WAS LUCKY ENOUGH TO GET A FEW THINGS SIGNED AS MOST OF THE FANS DID AT THE TIME.
I WOULD GET THEM TO SIGN ANYTHING I HAD TO HAND, INCLUDING MY HANDBAG!

THE BEATLES' GROWING POPULARITY

As the group's popularity grew, they would play bigger and better venues. Sometimes we would go 'over the water' on the ferry to The Tower Ballroom in New Brighton. The Beatles supported some huge names there, including some of their heroes such as Little Richard and Jerry Lee Lewis. I remember it would sometimes get really busy and Joan and I once got badly crushed by the crowd when we were standing near the front!

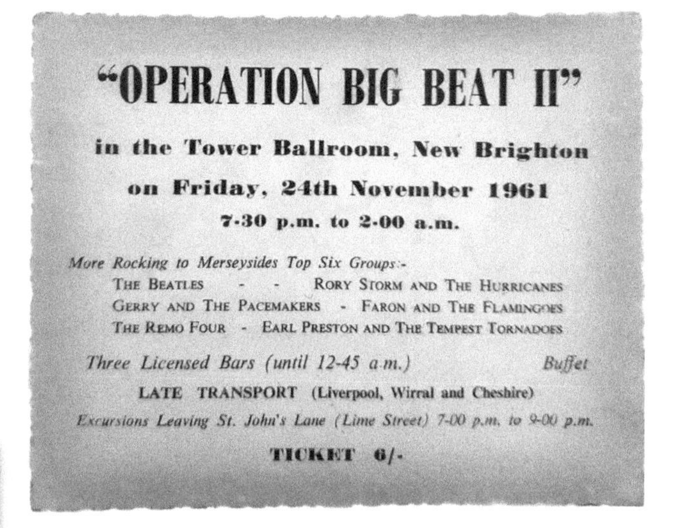
"OPERATION BIG BEAT II"

in the Tower Ballroom, New Brighton

on Friday, 24th November 1961

7-30 p.m. to 2-00 a.m.

More Rocking to Merseysides Top Six Groups:-

THE BEATLES - - RORY STORM AND THE HURRICANES

GERRY AND THE PACEMAKERS - FARON AND THE FLAMINGOES

THE REMO FOUR - EARL PRESTON AND THE TEMPEST TORNADOES

Three Licensed Bars (until 12-45 a.m.) *Buffet*

LATE TRANSPORT (Liverpool, Wirral and Cheshire)

Excursions Leaving St. John's Lane (Lime Street) 7-00 p.m. to 9-00 p.m.

TICKET 6/-

"Operation Big Beat I" *(last Friday, Nov. 10th) was such a phenomenal success, that by public demand we now present*

"OPERATION BIG BEAT II"

at the TOWER BALLROOM, NEW BRIGHTON

on FRIDAY, 24th NOVEMBER 1961

7-30 p.m. to 2-00 a.m.

THE "BIGGEST BEAT" *LINE UP EVER*

The Beatles - Rory Storm and The Hurricanes

Gerry and The Pacemakers - The Remo Four

Earl Preston and the Tempest Tornadoes

Faron and The Flamingoes

Three Licensed Bars *(until 12-45 a.m.)* Buffet

TICKET 6/-

TRANSPORT ARRANGEMENTS:-

Excursions (to Tower and Return) from St. John's Lane, (Lime Street) 7-0 p.m. to 9-0 p.m. Friday 24th November

(Ring Crown Coachways CENtral 6107)

ALSO LATE TRANSPORT

From Tower Ballroom to the following:-

To LIVERPOOL *Circular Trip to All Areas.*

To WIRRAL, *Wallasey, Seacombe, Birkenhead, Hoylake, W. Kirby, Leasowe, Moreton, Heswall, Bidston, Ellesmere Port, ETC.*

It was always a race after the shows ended to catch the last ferry back to Liverpool, or we would end up stranded on the wrong side of the Mersey. Occasionally we would get a lift back with one of the support bands who we knew on the scene. Billy Hatton from The Fourmost was a friend with whom we used to have a laugh and joke, and he once gave us a lift back.

In the autumn of 1962, I remember George started offering me a lift home after the Cavern sessions. I was on a different bus route to my friends and had to wait on my own on Church Street. One day, a blue Ford Anglia pulled up and it was George. He wound the window down and offered me a lift home and of course, I accepted. A lift home from a Beatle and a chance to escape the cold! He was always very polite, and we'd talk about the show and what they had been up to, but he didn't ask me out. Strangely, I can still remember that number plate as I'd look out for it when he was coming to pick me up - 935 MPF.

My older sister Maureen was very friendly with Jimmy Tarbuck, who was a well-known comedian by this time, and his wife Pauline. Jimmy was moving in celebrity circles as he had shot to fame quite quickly. He knew that I was disappointed not to have been able to get a ticket for a big show that NEMS was putting on at the Liverpool Empire one evening. It was to be headlined by Little Richard with support from The Beatles and several other acts including Kenny Lynch.

EMPIRE TICKET STUB FOR LITTLE RICHARD SHOW WHICH FEATURED SUPPORT FROM THE BEATLES

Jimmy was very friendly with Kenny and said he could get me in if I wanted to go. Naturally, I jumped at the chance, and not only did I get to see the show, but I was taken backstage to meet some of the artists afterwards. Strangely, I don't recall much of the evening, except that I was very pleased to get to hang around with The Beatles and some of the other acts!

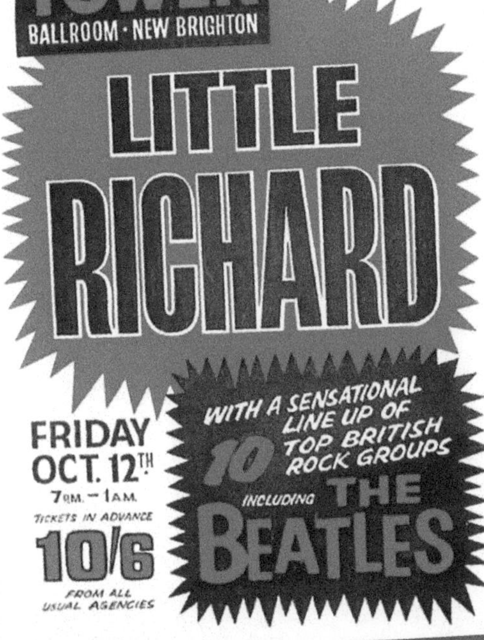

GEORGE AND HIS BLUE FORD ANGLIA

THE BEATLES WITH ONE OF THEIR HEROES, LITTLE RICHARD, AT THE TOWER BALLROOM, NEW BRIGHTON

PAUL

One night after a show at The Cavern, Marianne, Joan and I were walking up Mathew Street to catch the bus home. A green Ford Consul Classic car pulled up alongside us and inside Paul was driving, with John in the passenger seat. Paul leaned out and offered us a lift home. We were very pleased, as not only did we not have to get the bus, but it was two of the Beatles! We dropped the other two off first, and I was last. When we pulled up outside my house, John bluntly announced, "Paul will be around to pick you up tomorrow night!"

"Well he's not asking you to marry him!"

I was taken by surprise and replied, "Oh, I can't. I'm working." John's bizarre retort was, "Well he's not asking you to marry him!"

I think Paul was too shy to ask me out, so John took the matter into his own hands. It was such an odd encounter, and I didn't know what to make of it, but Paul walked me to the front door, and we arranged a suitable time for him to collect me after work the next day.

"that fella who nearly burnt the house down!"

Paul arrived promptly the next day in a very smart, dark, three-quarter, velvet ribbed overcoat. He was carrying a box of Maltesers for me, which I thought was a very nice gesture. While I finished getting ready, I told him to wait in the lounge where my dad, Bill, was lighting a coal fire. He asked Paul to help get the fire going by holding up a newspaper to the opening. This is something we used to do to help draw the draught up the flue. Unfortunately, the paper caught light and went up in flames. I heard my dad's choice language from upstairs and ran down to discover a room full of smoke and charred bits of newspaper floating around the room. Paul was stood there looking flustered and apologising and I doubt this is what he had in mind, especially when wearing his best coat. Whenever my dad heard Paul's name after that, he would be known as "that fella who nearly burnt the house down!" (Or more colourful words to that effect!)

He took me to the ABC Forum Cinema in Lime Street where I remember him being shocked to see me wearing spectacles. Straight away he said, "I didn't know you wore glasses!" He bought me an ice cream that I managed to drip down my front and I remember feeling very self-conscious for the rest of the film.

FORUM CINEMA IN LIME STREET WHERE PAUL TOOK BERNADETTE ON THEIR DATE

BERNADETTE'S SIGNED COPY OF 'LOVE ME DO'

After the cinema, we went to the Blue Angel for a drink, then he drove us back to Rory Storm's house, or as it was known, 'Stormsville'. All the bands went here after shows for their supper, as Rory's Mum, Vi, would make them egg and chips. When we got there, George was already settled in an armchair eating his supper. By now, I knew him quite well to chat to, because he'd given me a lift home quite a few times from various venues.

So I got to spend a lovely evening, chatting with Paul and George. It was just before they headed back to Hamburg for the last time, and I recall them saying that they didn't want to go as things were really starting to happen for them in Liverpool. But I think they were resigned to it and were professional enough even then to honour their commitments.

As we came out of Rory's house, there was snow on the ground, and for some unknown reason, George ran up behind me and tried to lift me up, but as he did, he slipped, and we both fell flat on our backs. I was surprised and embarrassed but saw the funny side and we both had a good laugh about it. However, Paul just looked at George, seemingly irritated at such childish behaviour, and probably wondered what on earth he was doing! It's funny to think back now.

After this, Paul and I just became friends who would see each other around the clubs and bars of Liverpool.

In November 1962, not long after 'Love Me Do' had been released, they went off on their last trip to Hamburg. Many fans, including me, bought the single and got them to sign it at one of their Cavern shows.

There was a feeling amongst fans that this success would take them away from Liverpool and some fans wrote to them, asking them not to go.

GEORGE

Shortly after they returned from Hamburg, I got a note through my front door from George asking me to call him. (I've still got that note. I must have known it might be of interest one day!) I was quite surprised but very pleased, and nervously called him back the next day. He asked me if I'd like to go to the pictures and we arranged it for his next night off.

He arrived as planned in his blue Anglia and we went to the Abbey Cinema in Wavertree, and afterwards he took me to The Cabaret Club where we saw Tessie O'Shea play. I don't know if it was a scheduled performance or she was simply there as a guest who ended up doing a performance. She was an accomplished ukulele player and would go on to be a guest on the same Ed Sullivan Show as The Beatles. We had a lovely time that evening and started dating.

His diary was extremely busy as they had a lot of touring commitments but when he had a rare night off we would usually go out to clubs and bars in town, or back to the Abbey Cinema as he loved films. (This was later referenced in the original handwritten lyrics of 'In My Life'.)

We would sometimes go to the Odd Spot Club on Bold Street, a late-night, narrow basement bar where The Beatles had played a couple of times in the past. It was a less popular venue, which appealed to George as they were starting to get more well-known at this time and he liked to avoid the attention.

He drank whisky and coke, and I'd have a gin and lime. In fact, I remember him saying that my Blue Grass perfume smelled like gin! He used to smoke all the time; the brand was Peter Stuyvesant, I think. Even though I wasn't a smoker, I didn't mind as it was so commonplace and fashionable in those days.

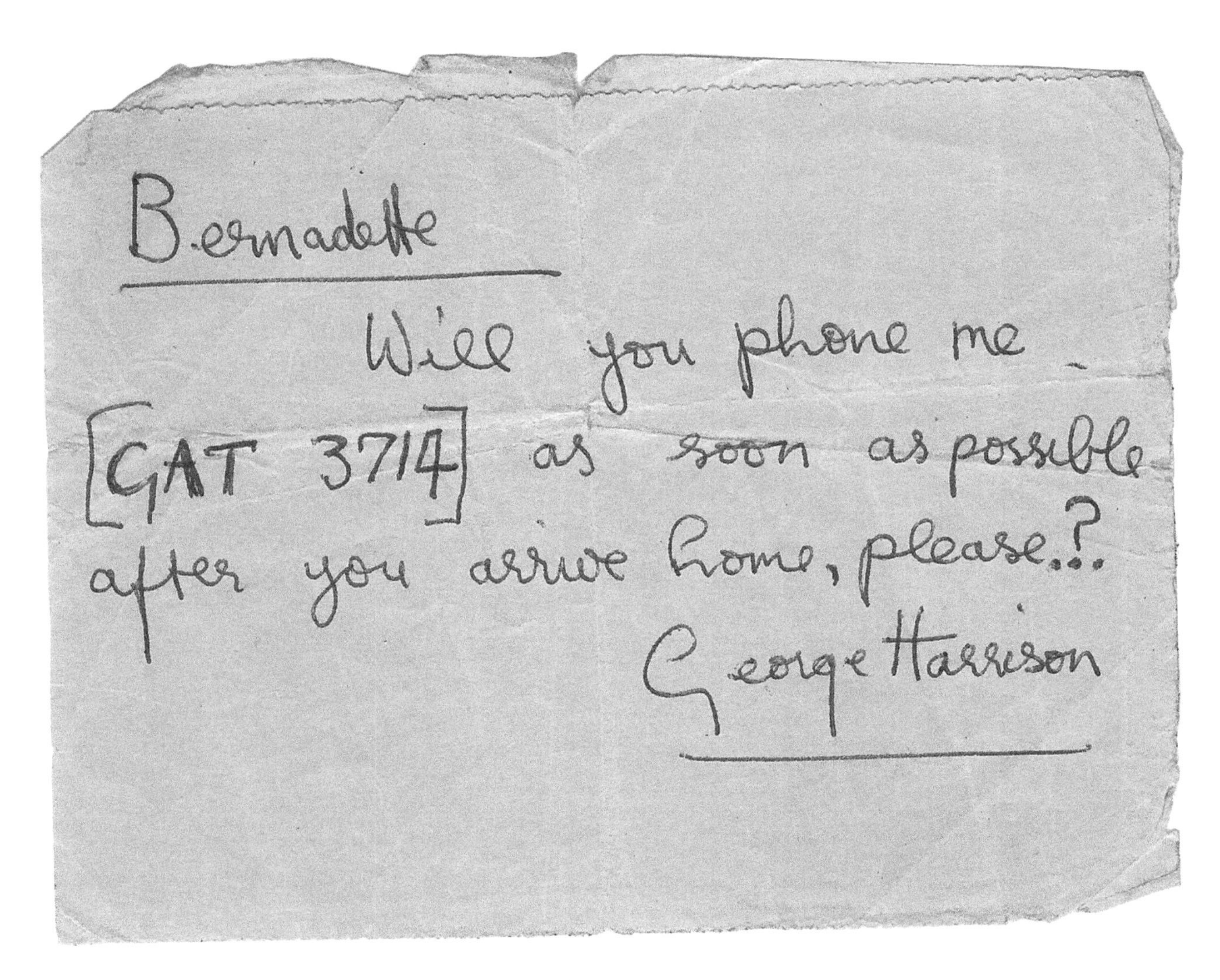

Bernadette

Will you phone me [GAT 3714] as soon as possible after you arrive home, please.?.

George Harrison

NOTE FROM GEORGE HARRISON ASKING BERNADETTE TO CALL HIM

A POLAROID PHOTO OF BERNADETTE AND GEORGE TAKEN BEFORE ONE OF THEIR DATES.
NOTE THE DETERIORATION AFTER 6 DECADES!

THE ABBEY CINEMA IN WAVERTREE, WHERE GEORGE TOOK BERNADETTE ON SEVERAL DATES
(N.B THIS WAS TAKEN IN 1972)

One night we decided to go to the Blue Angel, which was owned and managed by Allan Williams. Allan had been The Beatles' first manager, who sent them to Hamburg, but he subsequently fell out with them over non-payment of commission. He was a successful businessman and owned the Blue Angel as well as the Jacaranda on Slater Street. The Blue Angel, or 'the Blue' as we called it, was the club of choice for celebrities who had performed in the city that night. So although George was more likely to be recognised there, he didn't mind going as people didn't bother him too much. He was often not the most famous person there.

"You behave yourself with her... I know her mother!"

To gain entry, you would have to knock on the door, and the doorman, Dave Beatty, would open the door and let you in. Funnily enough, when Allan first opened the Blue, he had high aspirations for its clientele and said he didn't want any local riffraff or musicians coming in, but he'd obviously changed his mind by the time The Beatles were becoming rising stars! As we made our way to the bar, we bumped into Allan, who said to George, "You behave yourself with her... I know her mother!" Our families went back years, and we spent many family occasions together. George just laughed the comment off and ordered our drinks.

VISIT
THE ODD SPOT CLUB
89 BOLD STREET

January
6th—PHIL MORGAN'S JAZZ BAND
7th—ROYAL CARIBBEAN STEEL BAND
11th—LEO RUTHERFORD QUARTET
12th—DAVE LIND JAZZ BAND
13th—ART REID JAZZ BAND
14th—RON PARRY INC.
18th—DIXON HALL QUARTET

I also remember that night he mentioned he had seen a band called The Rolling Stones while he had been in London. He said they were good but not as good as the Liverpool Roadrunners! (Ironically this was the band Mike would join a couple of years later.)

As The Beatles' fame grew, during the early part of 1963, he was getting noticed more frequently and we were aware that people were looking in our direction when we were out. He would keep his head down and try to remain inconspicuous, and I tried not to ask him too many questions about The Beatles' increasing fame and popularity. I sensed that he wasn't overly comfortable with it, and it was quickly gaining momentum. I tended not to go to as many Beatles shows while we were dating as they were under so much pressure to meet and greet fans and press and I didn't want to add to this.

He was also aware that as their popularity grew, it would be the last time that they would be able to play some of the smaller venues they were booked at. This show at Queen's Hall in Widnes was billed as a 'Sensational Farewell Showdance'. I couldn't go that night as I was at night school, though I did see them play the next night at The Cavern, and afterwards George came back to our house for tea and toast.

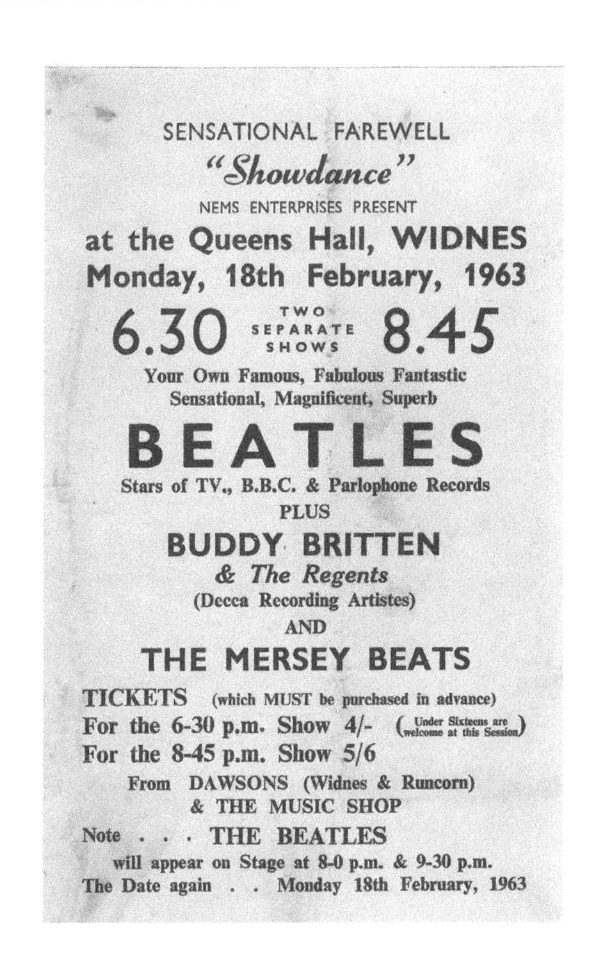

One thing George did enjoy about their increasing success was the fact that they were earning good money, and he was able to invest in one of his true passions - cars. It wasn't long before he traded in his Anglia for a beautiful green Jaguar. He called me and wanted to take me out in it, but I was busy bleaching my sister's hair. He was so excited to show it off that he came over to my sister's house and while I finished her hair he gave her husband a guided tour. We were all very impressed, not least by its walnut dashboard and electric windows, then we all went for a drive in it. It was certainly a step up from his Ford Anglia.

GEORGE WITH BERNADETTE AND HER SISTER MAUREEN – SADLY THE QUALITY IS DIMINSHED AFTER 6 DECADES

He was mad about cars and liked to drive fast. He decided to introduce me to his brother Harry, and his family, who lived in Ellesmere Port. This was a good distance from Liverpool and allowed him to give his Jaguar a good run. On the way there, he was going so fast we hit the kerb on a bend and the car nearly turned over. I was terrified but he seemed quite unperturbed; in fact, he seemed to enjoy the thrill. I was relieved to make it to his brother's house in one piece, where he introduced me to his niece, Janet, and nephew, Paul, and I played with them while we had a cup of tea.

I remember one time in April 1963, he arrived outside my house, having driven straight back from London after their first appearance at the Royal Albert Hall. I wasn't expecting him, and it threw me because he was in Paul's car, a Ford Consul. He told me that Paul had decided to stay in London as they had met Jane Asher at the show and Paul was keen on her!

In March 1963, 'Please Please Me' had been released, and by the April of that year, it had sold 250,000 copies. One night in April, I remember him coming to our house and being full of beans as he pulled out a silver disc in a presentation box. Each Beatle had been presented with a silver disc because the single had sold 250,000 copies. My mum wanted to know if it would play on our record player! Such happy memories.

He would also bring LPs like The Cookies and The Marvelettes to play on our record player. He'd picked them up on a trip to the US to visit his sister. I feel I was there at such a special time to see him getting excited about silver discs and new cars but there were already signs of what was to come in terms of fame, attention and success.

One time, they were recording in Manchester for the BBC Light Programme's radio show called Here We Go. We didn't have tickets, and I certainly wasn't going to ask George for any, but I was interested to hear the performance live, and Bob Wooler encouraged people to go and support them. So instead of asking George, a friend and I got the train over early afternoon and turned up at the stage door of the Playhouse Theatre in Hulme. We told the doorman that we had been invited (well, it was a broad invitation!).

As luck would have it, Paul walked past the doorway, saw us outside, and told him to let us in. We got to see the rehearsal from the theatre circle along with the invited press pack, but I didn't even try to speak to George as they were busy trying to work out the ending of a new song they had written, which turned out to be 'Do You Want to Know a Secret'. They were due to perform it for the first time live on air. I remember they were struggling to get it right, but we didn't mind. We stayed to watch the full recording and caught the last train back to Liverpool.

George's tour diary was getting busier by the day, and they were frequently travelling from the north to the south several times a week at this point. Sometimes, if I hadn't been able to see him for a while, he'd just call in for supper after a show, or on his way to another part of the country for the next one. One night, after a show in Stoke, in April 1963, they had broken down on their way back to Liverpool. Even though he was exhausted, he made time to bring a couple of signed photographs which my colleagues at work had asked for.

He stayed for some supper and talked to my mum and me before heading home. The next night they had a show in Frodsham, after which they were heading to the NME Poll Winners' Concert in London, where they were second on the bill after Cliff Richard. He arranged to pick me up from night school the following Monday, 22nd April, when they had a rare night off.

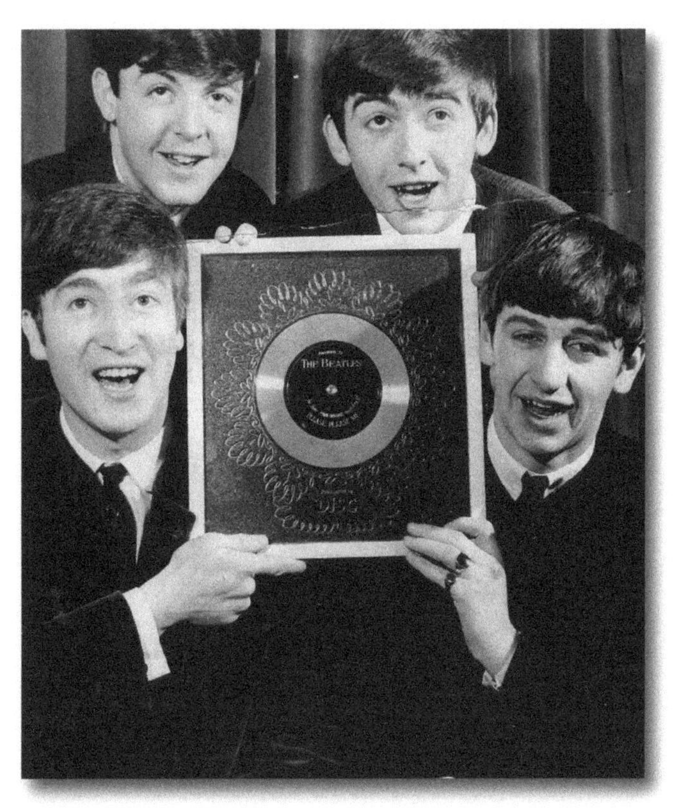

My mum asked George if the silver disc would play on our record player!

THE BEATLES AT THE DOCKS WITH PAUL'S FORD CONSUL 315 CLASSIC - GEORGE DROVE BACK FROM LONDON IN THIS TO SEE BERNADETTE

THE START OF BEATLEMANIA

On 23 April 1963, they had a show at The Floral Hall in Southport, and George had arranged to leave tickets on the door for me. He said that if I could get a lift there, he'd drive me back with his mum afterwards. So my sister and her husband took me there and we all watched the show from the back of the hall. It was hard to hear them over the screaming girls, but the atmosphere was incredible.

After the show, my sister went home as I was going back to George's house with him and his mum, Louise. Tony Bramwell, who was a close friend of George's and went on to work closely with them, met us in the foyer and took us out of a side entrance to where George's car was parked, hidden from the public. At this stage in their career, they were besieged by fans wherever they went, and the fans were getting increasingly persistent and numerous.

With Louise and me safely seated in the back of the car, the plan was for Tony to drive us to the stage door at the back of the theatre, jump out and let George get into the driver's seat. Unfortunately, as we approached the stage door, we could see a crowd of fans waiting, and we had no choice but to drive up to collect George (there were no mobile phones in those days to make an alternative plan!). As we pulled up to the door, George came out and was mobbed by screaming girls asking for autographs and trying to touch him. He pushed his way to the car as fast as possible, and Tony jumped out, leaving the engine running, but in the kerfuffle, as George climbed in, his arm got trapped in the door. I think Tony had slammed it too soon in the mayhem.

Despite being pretty shaken up, and with a sore arm, he had to cautiously drive away with the car surrounded by fans. We had all locked our doors, but it was still quite frightening, and he was pretty angry at the time. Fortunately, there was no permanent damage, and he had a lucky escape; this was certainly an early sign that Beatlemania had begun and that they were going to have to increase security and make better plans in the future for getting to and from venues.

At the end of April 1963, George went on holiday to Tenerife with Paul and Ringo. They stayed with their friend, Klaus Voorman, whose family had a villa there, and Astrid joined them. At the same time, John Lennon went away with Brian Epstein to Barcelona (controversially just a few weeks after Cynthia, his wife, had given birth to their son, Julian).

I was pleased for George that he had managed to get a break after such a busy and chaotic few years, and in hindsight, this was the last time they were able to get away and really relax, without being recognised. He sent me a postcard from their trip, addressing it to 'Bernydet', which was his pet name for me. He was keen to inform me that they had seen "many bullfights and onions, but not a senorita anywhere!"

He signed it from George [A BAND] – his tongue-in-cheek joke in case I wasn't sure who it was from!

"many bullfights and onions, but not a senorita anywhere!"

I was very happy to receive such a nice postcard from George, and we had arranged to go out on May 10th, which was the night after he got back. They had a couple of nights off before they were back out on the road again. But to my surprise and embarrassment, he decided to come and see me as soon as he got home. I was sitting in the living room, with my hair in rollers, hoping to look my best for his return the next day. My younger brother answered the door, and without any warning, showed him straight in.

I can still picture him now, walking in with a nice tan and wearing a lovely beige suede jacket that he had bought on holiday. He took one look at me and said, "So... this is the Face of Beauty!"

He was referring to a weekly article called 'The Face of Beauty' that Bill Harry had decided to run in Mersey Beat. It featured girls who went to popular music venues and dance halls around Liverpool. While George had been away, Bill chose me to appear, and George's mum had spotted it and told him about it. I was absolutely mortified and though I was very happy to see him, ran straight up the stairs to take my rollers out!

It was around this time that I was asked to do some modelling and it was fashionable to photograph girls out and about on the lively Liverpool music scene. The Beatles and the Merseybeat scene were attracting nationwide attention.

We carried on seeing each other when we could, but I accepted that fame was starting to take hold, and work commitments were taking them all over the country. He had to cancel one of our dates as he unexpectedly had to judge an amateur band contest at the Philharmonic Hall.

Dear Bernydet, [MAY]

Hi. Tis very rainy and bananas here in Tenapenny but the natives are very friendly. We have see many bull fights and onions but not a senorita anywhere. It feels quite healthy with the wind and the rain, but apart from that its great. Dont believe the picture on the card, I haivent seen such a thing here, it looks good tho'. tara

love frae

George [A BAND]

MRS BERNADETTE FARREL

79, CHILDWALL LANE

WOOLTON

LIVERPOOL 25.

ENGLAND

THE POSTCARD GEORGE SENT TO 'BERNYDET' FROM TENERIFE

PAGE 4 — MERSEY BEAT — May 9—23, 1963

The Face of Beauty

Miss Bernadette Farrell of Childwall Lane, Liverpool, leading junior hairstylist at Ellison Lea's (Great Charlotte St. and Prescot Road) models the teenagers' favourite style for Spring, 1963. The colour is Starlight Silver, the line dressed upwards from the neck into cascading curls from the crown of the head.

Bernadette is a pioneer habitue' of The Cavern, The Mardi Gras and Downbeat Clubs and, in company with her many staff associates, an ardent Beatle fan.

TV STAR— THE CAVERN

The Cavern Club featured in two television programmes last week-end. On Saturday evening the ABC At Large team moved into the club to televise excerpts [illegible] appeared on the air later that evening.

On Sunday, The Cavern featured in the Sunday Break Programme. Between 6-15 and 7 o'clock, camera men were in the club and members were being interviewed whilst the programme was being broadcast 'live.'

The interviewer was Jeri Matos, an American, who has appeared on numerous TV programmes. She was discussing church music in relation to the type of musical entertainment youngsters enjoyed.

The Dennisons were the group who were playing at the time of of 'The Sunday Break' programme which was networked and has a high viewing audience in all parts of the country.

READERS LETTERS

LIVERPOOL TV

I am glad to see that the campaign being waged by your paper to bring proper recording studios to Merseyside has had some effect, but it is also important to remember Liverpool's need for local sound and television studios and there is no practical reason for Merseyside not having them.

The Tyneside area, a far smaller region that that of Merseyside, has its own Tyne-Tees ITV station, BBC transmitter and studios and local BBC radio network. Surely it has no more talent than that which abounds on Merseyside.

I can see no reason why the ITA would not allow a local ITV station to operate here, except for a protest from Granada that it would be competition. This could be defended by pointing out that the ITA has already allowed competing stations to [illegible]

[illegible] Granada cease [illegible] Manchester and [illegible] operate in part from [illegible] This has been done by programme company [illegible] stations in both [illegible] Bristol.

Pressure must be [illegible] the BBC to make [illegible] that Merseyside is [illegible] its own account and no[illegible] of Manchester.

RAY PR[illegible]
8 Montrose [illegible]
Wallasey

BEATCOMBER

GUITAR REVOLUTION

by R. Sadleir

Rock groups, by their wholesale adoption of solid body guitars, virtually revolutionised the guitar business. Established [illegible]

THE BANDWAGON BO[illegible]

GUITAR

JAZZSHOWS PRESENT THE MERSEYSIPPI JAZZ BOAT —1963—

Mr. ACKER BILK and his PARAMOUNT JAZZ B[illegible]AND

KE[illegible] BALL [illegible]IEN

AL[illegible]WELSH [illegible] BAND

[illegible]UNSHINE [illegible]AND

THE 'FACE OF BEAUTY' 1963 MERSEY BEAT ARTICLE

PHILHARMONIC HALL PROGRAMME FOR THE BEAT GROUP COMPETITION

BERNADETTE MODELLING WITH MERSEYBEAT GROUP THE DENNISONS

MEET THE BEATBIRDS! (GIRLS WHO DATE THE BEATLES)

by Terry Smith

In a city of proud youngsters they walk with extra pride. In an age of uniformity they stand apart.

Ordinary girls from ordinary homes and doing ordinary jobs . . . but with a rare secret that makes them the envy of millions of teenagers the world over.

They were Beatles' dates when a night out with one of the boys meant a cheap seat in the stalls at a local cinema or a chat over a coffee.

Just an ordinary date with an ordinary guy. But now every word, every second and every kiss – especially the kiss – is locked away and cherished and only brought out for Very Special Friends.

Twenty year-old Pauline Matthews, a pert, gay receptionist in a Liverpool city centre store, was a Beatles' date.

So was Bernadette Farrell, 19, who works in a fashionable Liverpool hairdressing salon. Bernadette, a tall and willowy blonde was dated first by George Harrison and later by Paul McCartney.

Pauline, small and dark, with large expressive eyes was Ringo's steady for a while.

There were other Beatle girls too. Among them 20-year-old Pat Davies, who dated Ringo, and Lorraine Flight who caught George Harrison's eye.

Now all the girls find that some of the Beatles' glamour and glory has rubbed off on them.

People point them out in the street and in dance halls.

Some Beatles fans even discovered Pauline's address and began to write and then call for the lowdown.

Pauline sipped a coke in the very club she and Ringo used to frequent and said: "That's how it is a lot of the time. People are always describing me as Ringo's girl.

"The Beatles were very popular on Merseyside long before they became famous and they had lots of fans and lots of girl friends. I was one of them. When I first met Ringo I was working in a coffee club in Liverpool. He came in one evening on his own and we got into conversation. Before he left he asked to take me out.

"After that we saw quite a bit of each other. Most nights he was playing with the group and I usually met him afterwards. W'd go for a late night coffee.

"On his few free nights we'd go to the pictures." Pauline smiled as she recalled: "Ringo was crazy over films but he always had a preference for horror pictures – the creepier they were the better he liked them."

Another glass of coke was successfully ordered and Pauline continued: "I liked Ringo a lot. The thing which attracted me to him most of all I think was the impression of loneliness he always gave.

"But I don't want to give the impression he was a miserable sort of fellow. Far from it. He had a very dry sense of humour and was great fun to be with on a date.

"Ringo never talked about the group much but I remember he was very excited when their first record looked like being a hit."

Bernadette spent her lunch hour break talking about George Harrison and Ringo Starr.

"I used to follow the Beatles everywhere along with hundreds of other fans" said the girl with the elfin face.

"I got to know all the boys quite well and one night George asked if he could see me home. After that we had scores of dates together.

"George loved talking about beat music. He would go on for hours on the subject to anyone who was prepared to listen. I was a big fan of his and was only too prepared to hang on to his every word."

Bernadette nibbled away at a sandwich and scotched the idea about George being the quiet one. "He's not quiet at all," she said. "In fact, he has a bright and breezy sort of nature and is never stuck for conversation."

Of her dates with Paul Bernadette said: "Paul's personality comes across tremendously in a crowd. He thrives on a lot of company. On a date with just you and him he is quieter but I always found him a really friendly sort of person."

She recalled the Beatles favourite drink: "No doubt about that – it was always whisky and coke."

Blonde hairdresser Lorraine Flight was another of George's dates.

"I remember," she said, "when The Beatles were just starting to become famous and they were worried about the fans knowing they had girl friends, how he used to introduce me as his cousin wherever we went. It was all very secretive – but of course I understood. Girl fans were very fickle in those days."

Pat Davies who works for a Liverpool mail order firm had one very special memory of her dates with Ringo – his acute hatred of onions.

"He hated the sight and smell of them," she said. "Whenever we went anywhere near a restaurant he always steered clear of onions. He definitely had a thing about them."

Maralyin also had another keepsake from Ringo. A copy of the Beatles first record signed "With love from me to you" on it.

But being a Beatle date can pose its problems – just as it did for 18 year-old Elva Jamieson. Elva was friendly with Ringo who visited their home regularly when the full blast of Beatlemania was still to come.

But when the Beatles arrived with a bang on the beat scene rumours swept Britain that Elva and Ringo were to be secretly married.

They were so strong and went on for so long with newspapermen and TV cameramen constantly outside Elva's home that finally her parents had to pay for an advertisement in a local newspaper denying that the couple were engaged or were to be married.

Said Elva "Once you've been a friend of a Beatle you can be pretty sure people are going to know about it and remember you for a very long time."

But none of the Beatle girls will really want to com-

ARTICLE IN U.S. TEEN MAGAZINE – FEATURING THE HEADLINE 'MEET THE BEATBIRDS'

COVER OF U.S. TEEN MAGAZINE – FEATURING THE ARTICLE 'MEET THE BEATBIRDS'

He invited me along, but I couldn't go because I'd caught German measles, presumably from him as he'd had them the week before, so I shouldn't have been going out anyway. (Little did I know that Mike, my future husband, had entered that competition!)

As The Beatles grew more popular, George's fame started having an impact on my life in some ways. Colleagues would ask me to get his autograph, but I was reluctant as I really didn't want to bother him with that sort of thing. I think he saw our relationship as an escape from the madness of Beatlemania and I didn't want to seem like a fan.

I was surprised when I started getting phone calls, in the salon where I worked, from American newspapers asking me about George. The receptionist would come into the salon while I was with a client and tell me there was a journalist on the phone, asking to speak to me. I think they had found out my name because there had been a feature in a US teen magazine which printed a picture of me as one of The Beatles' girlfriends! That's when I truly started to realise the extent of The Beatles' fame. I started receiving letters from disgruntled Beatles fans who knew I was dating George and weren't very happy about it. Some were sent to my house, some to work. I'm not sure how they found out where I lived, but it was a bit unnerving at the time.

I don't remember things ending with George exactly. It just became harder and harder to see each other due to his hectic schedule, and eventually we drifted apart. Of course, the media coverage of their progression meant that I was very aware of where they were a lot of the time.

By the time he was making the film A Hard Day's Night in 1964, I hadn't seen or spoken to him for quite a while. I wasn't surprised when it was reported that he was dating Pattie Boyd, who he had met while filming. A lot of the girls who had hung around with The Beatles in Liverpool followed them down to London, to try to be able to see them, but I was too proud to follow and wanted to keep my job, so I stayed in Liverpool.

When I think back, I remember him as a very gentle person; funny, happy, and attentive. When we talked, he would listen and look right at you as if he was really taking in what you said. You could tell he was a deep thinker, but there was no sign of him being religious in any way at this time. He was just an ordinary Liverpool lad, trying to keep his feet on the ground while being in the eye of the storm that was Beatlemania.

"So what are you doing now?" as if the whole world didn't know!

I didn't see George again until 1966, by which time I was with Mike. We bumped into each other at the back of Church Street in Liverpool one night. He was walking along with Mal Evans, and I was with Mike. I remember making small talk and saying, "So what are you doing now?" as if the whole world didn't know! They had released over 10 albums, toured the world, and made two films, but it was the only thing I could think of to say! I also recall I had an awful hat on at the time.

The last time I spoke to George was in Liverpool in 1969, when he was on tour with Delaney & Bonnie and they played at the Empire Theatre. We were in the Lord Nelson pub behind the theatre when he came in with his entourage, wearing white robes and long hair. He sat down opposite us, spotted me, and waved his hand as a sort of summons to come over to sit next to him, along with the assortment of interesting characters. I went over and sat next to him, but it felt a bit awkward, so I made my excuses and left. I didn't want to make small talk again about what he had been up to, as though I didn't know!

Mike and I had met in 1965, and by 1967 we were married. Funnily enough, it was the custom to announce weddings in the local newspaper, and on the day ours was announced, there was an article about The Beatles directly below! In 1970, our son Matthew was born, and in 1973 Alison came along, so life settled down to some degree. I continued hairdressing and Mike built his career in show business, eventually having a compering residency in both the Shakespeare Theatre Club and Russell's nightclub, working with some of the biggest stars of the time such as Tommy Cooper, Olivia Newton-John and Ken Dodd.

The Beatles had gone on to conquer America, tour the world, break countless records, dominate charts internationally, and eventually break up in 1970 to pursue solo careers. They had moved on from their Liverpool roots, but the impact they had on the world was undeniable.

32, of 17 Grove Street, New Ferry was placed on probation for two years after pleading not guilty to stealing a tee short, a cardigan, three pairs of knickers and other clothing belonging to her next door neighbour, Mrs. Margaret Chase.

Inspector Kenneth Shield, said at 9 p.m. on July 23 Mrs. Chase washed some clothes and hung them out to dry on the clothes line in her back yard. At 9 a.m. next day the clothes were missing.

2.30 A.M. VISIT

Diane Dale, agen nine, of 18 Grove Square, New Ferry was a friend of Mrs. Smith's son and slept at the accused's home on the night of July 23. At about 2.30 a.m. Mrs. Smith and Diane went out of the house together and Mrs. Smith took the washing from Mrs. Chase's yard. She then ...

been stolen. Inspector Shield said she was aged 17, one of a family of eight. She was married last year but was separated from her husband, and was expecting a baby in December.

The police officer came up just as he had got out of the car.

"That would take you five seconds," said Mr. J. H. Cullen, the Magistrate's Clerk.

SPEED CAUSED BROADSIDE-ON DEATH CRASH, SAYS CORONER

Speed was only explanation for an accident involving two cars on the Queensferry to Helsby Road, resulting in the death of the driver of a Volkswagen and causing serious injuries to the driver of the other car.

This view was taken by Chester Coroner, Mr. H. O. Jones, recording a misadventure verdict at the inquest on William Frederick ...

travelling at about 60 "It is possible that it was going at too high a speed for the conditions."

HEIRESS CALLS OFF NINTH WEDDING

South Africa's most ...

Christ Church, Hampstead, London.

Miss Bernadette Farrell, daughter of Mr. and Mrs. W. Farrell, of ... Childwall Lane, Wavertree, Liverpool, and Mr. Michael Byrne ...

The latest addition to the cast of the new Beatle film "Magical Mystery Tour," currently in production ... tease artist, Jan Carson, who works at Raymond's Revue Bar where the sequence was filmed. Choreography was by Raymond's wife Jean. "Magical Mystery Tour," devised and directed by the Beatles, is a one-hour production intended for world wide TV distribution. Our picture shows Jan performing in front of the Beatles.

MIKE AND BERNADETTE'S WEDDING ANNOUNCEMENT WITH ADDED BEATLES!

These early memories of growing up in Liverpool in the 60s, experiencing Merseybeat and seeing the birth of The Beatles, never left us, and eventually formed the foundations of The Beatles Story.

A DREAM IS BORN... POST SIXTIES LIVERPOOL AND THE GROWTH OF BEATLES TOURISM

Mike: In December 1980, Bernadette and I were in the kitchen on what was a sunny day in Liverpool, and the terrible news came on the radio that John had been shot. We simply couldn't believe it. It made no sense. He was a pop star, not a politician.

Bernie: I think John's death was the catalyst for generating an increase in Beatles tourism. After that, people from Japan and America started visiting Liverpool trying to track down Beatles sites and find ways of paying homage to The Beatles, and particularly John.

John was now an icon and fans wanted to see where it all began and make their pilgrimages to Liverpool. But when they arrived in 1980, there wasn't a lot for them to see, apart from the Arthur Dooley Beatles statue in Mathew Street, Cavern Mecca, their childhood homes, and some of the famous locations featured in their songs.

THE ARTHUR DOOLEY STATUE IN MATHEW STREET

THE PENNY LANE STREET SIGN – THIS HAD TO BE PAINTED ON THE WALL AS IT HAD BEEN STOLEN SO MANY TIMES BY OVER-ZEALOUS BEATLE FANS

Liverpool City Council had no interest in promoting The Beatles or harnessing the potential value of Beatles tourism; in fact, there wasn't a huge focus on tourism at all. It felt that as far as the Council was concerned, The Beatles had made their money in the 60s and abandoned their roots. This sentiment was shared by many Liverpudlians at the time, and it continued to be this way for years.

"John's death was the catalyst for generating an increase in Beatles tourism"

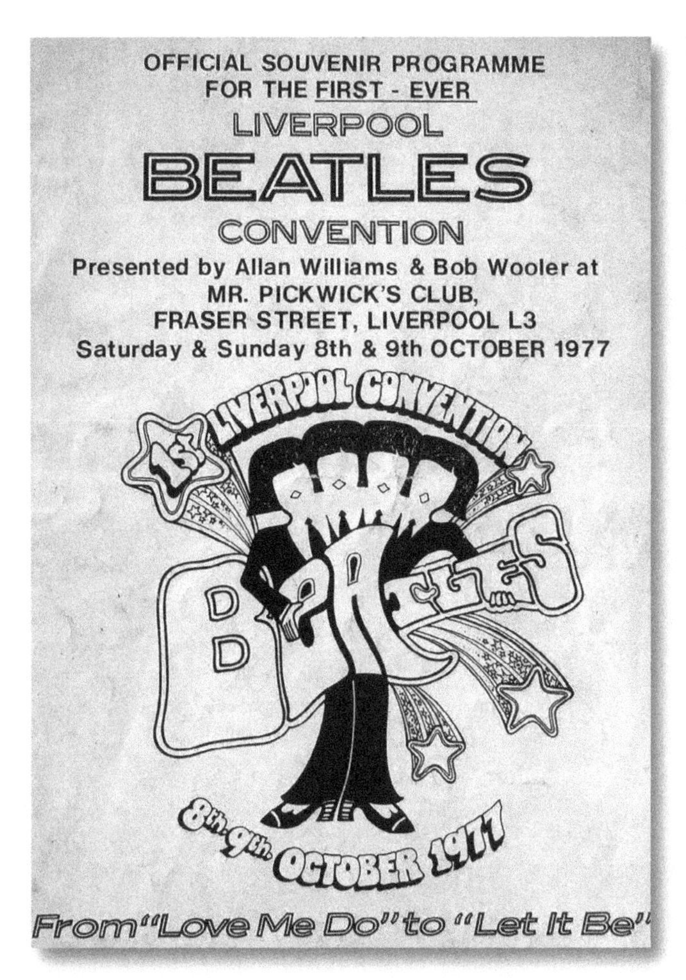

MR PICKWICK'S 1977 BEATLE CONVENTION TICKET

Mike: In 1977, Ron Jones, who was the Deputy PR Officer for Liverpool City Council, persuaded the North West Tourist Board to give Allan Williams and Bob Wooler a grant to help stage Liverpool's first-ever Beatles convention. According to Allan and Bob, they spent most of it on beer, but the convention did go ahead, at Mr. Pickwick's, and I was the compere.

It attracted around 200 fans from across the UK and featured special guests, a Beatles quiz, a fancy dress competition, and live music from Mojo Filter, who were probably the first Beatles tribute band. This would be the beginnings of what would eventually become the hugely successful International Beatle Week and Mathew Street Festival.

Bernie: After the demolition of the original Cavern in 1973, Beatle fans felt that there should be a tribute or memorial to them in Mathew Street. However, there wasn't a tourist board in the 1970s, despite clear opportunities to capitalise on The Beatles' success and bring tourists to the city. Ron Jones worked with rock musician and journalist Mike Evans to put together the first official Beatles souvenir package for fans, published in 1974. It came in the form of a double album with a map, showing for the first time the city's Beatles haunts.

Ron lobbied the English Tourist Board for funds to develop tourism in Liverpool and Merseyside, and they agreed to pay for a series of 'Discover Merseyside' tourism campaigns. He launched the first campaign in 1977 by sending out a press release with a photo of people sitting on deckchairs in Birkenhead docks with the Liverpool waterfront in the background, wrapped around a bar of mint rock. In an effort to promote Liverpool as a tourist destination, Ron attended a tourism event in London and distributed his 'Liverpool Rock' (normally associated with Blackpool).

Many people just laughed at him - because who in their right mind would want to "see Liverpool"? Despite this reaction the next day all the newspapers covered the story. Pam Wilsher was brought in to assist him, and working alongside him provided support and research to back up his belief that The Beatles could bring in visitors from all over the world.

In 1981 Ron and Mike Evans produced *In the Footsteps of the Beatles*, the first official Beatles guide to Liverpool.

Many people just laughed at him - because who in their right mind would want to "see Liverpool"?

HOLIDAY MAKERS ENJOYING LIVERPOOL'S WATERFRONT

PAM WILSHER AND RON JONES – TRAILBLAZERS OF EARLY BEATLES TOURISM

THE FIRST OFFICIAL BEATLES GUIDE TO LIVERPOOL

CAVERN MECCA

Jim and Liz Hughes were a couple of staunch Beatles fans who could also see the gaping hole in Liverpool's offering for fans like themselves.

Initially, they opened The Magical Mystery Store in North John Street, which was mostly a shop selling merchandise, but eventually it also became a meeting place for like-minded fans to gather and share their love of The Beatles. Following this, in 1981, they opened Cavern Mecca on Mathew Street, with the help of a grant from the English Tourist Board. This was a friendly haven for fans and tourists alike, with a small, mocked-up Cavern stage and a TV showing footage of The Beatles on repeat. Sadly, it closed in 1984 due to lack of financial help and ill health, and although it briefly reopened in Cavern Walks, it struggled to recreate the atmosphere of the original and closed for good. Jim and Liz are widely credited with kick-starting Beatles tourism in the late 70s and early 80s. They did it for the love of the group, not to make money.

Mike: In 1983, an American entrepreneur called Charles Rosenay ran hugely successful Beatles Conventions over in the US which attracted around 5,000 people each time.

He describes Mathew Street as "a ghetto street"

He started bringing groups of Americans over to Liverpool on Beatles pilgrimages, but recalls feeling embarrassed to discover Liverpool's lack of appreciation of The Beatles when he arrived with his first group. He describes Mathew Street as "a ghetto street" – everything was boarded up and there was no indication of where The Cavern had once been. He and his tour group would put their ears up to boarded up buildings – trying to imagine music coming from them – because there was nothing there to commemorate where The Beatles had played 292 times! He was grateful at least for Cavern Mecca – a place where Beatles fans were welcomed and understood.

Charles persevered over the years, continuing to bring groups over from the US, and he would eventually be recognised by Liverpool's mayor as an unofficial tourism ambassador. He also became a long-time friend and supporter of The Beatles Story.

JIM AND LIZ HUGHES WITH VICTOR SPINETTI AT THE OPENING OF CAVERN MECCA IN 1981

MATHEW STREET IN 1983 - THE BOARDED UP SITE OF THE CAVERN

RIOTS, DEPRIVATION AND REGENERATING THE CITY

Mike: In the early eighties, the Toxteth riots erupted as a consequence of racial tensions between the local community and the police; this gave Liverpool national publicity for all the wrong reasons. The image of a burning city was splashed across the headlines and Liverpool's already tarnished image was further damaged.

Michael Heseltine, the Environment Secretary of the time, was tasked (by the Conservative government under Margaret Thatcher) with reviving the city's fortunes. One alternative was to 'manage its decline', but Heseltine had become captivated by Liverpool's once-great trade and merchant history, thanks to the River Mersey's accessibility on the western coast of the country. He didn't believe it should now be left to deteriorate any further.

He recognised the economic difficulties Liverpool was facing, the social deprivation, lack of investment, and subsequent inability to attract tourists. He spent three weeks in the city, looking for opportunities to change its fortunes, and decided that huge potential lay in the redevelopment of the Albert Dock as the 'Covent Garden of the North', on the banks of the River Mersey. To do this, he used his substantial political weight to create the Merseyside Development Corporation and obtain public funds. He also recognised that the inaccessible, silted-up Salthouse and Albert Dock was thick with mud, and there was no way it would succeed if this wasn't dredged and cleaned up.

Albert Dock - 'the Covent Garden of the North'

THE SALTHOUSE DOCK WITH ALBERT DOCK BEHIND, WAS FULL OF SILT AND MUD

1984: A PIVOTAL YEAR FOR LIVERPOOL TOURISM

Bernie: In 1982 I saw an advert looking for Beatles guides – a brand new concept initiated by Ron and Pam. They were recruiting people to take visitors around the most famous Beatles sites in Liverpool. I knew I could do that and underwent months of training and examinations to become one of the first group of qualified Beatles guides in the country.

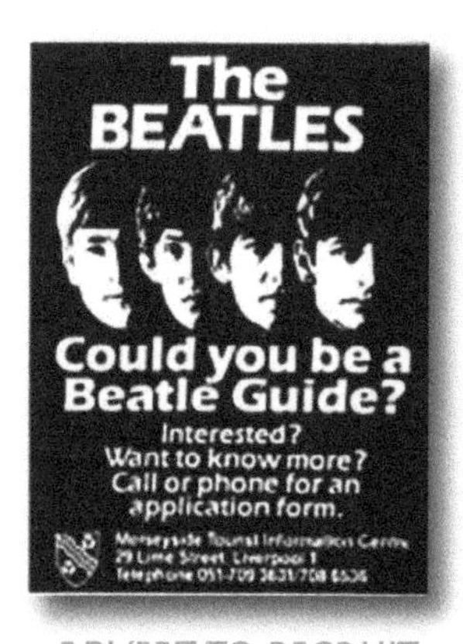

ADVERT TO RECRUIT BEATLES GUIDES

The idea was that our tours would get away from the traditional academic guided walks and deliver a more personal and entertaining experience. I trained with a team, and we planned the best routes across the city to take in the most important Beatles landmarks. Another of Ron's initiatives was to organise Mersey Beatle Weekends which included an overnight stay, guided tours, a Beatles-themed evening with a tribute band, and quizzes across two days.

'In the Footsteps of The Beatles' was one of the first tours we did on foot, but a little later they hired coaches to allow us to visit Beatles sites that were further afield. One of the locations was The Casbah in West Derby, where occasionally fans would be lucky enough to visit when Pete Best and his mum were in residence!

I realised it would help if I knew more about the city, so I went on to qualify for the full Blue Badge national guiding qualification. Around this time, I also worked part-time for Cavern City Tours, which had been set up in 1983 by Bill Heckle, Dave Jones and Ron Jones (a different Ron Jones from the MTB), three of my fellow Beatles guides. Their aim was to provide tour packages for international fans.

By 1984 things were beginning to snowball and the tourist board bought a minibus, for which we had to gain a PSV driving licence to be able to drive. It was a bit of a nightmare to drive a bus full of tourists, whilst guiding and playing music, but this was all part of being a guide at that time!

THE NEWLY QUALIFIED BEATLE GUIDES CELEBRATING THEIR SUCCESS

1984 MERSEYBEATLE WEEKENDS FLYER

BERNIE FEATURED IN AN ARTICLE ABOUT SUITABLE FASHION FOR GUIDING! SITTING WITH THE ELEANOR RIGBY STATUE IN SIR THOMAS STREET, CLOSE TO MATHEW STREET – SCULPTED BY TOMMY STEELE – HE WAS FORMERLY A POP STAR AND ACTOR IN THE LATE 1950s

LITTLE YELLOW BUS LEAFLET EXPLAINING GUIDED TOURS AVAILABLE BY MINIBUS, CAR OR ON FOOT

BERNIE'S BEATLE GUIDE BADGES

BERNIE WITH PETE AND MONA BEST AT THE CASBAH DURING A GUIDED TOUR IN 1984

INTERNATIONAL GARDEN FESTIVAL

As well as investing in the Albert Dock area, Heseltine chose Liverpool to host the International Garden Festival on what had been derelict land further along the banks of the Mersey. It was the first and only UK city to do this and it comprised of fifty international and themed gardens. It was opened by the Queen and Prince Philip and was so successful it attracted over three million visitors.

THE QUEEN AND PRINCE PHILIP ON WALKABOUT ON THE OPENING DAY - MIKE MANAGED TO ATTRACT THEIR ATTENTION (BY COUGHING!)

THE QUEEN BEING ESCORTED ON THE OPENING DAY

INTERNATIONAL GARDEN FESTIVAL SHOWING THE CHINESE GARDEN AND LAKE

The Most Spectacular International Event Anywhere in the World *2nd May–14th Oct 1984

SPECIAL TRAVEL & ENTRANCE RATES

NATIONAL EXPRESS
Details from your local National Express enquiry office or Travel Agent.

LOCAL COACH COMPANIES

BRITISH RAIL
Details from your nearest British Rail Main Station or BR appointed Travel Centre

**Special admission times to be announced for May 2nd 1984*

FREE TRAVEL FROM ANYWHERE IN MERSEYSIDE

International Garden Festival All Day Saveaway Tickets from

Merseyside Transport
051-236 7676

DAY TICKETS AVAILABLE AT MOST CROWN POST OFFICES

nationwide from April 1984.

Organised and Promoted by Merseyside Development Corporation

INTERNATIONAL GARDEN FESTIVAL POSTER

MILITANT COUNCIL CHALLENGES

Heseltine had to work with the Merseyside Development Corporation to get things done because the Militant Labour council had no interest in tourism, having stated "We want jobs, not gardens." The local council was so Militant that a non-political rally was organised at the Pier Head in 1985, to try to improve the city's prospects and get them removed from power. Tens of thousands of concerned Liverpool residents gathered to join the protest. Mike was tasked with writing a protest song, which was subsequently released!

Mike: Despite the council's apathy, tourism started to flourish as the first phase of the Albert Dock, The Edward Pavilion, opened, with specialist shops and an International Food Court. It was at this time that I met Tony O'Leary, who was well connected at The Albert Dock as he chaired the Shop Tenants Association, and had a business based there, with a well-known local artist named Frank Green. Tony and I became good friends and in later years he became a great supporter and sounding-board. The International Tall Ships Race was brought to Liverpool for the first time and the boats that could fit into the dock were moored there. This really brought the dock to life and introduced many new tourists to Liverpool and its magnificent waterfront.

LIVERPOOL AGAINST MILITANT

MASS RALLY

AT THE PIER HEAD

SUNDAY

6th OCTOBER

at 3 p.m.

SAVE LIVERPOOL FROM THE MILITANTS

NOW IS THE TIME FOR THE SILENT MAJORITY OF THIS ONCE GREAT CITY TO MAKE THEMSELVES HEARD BY THE NATION.

STAND UP AND BE COUNTED BEFORE MILITANT DESTROY OUR CITY COMPLETELY.

Above:
'LIVERPOOL AGAINST MILITANT' FLYER INVITING PEOPLE TO A MASS RALLY

Left:
'LIVERPOOL AGAINST MILITANT' PROTEST SINGLE

THE BEGINNINGS OF BEATLES TOURISM

Beatles tourism was starting to show signs of life. A dedicated Beatles shop opened in Mathew Street, with a retro jukebox full of Beatles singles, and selling all kinds of merchandise and memorabilia. An 'Art of The Beatles' exhibition was organised at the Walker Art Gallery by Ron Jones and Mike Evans. It featured contributions from many artists and photographers as well as people they knew personally, including Stuart Sutcliffe, Astrid Kirchherr, Mike McCartney and Peter Blake.

It was also the year that Cavern Walks opened, alongside the newly reconstructed Cavern Club which used some of the bricks from the original Cavern. On the 28th of November 1984, Paul McCartney was awarded Honorary Freedom of the City of Liverpool and premiered his film 'Give My Regards to Broad Street' on the same evening, in the city.

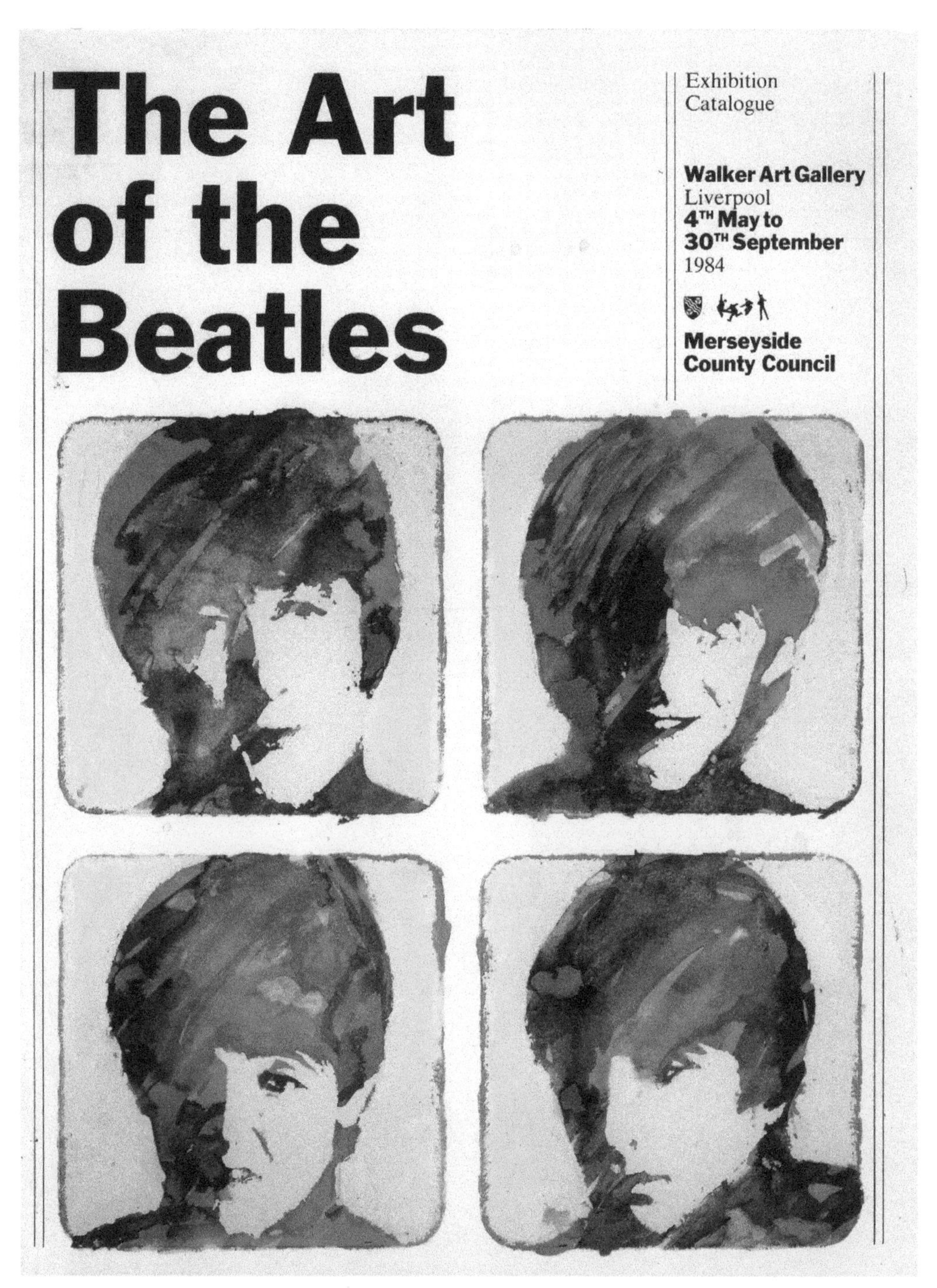

THE 'ART OF THE BEATLES' EXHIBITION CATALOGUE

GETTING A PROPER JOB

Mike: In the early 70s, I progressed from singing in groups to become a solo cabaret artist, which led to me becoming the host and compere at The Shakespeare Theatre Club, which was the top cabaret venue at that time. It hosted all the top comedians and singers of the time such as Tommy Cooper, Tony Christie, Bruce Forsyth, and Ken Dodd. I remember my first night as host and compere when Tommy Cooper, the most popular comedian of the day, was topping the bill. At the soundcheck, I told him it was my first night, and he was very keen to help me with my nerves. He invited me to his dressing room before the show, where he produced a bottle of Scotch whisky and got me drunk. I somehow got away with it despite my opening number being a piano rendition of 'Great Balls of Fire', where I came up out of the floor on a motorised stage! I wasn't a natural compere but learned very quickly how to work an audience by ad-libbing. I learned a lot from the acts who performed there.

After a year at The Shakespeare, I moved to Liverpool's newest cabaret club – Russell's. I stayed there for seven years and became entertainment manager so gained valuable experience in booking and scheduling acts as well as marketing and promotion.

After having two children, I decided it was time to find a more family-friendly job. My friend, Phil Birtwistle, had started Liverpool's first free newspaper, Merseymart, in 1978 after the Liverpool Echo refused to advertise his used car adverts. He offered me the position of promotions manager, which I accepted without much of an idea of what was involved. I didn't have a job description as such; my remit was to cover local news stories, organise charity events and sell the occasional promotional feature. It was my first day job since leaving my dad's shop and I enjoyed it because no two days were the same. It led to some fun and interesting experiences which I could write a separate book about. These pictures of me interviewing an escapologist 100 feet up in the air, at a Liverpool Family Show, whilst strapped to a mattress with a piece of rope, sums it up nicely!

ALL PART OF THE DAY JOB – INTERVIEWING 'THE GREAT CROSSINI' ESCAPOLOGIST – MIKE WAS ATTACHED TO A CRANE WITH ROPE, 100 FEET IN THE AIR

Over five years at Merseymart, I became immersed in all newsworthy aspects of Liverpool life including the Toxteth riots, the expansion of Liverpool Airport and the regeneration of the Albert Dock. When the International Garden Festival (IGF) opened in 1984, I saw a great opportunity for Merseymart. We produced a special monthly newspaper called Hello Tourist in conjunction with the Merseyside Development Corporation. This was a guide for visitors about art, culture, music and events taking place in the city.

THE IGF AND ITS IMPACT ON TOURISM

Mike: The IGF gave me a press pass which allowed me daily access to the festival site, and I could see Liverpool tourism developing before my eyes. Bernie was coming home from her tours and telling me about her encounters with tourists and their reactions to the city – mostly that they were pleasantly surprised after seeing a lot of negative press. I started looking for any opportunity to promote Liverpool as a tourist destination and realised that this was what I wanted to do.

"The Ambassador was not impressed and after five minutes stormed out"

Bernie: The IGF attracted visitors from all over the world and many VIPs. One day, in my capacity as a Blue Badge guide, I was asked to take the Venezuelan Ambassador and his entourage to the site where we would be greeted and taken on a VIP tour of the whole site. Unfortunately, the staff hadn't been briefed and sat us in a basic portacabin while they tried to find management. The Ambassador was not impressed and after five minutes stormed out!

CHINESE DANCE TROUPE

WORZEL GUMMIDGE AND THE CHINESE DRAGONS

Throughout the course of the festival, the participating countries would stage their own themed events such as, Canadian tree felling, cheese-tasting from Holland and a spectacular dragon dance display from China.

The organisers recognised that The Beatles were an attraction for international visitors, and arranged for a giant Yellow Submarine to be built by a group of 80 apprentices at Cammell Laird's dockyard. This was located just over the water on the Wirral, so once it was ready, it was floated down the Mersey to the IGF site. (It now resides at Liverpool John Lennon Airport.)

In front of this was an Apple maze filled with water in between the maze path which was great fun for children.

They also featured a bronze statue of John Lennon by the sculptor John Curran – the world was still reeling from his murder only four years earlier.

Hello Tourist!

Welcome to Merseyside!

There's never been a better time to be here. With a whole host of events taking place, including the International Garden Festival, there is something for everyone to enjoy.

International Garden Festival LIVERPOOL '84

OFFICIAL FESTIVAL GUIDE

FESTIVAL GUIDE

On sale at both Festival entrances and throughout the site. Price £1.50

INTERNATIONAL GARDEN FESTIVAL 1984

Flowers, fun and fantasy . . .

Centrepiece

Key Features

FULL FESTIVAL EVENTS PROGRAMME INSIDE

HELLO TOURIST – NEWSPAPER WHICH WAS A GUIDE FOR VISITORS TO MERSEYSIDE

DAVID YIP – ACTOR FROM THE TV SERIES 'THE CHINESE DETECTIVE' – ON A VISIT TO THE INTERNATIONAL GARDEN FESTIVAL

THE DUTCH GARDEN

I.G.F. TOUR GUIDE BADGE 1983

I.G.F. STAFF BADGE 1984

A NEW BEATLES ATTRACTION

The IGF's presence was a huge boost to Liverpool's tourism and the guides were getting busier as a result. Visitors came from all over the world and perceptions of Liverpool were starting to change for the better.

Mike: While the IGF was wowing tens of thousands of visitors every day, Radio City, Liverpool's commercial radio station, opened Beatle City, a museum of Beatles memorabilia. The opening day welcomed special guests Queenie Epstein (Brian's mum), Gerry Marsden and Liverpool's Lord Mayor, Hugh Dalton. It had been estimated that ten percent of the footfall from the Garden Festival would visit it - that's easily three hundred thousand people across the summer. But the Garden Festival was so vast, and there was such a variety of things to do, that day-trippers could easily have spent two or three days there and barely had time to see it all, never mind going to see Beatle City at a completely separate location. So, unfortunately, Beatle City didn't benefit much from IGF visitors, and it only attracted hardcore Beatle fans. In its first year, it lost money, and by October 1985 its doors had closed as the owners tried to find a buyer.

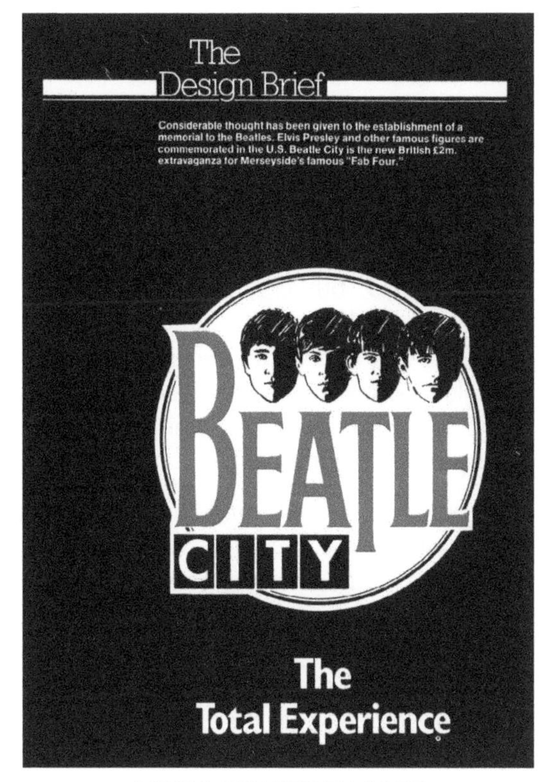

BEATLE CITY DESIGN BRIEF

BEATLE CITY MUSEUM ON SEEL STREET IN 1984

TRANSWORLD FESTIVAL GARDENS

Meanwhile, when the International Garden Festival came to an end in 1984, the council was offered the chance to take over the site and benefit from its success and the foundations that had been laid, but they turned it down. The Merseyside Development Corporation had no alternative but to continue running it themselves the following year, operating a scaled-back version where the gardens were maintained alongside a smaller events programme.

This was never a long-term solution, and the site was eventually leased to Transworld Leisure Plc, who were already undertaking the redevelopment of New Brighton waterfront on the other side of the Mersey. They had grand ambitions to turn it into the Alton Towers of the North and renamed it Transworld Festival Gardens.

MIKE ON THE OPENING DAY OF TRANSWORLD IN THE FESTIVAL HALL - PREPARING TO PRESENT A MINI-BUS TO THE VARIETY CLUB OF GREAT BRITAIN

WORKING AT TRANSWORLD FESTIVAL GARDENS

Mike: In 1985, two new free newspapers had appeared in competition with Merseymart. This put a lot of strain on the paper, and Phil called me into his office to inform me that I had a new job – selling advertising. I threw myself into it for at least six months but realised it wasn't the job for me and I felt it might be time to move on. In March 1986, I saw an advert for events manager at Transworld Festival Gardens and jumped at the chance of getting involved full-time with event management in a tourism capacity.

It combined my background in entertainment management with my newfound passion for tourism. I got the job and only had a few weeks to book entertainment for the whole season across several event areas and stages.

Fortunately, I knew agents and promoters who I could call on to provide a variety of acts at relatively short notice. I arranged a packed schedule of family entertainment every single day, which included a grand parade, circus acts, all kinds of bands, majorettes, comedians, and children's entertainers. There were one-off special events such as a Barracudas Parachute Display and we built a special stage for the roller-skating Muppet Show Tour. I even arranged a fly-past by the famous Red Arrows Display Team.

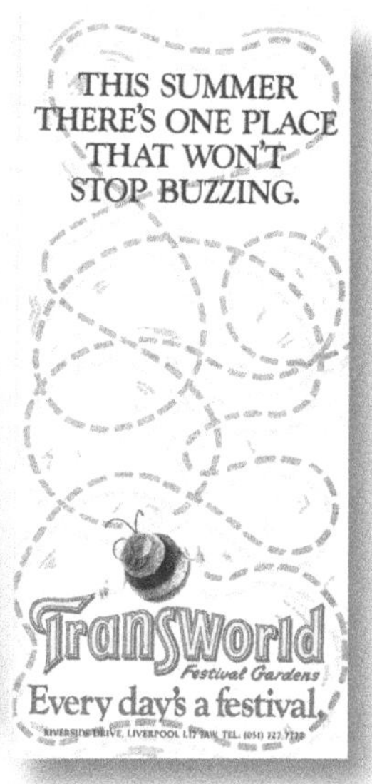

TRANSWORLD YELLOW SUBMARINE FEATURE

BEATLE CITY - LIVERPOOL

Mike: In 1986, the chairman of Transworld bought Beatle City from Radio City, with the plan to move the exhibition over to the festival site the following year. However, this ambitious plan didn't come to pass, as sadly, Transworld Festival Gardens got into financial difficulties. This was down to a number of factors including poor publicity and weeks of bad weather.

AERIAL VIEW OF BEATLE CITY PRE-OPENING

The management team was called in by the CEO for an emergency meeting, informing us that the venture would have to close mid-September 1986, and that we would all be out of a job. However, with the purchase of Beatle City, there was one position available - as its manager.

I put my hand up. *"I'll have it!"*

A week later, on the 18th of September, I found myself in charge of Beatle City. Keep in mind, I had no prior experience of managing an exhibition on this scale. I didn't know how to do cash projections, calculate wages, run a café or manage a team of staff. But I was good at promotions so focused all of my events and marketing experience into raising awareness of the exhibition to get people through the door.

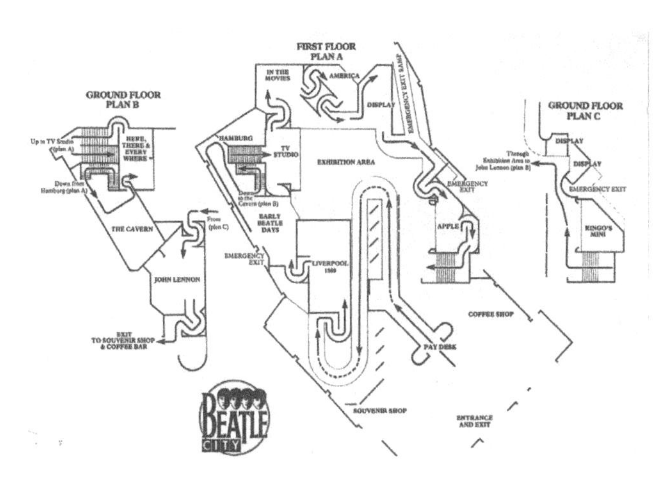

BEATLE CITY FLOOR PLAN

TRANSWORLD FLYER FOR BEATLE CITY

The exhibition was very nicely designed and had some incredible memorabilia including Ringo's customised Mini, John's moped, and Apple's front door. We also had the original Magical Mystery Tour bus parked outside which was used for Beatle tours every weekend.

CAVERN STAGE MOCK UP

RINGO'S CUSTOMISED MINI COOPER AND JOHN LENNON'S MOTORCYCLE

MAGICAL MYSTERY TOUR BUS WHICH WAS OWNED BY BEATLE CITY – THERE WERE DAILY TOURS WITH QUALIFIED BEATLE GUIDES

JOHN LENNON STATUE BY JOHN CURRAN – ON DISPLAY IN BEATLE CITY

Transworld decided to take the John Lennon statue that had been on display at the International Garden Festival and put it on display at the entrance of Beatle City.

It held a lot of interest for real fans and even attracted some high-profile guests including one of the Doobie Brothers, Michael McDonald, who visited us during his UK tour. I took him on a personal tour of the exhibition, and discovered after he had left that he had accidentally left his wallet behind. I called his manager and they invited myself, Bernie and the kids over to Manchester the next night to see his show (and return his wallet). We had a fantastic evening and were invited back to the dressing room after the show to meet Michael, his wife and the band.

To be financially successful, it had to appeal to more than just Beatle fans

Sadly, I soon discovered that the exhibition was struggling to make money. Bernie and I had a theory as to its lack of success. One factor was the location – the other side of town from Mathew Street, miles away from the key Beatles sites. Another reason was that although the exhibition was a big draw for the die-hard Beatle fan, with over a million pounds' worth of memorabilia, it didn't offer a lot of entertainment value to the average day-tripper, who might have wanted more of an experiential day out, taking them back to the sights and sounds of the 60s. To be financially successful, it had to appeal to more than just Beatle fans.

The Greatest Beatle Show on Earth!

Featuring over 1,000 priceless exhibits and ten superb sound and video shows

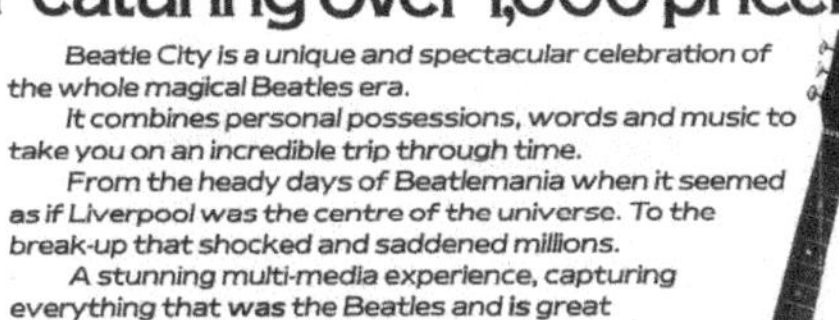

Beatle City is a unique and spectacular celebration of the whole magical Beatles era.

It combines personal possessions, words and music to take you on an incredible trip through time.

From the heady days of Beatlemania when it seemed as if Liverpool was the centre of the universe. To the break-up that shocked and saddened millions.

A stunning multi-media experience, capturing everything that was the Beatles and is great entertainment.

LIVERPOOL IN THE '60's

It's fab, it's gear, it's here!

The new Mersey Sound has set everyone swinging. And the City's buzzing with excitement, energy and enthusiasm.

Kids like John Lennon are writing songs in living-rooms all over the City. And you can join them.

Reliving their hopes and aspirations. Sharing the unique mood of the time. Just being there.

Beatle City takes you back, with an amazing illuminated tableau and many evocative displays.

EARLY BEATLE DAYS

John Lennon forms a skiffle group. It's called The Quarrymen. And gradually it evolves into a group whose music is to rock the world.

Early posters, programmes and tickets chart the changes. Until eventually, with newest member Ringo, they burst onto the Cavern stage. The Beatles are born.

HAMBURG

The hard seaport city acts like a furnace. Helping the Beatles forge an individual style which attracts growing crowds to their shows.

You'll read their letters home – they capture the mood completely. And see a priceless guitar signed by the boys.

THE CAVERN

The excitement is incredible. Live music pulses through your body. Everyone's twisting to the beat.

You're back in the Cavern.

An authentic replica of the original site. Continuous video of the Fab Four's performances rekindle it all.

TV STUDIO

Ready. And action! The cameras roll. The Beatles sing. And you're at the control panel.

Watching their act on TV monitors. In at the beginnings of a national epidemic. Beatlemania.

IN THE MOVIES

John, Paul, George and Ringo break into films.

From the zany humour of 'A Hard Day's Night' to the touching honesty of 'Let it Be' they're a hit with all nationalities.

And Beatle City's got the weirdly worded posters to prove it!

Plus original animation stills from 'Yellow Submarine'.

AMERICA

1964 sees the Fab Four's greatest achievement – the conquest of America.

Hordes of screaming fans flock to the airports and over seventy-three million are glued to their TV sets for the group's appearance on the Ed Sullivan Show.

You share the excitement and magic. You follow their amazing progress. And you see the original, highly entertaining interviews.

In addition to this, at that time, there was huge apathy towards Liverpool and The Beatles, fuelled by hostile press coverage leading to a nationwide negative perception of Liverpool.

As if things weren't challenging enough, not long after I started managing Beatle City, there was a show on the BBC that incorrectly stated that the exhibition had closed. I called up the producer to complain, and he said he'd heard this from a local paper and continued on to tell me they were considering making a comedy about two Beatles guides who rip off tourists! He thought this was funny. I was furious and wrote a letter to the head of the tourist board to appeal for more help in combatting the negative attention that the city was receiving from the media.

This is just one example of how Liverpool was commonly portrayed in the 1980s and why Liverpool tourism was facing an uphill battle. It didn't take me long, as manager, to realise just how bad things were for Beatle City, and in an attempt to cut costs, we closed the café. Some days we were making more money from car park charges than ticket sales for the exhibition!

FANS USED TO SEND LETTERS FOR THE ATTENTION OF THE BEATLES TO THE EXHIBITION

BEATLE CITY DALLAS

A few months into my employment, out of the blue, a man walked in and said, "I'm John Symons, the new owner of Beatle City." I hadn't been informed that it had been sold, so was a little surprised, to say the least. He wasn't a Beatles fan, but he knew there was a market with international Beatle fans, so his plan was to take the whole exhibition on tour, firstly to America and then possibly on to Japan.

He told me straight away that he liked to be called JR so it was appropriate that the first stop would be Dallas, Texas! He had connections with Southfork Ranch, home of the famous TV show, 'Dallas', and they arranged a location in downtown Dallas. For a share of the profits they would help to promote the exhibition. I was surprised that of all the cities to choose from in America, he had chosen the bible belt city of Dallas, which had burnt Beatles records in the 60s owing to John's comment that The Beatles were bigger than Jesus.

He asked me to go with it as manager, and wanted Bernie to come along as an authentic link to The Beatles and official Beatle guide. Despite some reservations, we decided to go for it as we had nothing to lose, and it was such an exciting opportunity.

He told me straight away that he liked to be called JR so it was appropriate that the first stop would be Dallas, Texas!

In a matter of weeks, we closed the exhibition and packed everything into fourteen large crates of varying sizes; this included Ringo's customised Mini and John's Steinway piano - extremely precious cargo - bear in mind that in 2000, George Michael bought the piano for £1.45 million!

BEATLE CITY DALLAS BROCHURE

CLOSING THE EXHIBITION AND MOVING IT TO DALLAS

The day after we closed Beatle City, we blocked out the windows with brown packing paper to prevent the public from getting too curious. Radio City seemed to be unaware that it had closed and that we were preparing to pack it all up and take it abroad.

One day an irate Terry Smith arrived - he was the MD of Radio City - and upon seeing the windows covered he started hammering on the front door. I was in my office unsure what to do. I couldn't contact JR. The next day Terry Smith took out an injunction to stop us from moving it. It turned out that the promised payment to Radio City had not been made, and until this was sorted out, I couldn't pack another item. After some frantic phone calls and meetings, I presume some money exchanged hands, and we were allowed to finish packing everything up.

The whole exhibition was flown to Dallas in July 1987, and I flew over on August 3rd. Some of the bigger items had to be sent via boat into the Port of Galveston, which was the nearest port to Dallas.

The contents were delivered to West End Marketplace, the shopping mall that would become Beatle City's home for the foreseeable future, in Dallas' historic district.

We were situated on the fourth floor, which is where every single item had to be taken. Despite being exhausted after a fifteen-hour journey via Chicago, I was taken straight to the exhibition space to supervise the build and installation in 107-degree heat, with no air-conditioning! We had five days to get everything ready for the grand opening.

The cases were unpacked by a robust team of Mexican workmen and taken by goods lift to the fourth floor, then carefully carried to the exhibition area by hand under my close supervision. Most items fitted in the lift, but Ringo's customised Mini was too big and the only way to get it up there was to carry it. We realised it was impossible to get it to the fourth floor, so we had to settle for it being displayed on the first floor instead. The sight of fourteen men carrying Ringo's Mini up the escalators of a shopping mall is something I'll never forget.

All things considered, the move from Liverpool to Dallas went well apart from the accidental disposal of two bin bags full of original Magical Mystery Tour seat covers, which had been painstakingly cut into small pieces by one of Bernie's guiding colleagues, Mandy Webster.

The plan had been to sell them as merchandise for a not-insignificant amount, but they were mistaken for rubbish and thrown in the bin!

Media interest was growing, and a Dallas TV station wanted to come down before the official opening date to get an early interview, and footage of some of the exciting memorabilia that would be on show. However, on the agreed date for the interview, many of the items were still being held in customs and a plan B had to be hastily

Fort Worth Star-Telegram

Arlington

Rick Alvarez, left, helps Mike Byrne of Liverpool, England, general manager of the Beatle City museum, unload the letters spelling "love" yesterday at West End MarketPlace in Dallas. The letters were part of the Beatles' famed "All You Need is Love" sign. The exhibit of Beatles memorabilia opens tomorrow.

RINGO'S MINI WAS DISPLAYED ON THE FIRST FLOOR – IT DIDN'T HAVE A COVER OVER IT, AND AFTER ONE BOOZY SATURDAY NIGHT IN THE MALL, A FLYING BEER BOTTLE SOMEHOW MADE IT INTO THE CASE AND SMASHED THE REAR WINDOW!

NEWSPAPER ARTICLE SHOWING MIKE UNPACKING SOME OF THE ITEMS

arranged. We decided to ask for the help of three American Beatle collectors, Mark Naboshek, Mark Peterson and Doug Green, who had impressive collections and were based in Dallas. They saved the day by loaning their memorabilia so that there were some interesting items to show on the TV interview, and these items remained in the exhibition for the duration.

Mark Naboshek recalls – "I noticed that there were no tops to the many glass display enclosures throughout the exhibit, specifically the ones that contained the memorabilia contributed by the three Dallas collectors, including me. I was told that this was done because of fire codes. Glass tops simply weren't allowed. On the ceiling above those enclosures were sprinkler heads that were part of an elaborate sprinkler system. I asked someone from the West End Marketplace about them. I said, 'What if those sprinklers go off above the topless enclosures and soak all our memorabilia with water?' He smiled and said, 'I wouldn't worry about that! By the time the sprinklers go off, your stuff will be burned to a crisp.' If he wanted to unnerve me, he succeeded!"

'I wouldn't worry about that! By the time the sprinklers go off, your stuff will be burned to a crisp.'

We opened on August 7th, 1987, less than a month since packing everything up in Liverpool.

Mark Naboshek again remembers what a rush it was to get everything done on time: "I recall that some of the artefacts arrived from Liverpool so late that some were being installed on opening day! As the line of customers grew at the entrance to the exhibit, there were workmen and Southfork staff inside literally placing pieces into the enclosures and installing the glass at the very last moment. I even recall sweeping up building debris on the opening day!"

THREE U.S. COLLECTORS AND CONTRIBUTORS - MARK NABOSHEK, MARK PETERSON, DOUG GREEN

COLLECTORS MARK, MARK AND DOUG PUTTING FINISHING TOUCHES TO THE DISPLAY

MARK NABOSHEK
WITH SOME OF HIS BEATLE COLLECTION

Mike: On the opening day, while the owners were being interviewed at the entrance by all the major news channels, and having their pictures taken cutting the ribbon, the designers and I were frantically clearing rubbish, brushing floors, and applying finishing touches to the exhibits behind the scenes.

Publicity was very positive as this was an exciting new addition to Dallas tourism, and particularly the West End Marketplace. It even made the front page of USA Today.

Initial signs were promising as we welcomed visitors from across the USA to see what they saw as the only exhibit of its kind in the world. The appetite for Beatles tourism in America was thankfully a lot greater than it had been in Liverpool.

JOHN LENNON'S MOTORCYCLE

TOUR ARTEFACTS – JACKET, TWA AND BEA FLIGHT BAGS, CONTRACT & PROGRAMME

BEATLES JACKETS FROM TOURING YEARS

MARK IN CORRIDOR OF MEMORABILIA

DALLAS EXHIBITION ENTRANCE ON 4TH FLOOR – WITH BERNIE, HER SISTER MAUREEN AND DAUGHTER, ALI

'ALL YOU NEED IS LOVE' LETTERS IN THE YELLOW SUBMARINE SECTION

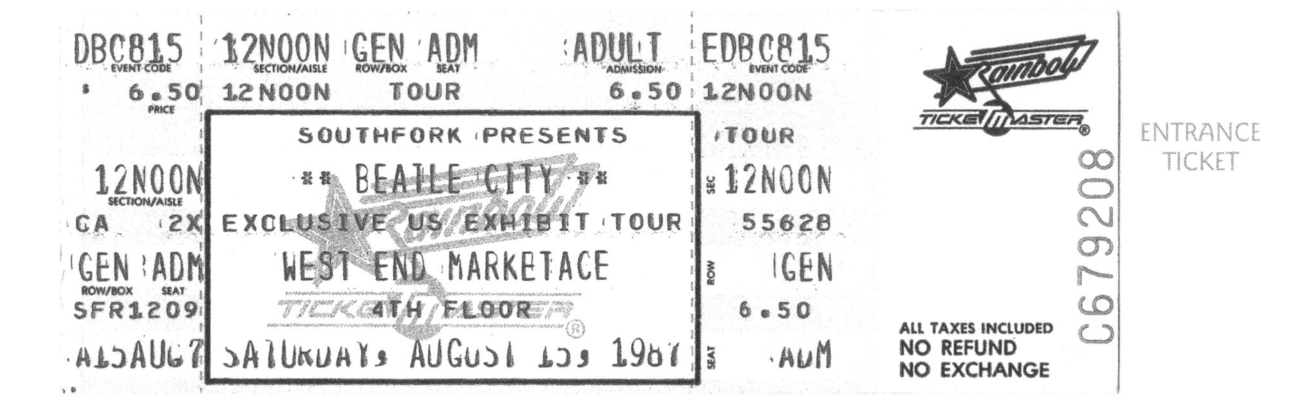

ENTRANCE TICKET

JOHN LENNON'S STEINWAY PIANO ON WHICH HE COMPOSED 'IMAGINE' AND HAMMOND ELECTRONIC ORGAN

BEATLE CITY BILLBOARD AT NIGHT WITH THE DALLAS SKYLINE IN BACKGROUND

'PAUL IS DEAD' LEAFLET PRODUCED BY MARK NABOSHEK

John Lennon/bag one

JOHN LENNON'S 'BAG ONE' BOOK

The successful launch was helped by the fact that one of the three partners was Southfork Ranch home of 'Dallas', the huge hit 80s TV show, and one of the biggest tourist attractions in Texas. As a result, they had fantastic access to the media, which we could take advantage of to promote Beatle City. There was a comprehensive marketing campaign including newspapers, billboards and radio, and it was featured on local TV news programmes. We also had the support of four sponsors, including Pepsi Cola, which shows what a big deal it was, having Beatle City in Dallas.

In terms of appealing to local fans, opening in New York, San Francisco or just about any other more cosmopolitan city would have been a better location. The Dallas locals were far more interested in country music and going to church. Despite this, we opened to great acclaim thanks to all the marketing contacts leveraged through Southfork Ranch. Following initial success, its opening was extended by an extra month and reviews were really positive.

The large majority of the exhibition mirrored the Liverpool version, but we did tailor it for the American audience in part. Mark Naboshek was integral to making sure that the descriptions and explanations were suitable for an American audience. Not only did he write the brochure for the Dallas exhibit, but he also produced a leaflet about the 'Paul Is Dead' phenomenon.

BEATLE CITY DALLAS BILLBOARD FROM STREET

Another exclusive addition to the Dallas exhibit was the John Lennon Bag One feature. This included a number of erotic drawings, and consequently, it had to be displayed in a private viewing area for over 18s only.

Bernie: I gave guided tours of the exhibition and fans were delighted to meet somebody who had actually been there in the 60s and had been friends with The Beatles. I was mortified to have to sign autographs and have my photograph taken regularly with Beatle fans. My sister Maureen visited as she had loaned some pictures to the exhibition and fans even wanted her autograph, just because she had met George a couple of times when I was dating him!

They were so enthusiastic to hear our stories of Liverpool, The Cavern, and The Beatles, and after the apathy we experienced in Liverpool, this really reinforced our belief that The Beatles were still popular and had the potential to bring thousands of visitors to Liverpool.

We were treated a little bit like celebrities during our time there, being invited to all the best restaurants, and the VIP area of the Hard Rock Café, and we also got VIP treatment at Southfork Ranch.

Mike: During our stay, we hosted several VIPs from various Texan radio and TV stations. They would usually be given a personal tour of the exhibits by myself or Bernie and loved to hear our personal stories of growing up in 1960s Liverpool.

One of our more surprising visitors was Pete Best. He was on a promotional tour in the States at that time and had heard about the exhibition. One of his entourage informed us that he would like to come the next day, so we arranged for a private viewing, after normal visitor hours.

The only other guests who were there were the three Dallas collectors, who I invited along as a thank you for their support.

BERNADETTE SIGNING AUTOGRAPHS FOR AMERICAN BEATLE FANS

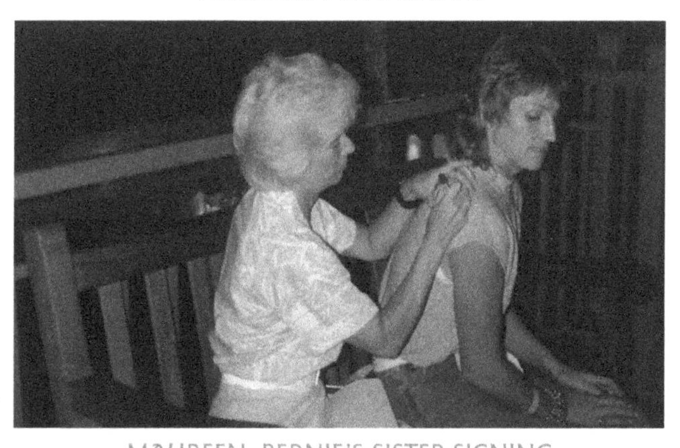

MAUREEN, BERNIE'S SISTER SIGNING A BEATLE FAN'S SHIRT

MIKE ADOPTING THE LOCAL FASHION!

MIKE AND PETE LOOKING AT SOME ICONIC EARLY BEATLES PICTURES – TAKEN IN THE CAVERN

MIKE, THE COLLECTORS AND PETE BEST AT THE HARD ROCK CAFÉ IN DOWNTOWN DALLAS

I remember feeling a little bit uncomfortable showing Pete around, although it was his choice to come, and he had clearly come to terms with his exit from the group. Nevertheless, there were parts of the exhibition I would have preferred to skip altogether!

Later that night, we took Pete out to the Hard Rock Café for dinner, where we spent a great evening with him, listening to his stories. Many fans were amazed to see the former Beatle at the restaurant and had their photos taken with him.

Everything was going well for the first month and we had lots of journalists and film crews arriving from all over America. However, behind the scenes, things weren't going quite as JR had planned. It had been agreed that ticket sales revenue would go straight to Southfork Ranch, and any profit was split three ways between JR (Beatle City), West End Marketplace, and Southfork Ranch. At the end of the first month, JR went to Southfork to pick up

THE FRONT DOOR FROM APPLE CORP'S OFFICE ON SAVILE ROW

They sent in the police, who arrested me in front of staff and customers

his share of the money but the owner, Terry Trippett, refused to hand it over. He was unhappy because JR had arranged for one of the main exhibits, the Apple front door, to be loaned to a Beatles museum in Japan. He had done this without Southfork's knowledge. This is when the partnership began to break down.

Under JR's instructions, I packed up the door to ship to Japan. This was done in good faith, but when Southfork found out, they sent in the police, who arrested me in front of staff and customers and barred me from the building until the situation was resolved. The Apple door ended up staying put, but the relationship between the three partners deteriorated rapidly. West End Marketplace was also unhappy and immediately stopped paying my hotel bill at the Sheraton.

I had twenty-four hours to find a new place to stay.

Despite the disagreements behind the scenes, the exhibition continued to do well. In November, I needed a break and flew back to Liverpool to see the family for a week.

I used the opportunity to meet with the head of the Merseyside Tourist Board, who informed me that JR hadn't been in touch with them, as had been agreed, about bringing the exhibition back to Liverpool. Alarm bells were ringing, and when I returned to Dallas, I confronted JR to find out his intentions.

It became clear that Beatle City would not be returning to Liverpool as promised, and he had been negotiating with his Japanese contacts about moving the exhibition to Tokyo. Although we had previously discussed Japan, I had no intention of going with it as I had been away from my family for long enough, and I wasn't happy with his way of doing business.

As a consequence of the in-fighting, I hadn't been paid for a month, and by December, I was owed $1,500 and could see the writing on the wall. I decided it was time to get out, take the money that was owed to me and book myself a flight home.

RETURNING TO LIVERPOOL – A CITY WITHOUT A PERMANENT BEATLES ATTRACTION

Mike: Getting back to Liverpool, we found a busy city with increasing numbers of tourists coming from all over the world. Having seen the international appeal of The Beatles first-hand, Bernadette and I were getting more and more frustrated by the lack of a permanent Beatles tribute in the city. We knew that The Beatles were to Liverpool what Shakespeare was to Stratford – but we felt very alone in this thinking, as we faced apathy from the council. They were blind to the opportunities that The Beatles gave to the city. In a jaw-dropping statement, the head of the Mersey Tourism Board at the time described The Beatles as "rubbish".

We felt compelled to do something about it and lobbied the head of the tourist board until he realised we would not give up. Eventually, he gave us £1,600 to do a feasibility study into why Liverpool needed a Beatles 'museum'. This seems laughable today, but that was how it was in 1988. The only trouble was, we hadn't a clue what a feasibility study was. So, I asked my dad, who asked his accountant, and between us we quickly figured it out! For the next three months, I worked on the study, collecting data on visitor numbers, the popularity of The Beatles, and fan statistics, until I had the evidence to show that this was a viable business proposition. Despite our findings, it felt like we were no closer to getting a new Beatles exhibition. At the same time, I was beginning to wonder why I was doing all this work in the vain hope that somebody else would set it up and reap the benefit. ***I woke up one morning and decided we would have to build it ourselves.***

Bernie: Our time in Dallas strengthened our belief that Liverpool needed a permanent tribute to The Beatles. As a Liverpool tour guide, I witnessed many tourists going away disappointed at the lack of a substantial focal point for fans - there was a glaring hole in the market due to the demise of Beatle City! Neither of us had any experience in creating a tourist attraction, but nevertheless, we decided to put our minds to it and find a way. After all, "Better to have tried and failed than never to have tried at all."

The major hurdle, of course, was raising the money to proceed with this germ of an idea. With little security behind us, Mike knew there wasn't much chance of a bank loaning us the necessary cash. He had already approached the tourist board and similar bodies to ask for help to get the venture off the ground, but they were facing financial challenges, and although they could provide us with statistics and research, they couldn't provide any funding. We were advised to approach the Merseyside Development Corporation (MDC) for financial support, but their remit didn't cover private commercial ventures.

Following the initial feasibility study, Mike produced a very impressive business plan. The MDC contributed a small amount to pay for Peat Marwick McLintock, part of KPMG (one of the largest, multinational, professional services companies in the world), to analyse our business plan. Based on their vast knowledge of other tourist attractions, they convinced us it would be a success.

FINDING THE IDEAL SITE

Bernie: As a tour guide, I was often taken to see new developments in the city. One time, we were invited down to the Britannia Pavilion at the Albert Dock, including the basement, which hadn't yet been developed. This was the old tobacco warehouse, and the smell was still in the air. When entering the basement, I was immediately struck by the similarity of the shape of the vaulted ceiling, which was arched, and it reminded me of the original Cavern. That evening, I went home and told Mike I'd found the perfect place for a new exhibition

Mike: In addition to the basement being the perfect shape to recreate The Cavern, the Albert Dock was well equipped with its huge adjacent free car park, which would be able to accommodate coach loads of tourists. It was also a leisure destination in its own right with the Maritime Museum and Tate Gallery already operating from there; we knew a tourist attraction would work well there and would benefit from passing trade. Prior to the American trip, I had held some preliminary discussions with the landlords at the Albert Dock regarding Beatle City being housed there on its return. We had also considered Mathew Street as a location because of its Beatle links but decided against it because of the lack of access and parking.

DARING TO DREAM

Bernie: As soon as we realised that we were going to build it ourselves, I began to write the story. Although the story of The Beatles was well known, it had to be written to complement the rough layout we had in mind. Long evenings were spent producing words, drawings, and plans, until we agreed on how we would like to see the concept evolve. We would sketch our ideas out wherever and whenever they came to us, sometimes in the middle of a family meal!

Mike began discussions with the landlords of the Albert Dock and was met with a certain amount of scepticism from people who felt he had no chance of bringing the project to fruition. There was also a sense of snobbishness about The Beatles not being quite the right 'fit' for the prestigious Albert Dock.

At the same time, we teamed up with a great architect called Steve Quicke who worked for the Franklin Stafford

BERNIE'S IDEAS AND PLANS FOR THE EXHIBITION, SCRAWLED ON A SERVIETTE DURING A FAMILY MEAL

EARLY IMAGES OF THE EERIE BRITANNIA VAULTS BASEMENT

FORMAT FOR EXHIBITION

Liverpool
Life History Birth etc
Influences
Quarrymen / Art college / stuart?
Merseybeat news / alter bands
Casbah
alter local clubs
Hamburg / stuart / allen w.
cavern / B. wooler
B. Epstein / stalls of stars
Peter Kaye
T.V. Studio
64 { America / H. days night
65 { Help / Beatlemania / MBE
66 { Touring / candlestick pk.
67 { Flower power / physchodelia / Drugs / Maharishi / sgt pepper / strawb. fields / Brians Dealt / Mag Myst tour.
68 { Yellow Sub. / Divorce John / Apple
69 (Paul is dead Theory

BERNIE'S EARLY HANDWRITTEN IDEAS FOR KEY FEATURES

1. Gift shop-
2. Exhibition entrance
3. Introduction to Liverpool
4. Beatles brief history (birth, family, homes)
5. Influences (skiffle, Elvis, Buddy Holly, Quarrymen, art school)
6. Casbah, Jacaranda
7. Hamburg. Clubs, tribute to Stuart Sutcliffe, Astrid
8. Merseybent office, Mathew Street Merseybeat
9. Cavern (video, Bob Wooler, memorabilia)
10. Nems (Brian Epsteins stars, records)
11. Peter Kaye E.M.I. audition.
12. TV. / Recording studio
13. Beatlemania, Tour, London Palladium, audio headphones
14 Fans bedroom
15 America
16 Temporary exhibition area
17 Sgt 1965 1966 1967.
18 Yellow Submarine
19 1968 1969 1970
20 Solo Years
21 Tribute to John.

MIKE'S EARLY HANDWRITTEN IDEAS FOR THE LAYOUT

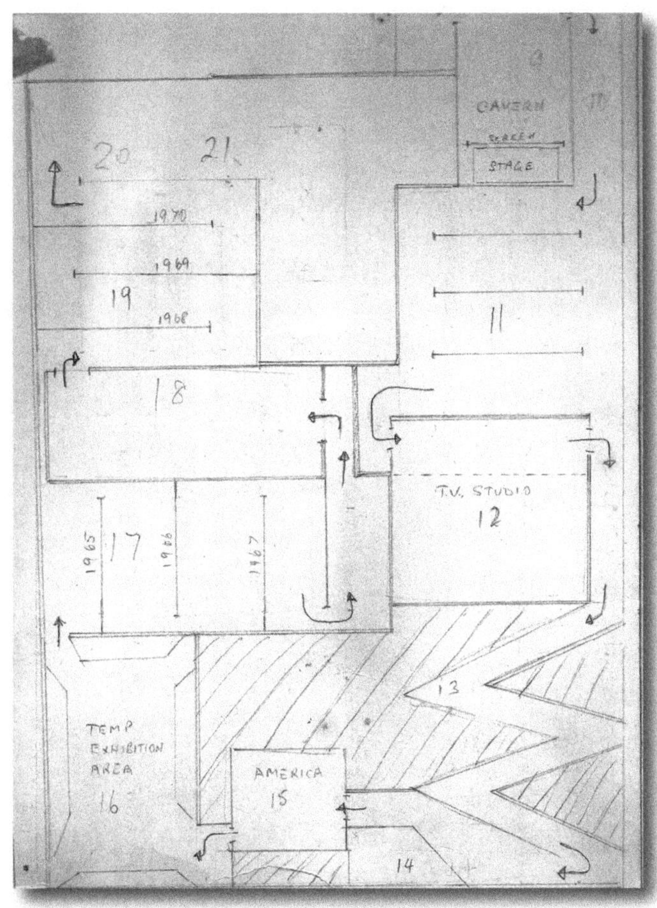

MIKE'S ROUGH DESIGN ON THE CARDBOARD INSERT FROM A SHIRT BOX - 1988

Partnership. They were a very reputable firm of architects, who were not only based at the Albert Dock, but had already converted some of its basement areas for bars and shops, so they knew many of the potential pitfalls before they arose. They provided us with preliminary plans and drawings to help Mike sell his ambitious project to the Albert Dock Company and potential investors.

Bernie: We were young and ambitious and determined to achieve our dream. We had approached an architect and a graphic designer to put some of our ideas before them; just to test the water and see if it all seemed possible. Positive answers came back from them both and we believed it might work.

Eventually, the Albert Dock Company was persuaded to see things Mike's way and a suitable site was agreed upon, which was the original basement of the Britannia Pavilion, which I had seen the year before. All we needed to do then was find the money to build it!

Mike: In the summer of 1988, although no contracts had been signed, letters of intent had been exchanged and we were allowed to access the site, with a view to start planning the layout. We had confided our ambition to a few close friends and family and were keen to show them what would become Liverpool's newest Beatles attraction.

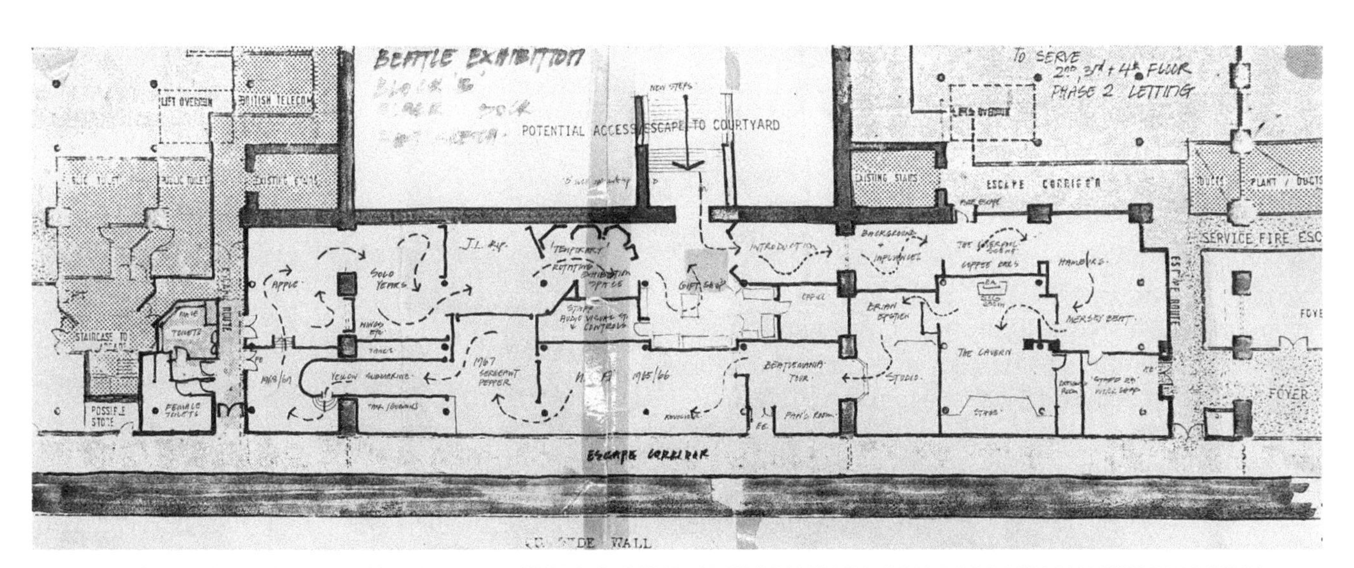

EARLY PLAN FROM FEBRUARY 1989 – THIS WAS THE FIRST DESIGN IN COLLABORATION WITH FRANKLIN STAFFORD – SHOWING HOW PEOPLE WOULD FLOW THROUGH

This included some Merseybeat friends, Don Andrew (Remo 4) and Johnny Guitar (Rory Storm and the Hurricanes), as well as their wives. We also took Charles Rosenay down – he was over for the Annual Beatle Convention, and we had become good friends.

Bernie: We recently spoke to our good friend and supporter, Charles Rosenay, about his recollections of Mike first taking him around the empty dock basement. This was in the August of 1988 when Charles was visiting from America for the Annual Beatle Convention.

THE BARE BASEMENT AS IT LOOKED WHEN MIKE GAVE EARLY TOURS TO FRIENDS AND FAMILY

He recalls: "Mike had taken me on a tour of the property when it was nothing more than an old, seemingly abandoned underground dungeon. He walked me around the dark, musty basement and said, 'This is where Abbey Road is going, and this space is going to be The Cavern.'

"I smiled and nodded my head and said 'Oh wow, awesome, sounds great' but in my mind I thought he was a nutter! I thought there's no possible way that this is going to happen. It was less than a year later it was in progress and less than two years later it was open."

Don Andrew recalls: "I remember the first time Mike took me down to the dark Albert Dock basement – he had laid out a pathway marked out of loose bricks which was meant to be the route that tourists would take through the various parts of the exhibition. He took me on a virtual tour and described what would eventually be in each section, but it was really just a load of dust at the time."

'Oh wow, awesome, sounds great' but in my mind I thought he was a nutter!

GIVING OUR DREAM A NAME

We had a lot of discussions about what to call the exhibition. One option was 'Beatlemania' which we felt encapsulated everything to do with the group, but we were worried it might misrepresent the fact that it covered the whole of their lives from birth to solo years. Other names in the mix were 'The Fab Four' and 'Magical History Tour'. But because the attraction was experiential, we wanted the word 'experience' to feature in the marketing. We also kept coming back to the story element that Bernie was writing to complement each section.

We eventually settled on *The Beatles Story – A Magical Experience.*

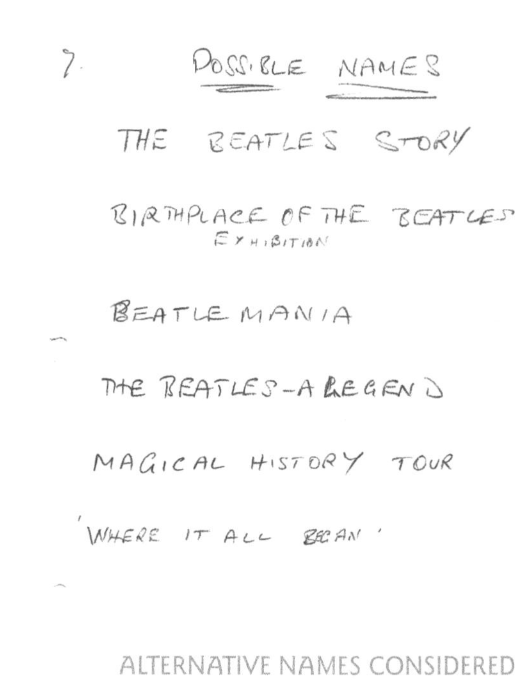

ALTERNATIVE NAMES CONSIDERED

MONEY

Mike: Initially we thought it would cost around £365,000 to build, but as we developed the concept, costs naturally increased. We eventually realised that if we were to create the ultimate audio-visual experience that we envisaged, we would need closer to £700,000. Our strapline was 'See It, Hear It, Feel It' and this vision didn't come cheap!

We were two complete amateurs, on the brink of trying to open a major tourist attraction. Personally, we had no financial backing and needed to raise the daunting sum of £700,000. The best we could do was re-mortgage our home for £25,000 and borrow £15,000 from my dad.

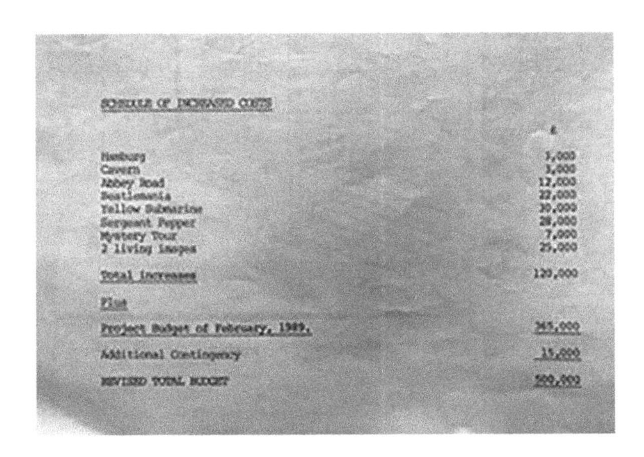

SCHEDULE OF INCREASED COSTS

	£
Hamburg	3,000
Cavern	3,000
Abbey Road	12,000
Beatlemania	22,000
Yellow Submarine	30,000
Sergeant Pepper	28,000
Mystery Tour	7,000
2 living Images	25,000
Total Increases	120,000
Plus	
Project Budget of February, 1989.	365,000
Additional Contingency	15,000
REVISED TOTAL BUDGET	500,000

THE SCHEDULE OF INCREASED COSTS DURING THE PLANNING PHASE

To find the remaining £660,000 we would have to sell shares in the business or borrow the money from a bank. I approached six banks, to no avail, though they thought it was a sound business plan. We then tried a few venture capitalists who couldn't offer us favourable terms, so we were left no other option but to sell shares to partners.

The first £100,000 came from my close friend, Phil Birtwistle, who was the first person who truly believed in our idea and showed his faith in it and in us by investing hard cash. This was such a critical moment in the journey towards success and it gave us momentum and a confidence that we might actually be able to pull it off. A few weeks later, he told us that he had secured another £150,000 from two local businessmen he knew. Without Phil's support, there's a high possibility that the exhibition would never have happened. With this foundation, I then managed to persuade the English Tourist Board to give us a repayable grant of £60,000. So together with our personal investment, we had raised a total of £350,000. Now we just had to find the remaining £350,000!

Through a chance meeting with the Merseyside Development Corporation, we found out that Wembley Stadium Ltd was planning to expand its empire into tourist attractions. The then Managing Director was very enthusiastic about our idea; he was from Liverpool, as was the Wembley Chairman, Sir Brian Woolfson, and he thought his company might be interested. We believe his Liverpool connections may have helped our cause, and they eventually agreed to invest, but it would be at a cost… they wanted the majority share and casting vote.

Bernie and I had to make a decision: accept their terms or forget the idea altogether. By that time, we had invested over a year of our lives researching, planning, and raising half the money; we couldn't give up at this point, so we reluctantly accepted Wembley's terms.

Bernie: Time was moving on and no other investors were forthcoming, so it was agreed by all to allow Wembley to have 50% of the shares and the casting vote, providing that major protection clauses were added to the contract to protect the minor shareholders.

Mike: All of a sudden, in the summer of 1989, the whole idea became a reality. Things began to move fast, and decisions had to be made as to who would run this exciting new tourist attraction.

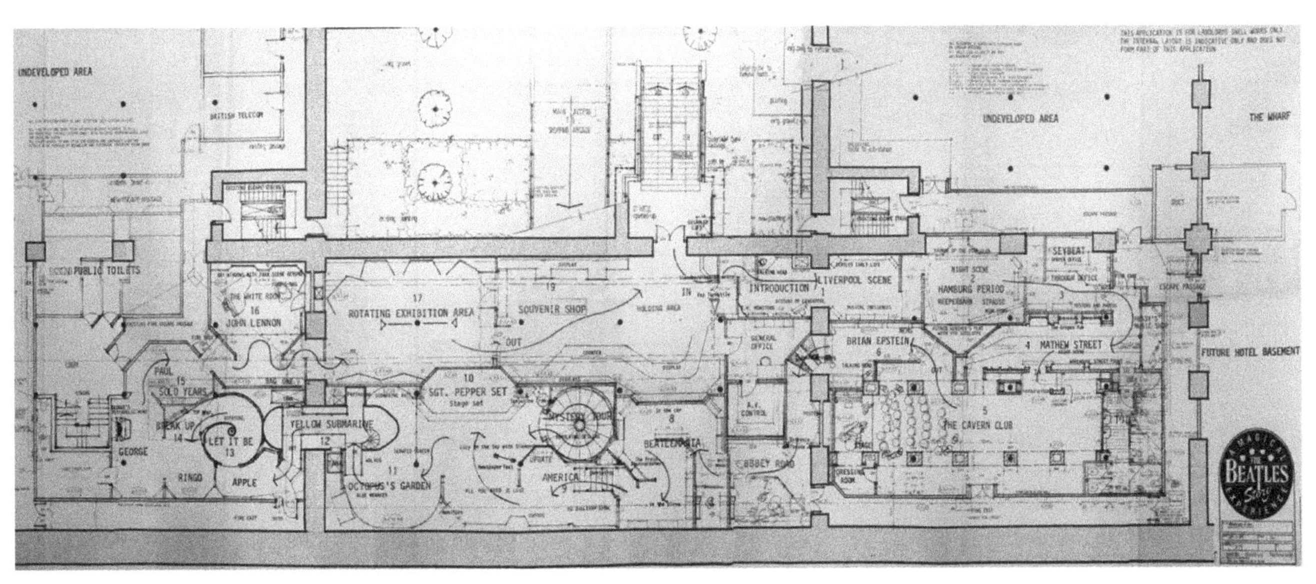

DECEMBER 1989 PLAN

> *"Mike was gigging, hosting the Annual Beatles Convention, and running aerobics classes to make ends meet"*

Bernie: An early meeting with the Northern directors agreed that Mike and I should both play a major role; not only with the set-up, design, and launch of the exhibition but also with day-to-day operations. Up until this point, Mike and I were still doing part-time jobs while planning the exhibition; I was doing guided tours, and Mike was gigging, hosting the Annual Beatles Convention, and running aerobics classes to make ends meet!

The Beatles Convention was a great source of contacts during this time when we were building and designing the exhibition. (It was at the 1989 convention that I met Charles Rosenay, who became a great supporter and friend who was there from the very beginning.)

Mike became Managing Director as soon as the company was formed, and I became officially employed in 1990. Mike and I worked together as project coordinators in every aspect of the design, alongside the architects, builders, and graphic designers.

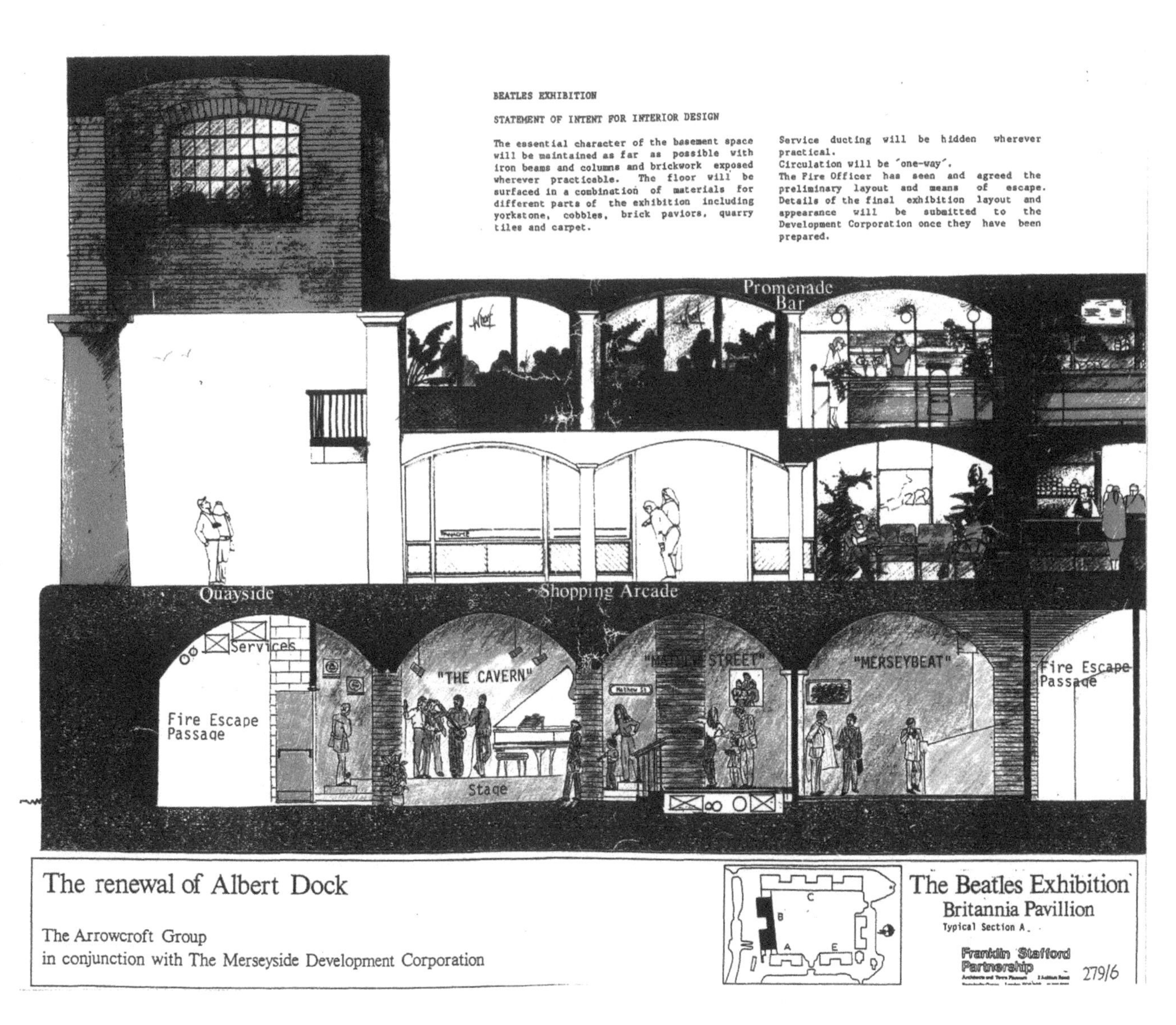

CROSS-SECTION OF ALBERT DOCK

PLANS AND DESIGNS

Bernie: Easter 1990 was the target date for opening, but there was a lot of work to do in the space of five months. The basement had been left untouched since the Albert Dock was restored in the 1980s and it had to be dug down and have a concrete slab laid, and fire passages built to allow construction to begin.

One of the problems we had at Beatle City was sound leakage. The layout created a cacophony of sound as you walked from one set to the next. We were determined, in our exhibition, to have the best soundproofing possible to avoid this, and we put a massive amount of money into soundproofing between each set.

We deliberately chose not to create a museum with cases full of memorabilia; that had been tried and failed, plus it would have eaten up our budget. We wanted to appeal to all ages, fans, and non-fans of The Beatles, and yet still tell the history of the group. Memorabilia could be added later if budget allowed.

We used the word 'experience' a lot because that's what we wanted to create, and we had been inspired by other experiential attractions such as Jorvik, Rock Circus, and the London Dungeons. Our gut feeling told us this was the right way to go.

We can't stress enough how important Steve Quicke's input was to the whole project. He worked with us every day to create the walk-through aspect of the exhibition.

We had no prior knowledge of designing an exhibition but knew exactly how we wanted it to look and were grateful to Steve and his staff, who tolerated some absurd suggestions that we put to them. They tried, on every occasion, to oblige and find a solution; in fact, in some cases, it was our naivety that produced results that would traditionally have been rejected.

Many versions of the layout were produced before a final working design was agreed upon toward the end of 1989, which culminated in a set of artists' impressions that we could work from. This example shows many features that didn't make the final version of the exhibition, such as Liverpool coffee bars, a fan's bedroom and a section dedicated to their films.

This was such an exciting time, but even now Mike and I were responsible for every stage of the design and build.

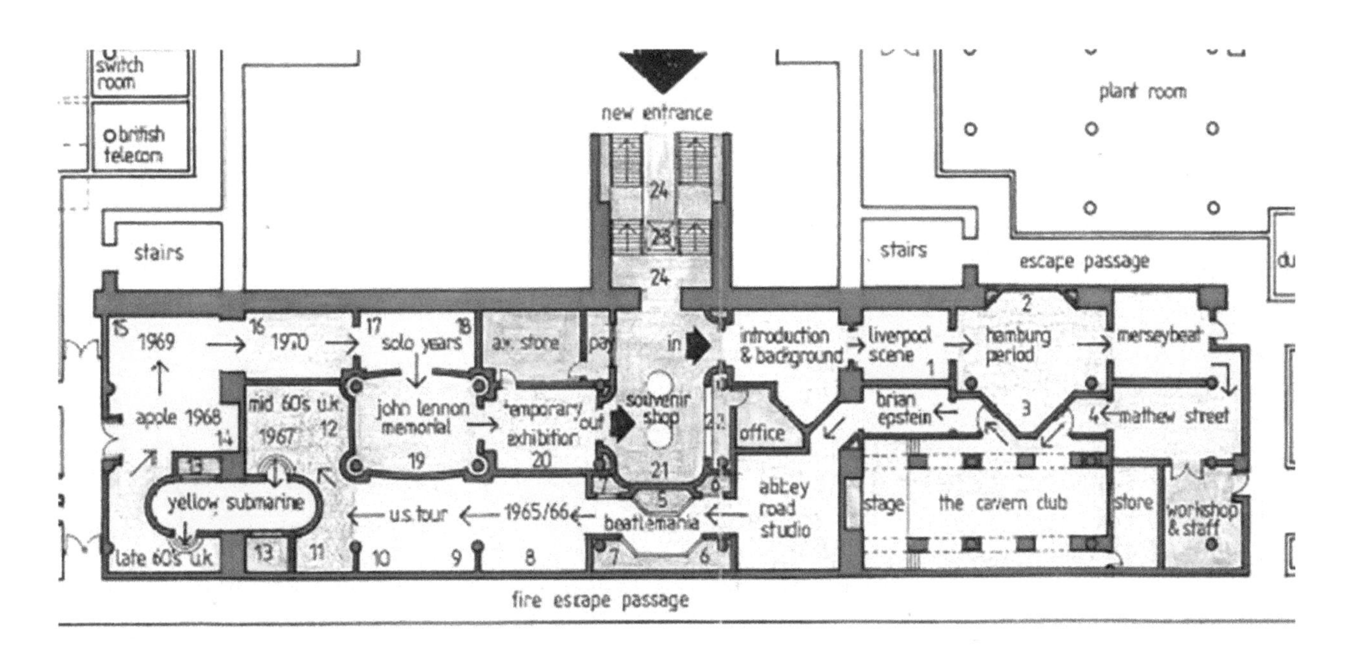

EARLY PLAN INCLUDING MULTIPLE FEATURES IN THE LEGEND THAT DIDN'T MAKE THE FINAL DESIGN INCLUDING A FAN'S BEDROOM AND SPECIFIC FEATURES FOR RUBBER SOUL/REVOLVER AND THE WHITE ALBUM

VERY EARLY YELLOW SUBMARINE AREA SKETCH

ARTIST'S IMPRESSION OF PEPPERLAND AND THE YELLOW SUBMARINE

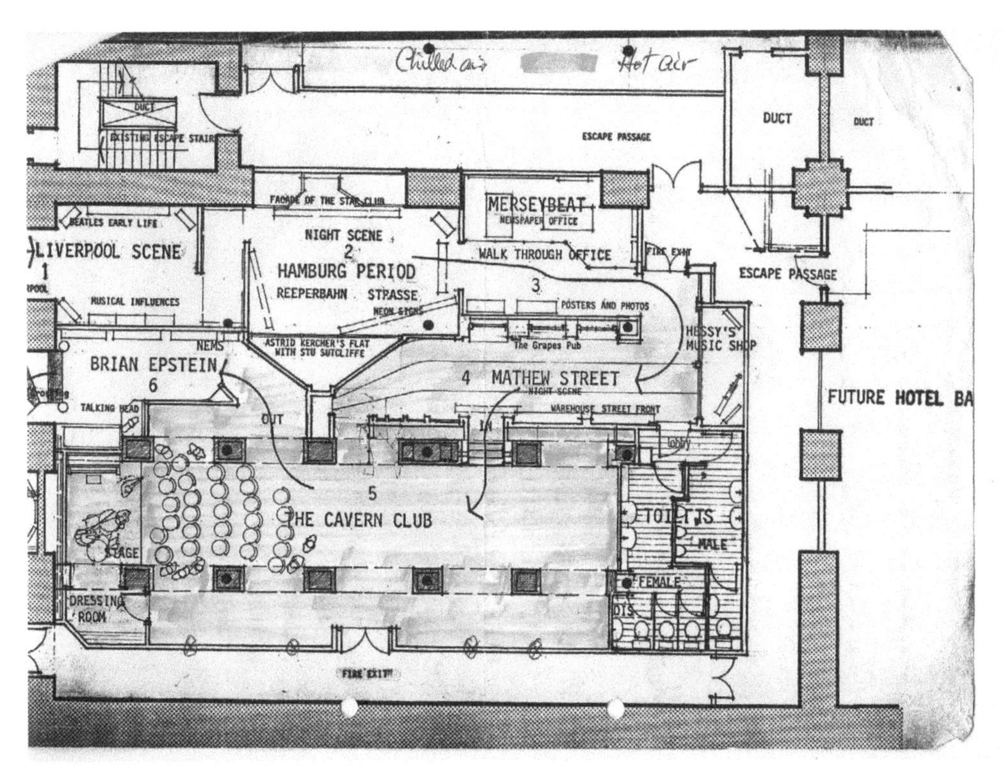

TEMPERATURE ZONES PLAN

APPLE

Mike: We couldn't create The Beatles Story without original photos, film clips, and Beatles music, and our success depended on getting permission from Apple to use them; we were also wondering if we needed Apple's approval to go ahead. Therefore, we had to talk to Apple Corps.

Back then, Apple was run by three people, Neil Aspinall, Derek Taylor, and Tom Hanley who looked after the photo library. I wrote to Neil, who was The Beatles' right-hand man.

He said I'd recognise him because he'd be carrying a rolled-up copy of The Guardian.

The letter was ignored. I tried ringing them and got a secretary who suggested I try writing. So, I wrote again, and included a copy of the intended plan of the exhibition.

This time I got a faxed reply from Derek Taylor, who suggested we meet in the crypt of St Martin's in the Field in London. He said I'd recognise him because he'd be carrying a rolled-up copy of The Guardian under his left arm.

I was told to bring a shortlist of questions to describe what we hoped to get from Apple, and he said he would rate them 'one to ten' as to the likelihood of them cooperating.

I got the train to London Euston and took the tube to Trafalgar Square. The closer I got to my destination, the more apprehension I felt. This meeting could make or break our dream and I had no idea how it would go. Making my way down to the crypt, I started looking for somebody carrying a newspaper as even though I had a vague idea of how he used to look, I knew his image had changed from his hippie days!

I spotted him sat at a corner table in a suit and tie, and made my way over to introduce myself. He was friendly and relaxed and wanted to hear all about our plans.

I explained our backgrounds and motivation for wanting to do the exhibition. I showed him some artist impressions and went through the plan with him in detail. I think we got on ok; he liked the fact that we were from Liverpool and not big business people, and he liked the look of our plans. But it was clear that he had to protect Apple's interests and he couldn't endorse it there and then. When I produced my list of questions, the first of which was "Would Apple endorse the exhibition?" the flat answer was "No."

However, he was more amenable with my next few questions and said the likelihood of getting photographs and memorabilia from Apple was an '8' and that they wouldn't stop us from using the music and selling merchandise. I also included a list of people who we would like to make a personal appearance such as Derek himself, Neil, George Martin and The Beatles. After me reading out a couple of names, he took the list from me, studied it, smiled wryly and proceeded to mark the names out of ten as to the likelihood of them coming. I was pleased that he had given my list some proper consideration and it wasn't all negative. He thought there was potential for at least some of our desired guests to show their support; however, this was just his opinion and he clearly noted that this was 'supposition'.

Our meeting lasted a couple of hours and as it concluded I had one final question, which was: "I don't think you can stop me, can you?"

He replied, "You'll have to discuss that with Neil!"

I came away from the meeting feeling optimistic that we hadn't been blocked outright, and after leaving Derek, went straight to a phone-box and called Bernadette to let her know how it had gone. However, there was still a hurdle to overcome - I would have to meet Neil Aspinall to get the green light.

The meeting happened two weeks later at Abbey Road. Again I was apprehensive because even though Derek had been quite encouraging, Neil could put an end to our dream in this next meeting. My nerves weren't helped by the fact that Neil was two hours late because he'd been out for a liquid lunch with Derek.

Once again, I went through the plans, showed him pictures, and explained our motivations for doing it, which was for the fans and Liverpool, not for our personal gain. His blunt response was, "I don't want you to do it." This was a big shock and not what I had expected after the mostly positive meeting I'd had with Derek. "Oh! Why?" I asked. He said, "Because if it fails, I will get the blame because I get the blame for everything that goes wrong in Beatleworld."

6th October 1989

Neil Aspinall Esq.,
Apple,
6, Stratton Street,
London,
W1X 5FD.

Dear Neil,

After speaking to Derek Taylor recently about the progress of the new Beatles' Exhibition in Liverpool, I would like you to know where I am up to, plus try to arrange a meeting to discuss the selling of 'Apple' related merchandise.

The name of the Exhibition is to be THE BEATLES STORY and as I have mentioned before, I have the support of the Liverpool City Council and the Merseyside Development Corporation, and I am involved annually in ensuring the smooth running of the Beatles' Convention with Cavern City Tours.

I am pleased to say that I have now raised the finance to put the project into operation and am now waiting for the final draft of the lease to be prepared and the copyright details to be worked out with E.M.I. and the other licensing bodies. I would appreciate any help or advice you could give me on that subject.

We hope to open the Exhibition by Easter 1990 and where possible, local firms are being commissioned to carry out the work. The Exhibition will be of the highest quality and our aim is to build something that Liverpool will be proud of and hopefully send visitors away with a more positive image of the area.

I hope that you share my wish to see a permanent Beatles' attraction in Liverpool and that you can see me soon, when I can show you the design in more detail and talk to you about selling your merchandise.

I would appreciate an early reply.

Yours sincerely,

Mike A. Byrne

P.S. I have enclosed a programme from a Merseybeat Reunion Night which I think might interest you.

encl.

He said that when Beatle City failed, he was one of the first points of contact for the media asking for an explanation. He wanted to avoid further problems of a similar nature, with another venture that he presumed would fail.

I reiterated my beliefs about why Beatle City had failed, and that our exhibition would be completely different, and I reinforced our findings from the feasibility study and all the other research and evidence that we had. I asked again "I don't think you can stop me, can you?" – and he confirmed, to my relief, that he couldn't.

I informed him that we were going to go ahead as we were so far down the road with it. So while we didn't exactly get their permission to open, they didn't block us, and we did get a 'silent nod' from Neil.

I had to make our shareholders believe that was enough. I think if we'd tried to open in New York or London, Apple would have found a way to stop us. But I sensed that Derek and Neil recognised that Bernie and I were doing it for the right reasons, in Liverpool. So that's how we navigated our way around Apple's red tape. Later on, we did hear that Neil visited the exhibition and liked it.

2ND LETTER TO NEIL ASPINALL FURTHER REQUESTING A MEETING TO DISCUSS PLANS FOR THE EXHIBITION

MEETING WITH DEREK TAYLOR   THURSDAY 9TH JUNE 1988

APPLE

AGREEMENT TO CO-OPERATE WITH NEW EXHIBITION.
ADVICE AND CONTACTS FOR SETTING UP OF EXHIBITION.
LOAN OF MEMORABILIA.
LICENCE TO SELL MERCHANDISE.
HELP IN OVERCOMING COPYRIGHT PROBLEMS, r.e.LOGOS, MUSIC, VIDEOS, FILM NEWSREELS etc.

CONTACTS

AGENTS, FILM DIRECTORS, PHOTOGRAPHERS,E.M.I. NORTHERN SONGS, etc.

PERSONAL APPEARANCES

DEREK TAYLOR, NEIL ASPINALL, GEORGE MARTIN, ROBERT FREEMAN, KLAUS VOORMAN, GEOFF EMERICK, PETER BLAKE, MICHAEL COOPER, DICK LESTER, TONY BARROW, HUNTER DAVIES, PETER ASHER, PETE SHOTTON, ANTHONY FAWCETT, EPSTEIN FAMILY, ASTRID KIRCHER, TONY SHERIDAN, WILLIAM MANN.
— Supposition.

EX BEATLES

ENDORSMENT FROM PAUL, GEORGE, RINGO, AND YOKO ?
Difficult. Credentials impeccable?

NOTES FROM MIKE'S MEETING WITH DEREK TAYLOR

MUSIC & LICENCES

Mike: Obviously it was crucial that we would be allowed to use The Beatles' music – without it, we wouldn't have an exhibition! The same went for film and pictures, so I set about the daunting task of getting permission from the relevant parties. This included Michael Jackson who, after buying Northern Songs at auction, owned the publishing rights to all of The Beatles' songs. Then, to use their solo releases, I needed permission from The Beatles' individual companies: McCartney Productions Ltd, George Harrisongs, and Yoko and Ringo's management teams. This was essential if we were to be able to go ahead; and somehow, following a flurry of trans-Atlantic phone calls and faxes, we secured the necessary approvals for free! This was incredible - I can't imagine that happening now.

The world of licensing is a minefield and can be very costly, but Neil and Derek recognised that we were on a tight budget and gave us their support to help smooth the way and minimise possible objections from record labels such as EMI and relevant film distributors, making it clear that they wouldn't get into trouble with Apple by providing us with Beatles music and footage. They also directed me towards their library curator, Tom Handley, and told him to provide us with certain pictures such as the Saville Row rooftop concert and the Apple Boutique.

Initially, we had hoped to be able to show the only piece of footage of The Beatles live at The Cavern - we wanted to project it onto the back wall of our replica Cavern - but it was being closely guarded and we weren't able to use it. We believed this was because of Apple's plans for the forthcoming Long and Winding Road film which later became The Beatles Anthology. We were, however, able to use film footage of UK and USA Beatlemania scenes, their arrival into JFK Airport in New York, as well as The Beatles reacting to the death of Brian Epstein.

Some of our features needed a narrator, such as the War Years section, so we approached Phil Sayer, one of the presenters on BBC North West Tonight, because we liked his voice. (He was also the announcer on the London Underground and was famous for the 'Mind the Gap' announcement!)

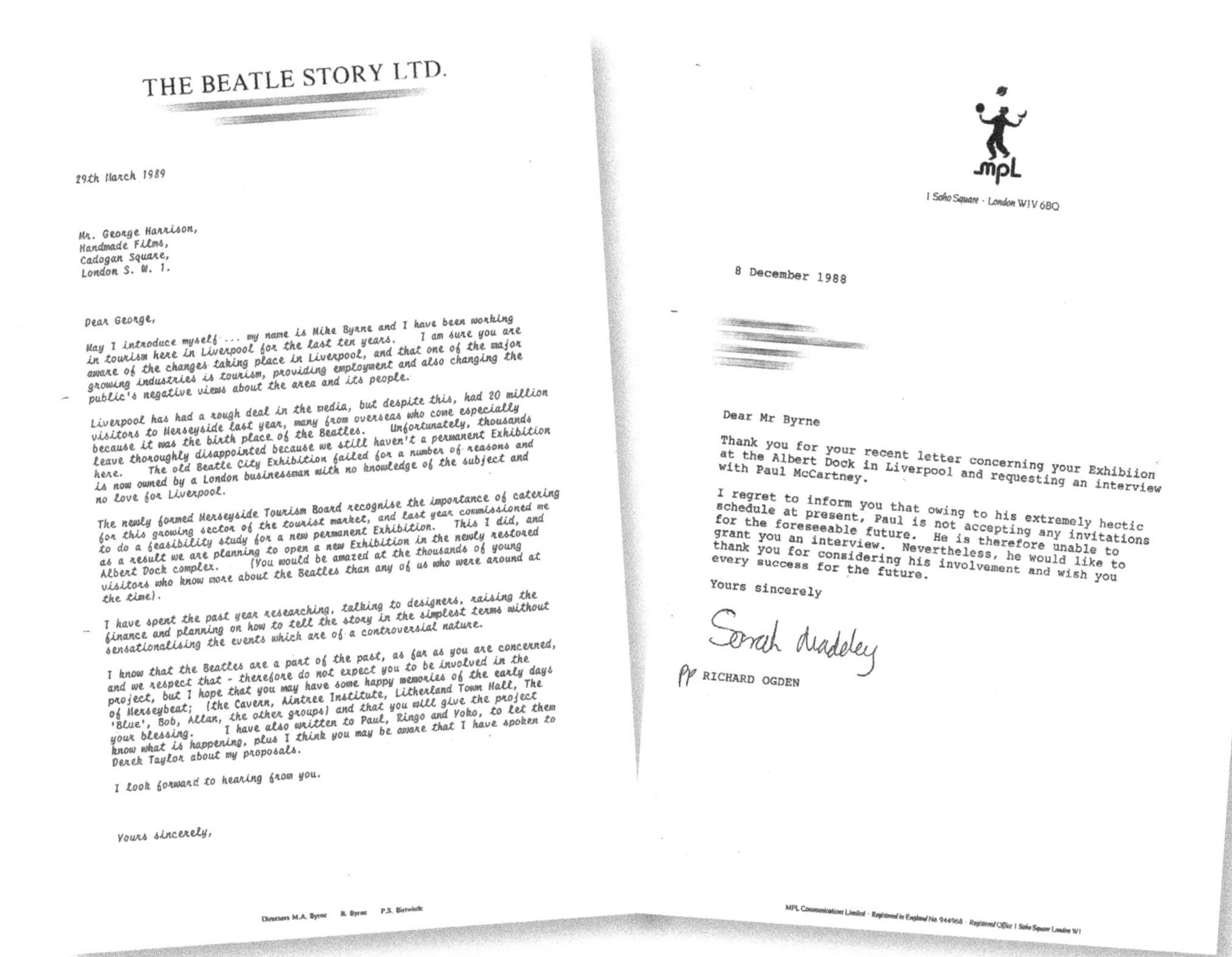

THE BEATLE STORY LTD.

29th March 1989

Mr. George Harrison,
Handmade Films,
Cadogan Square,
London S. W. 1.

Dear George,

May I introduce myself ... my name is Mike Byrne and I have been working in tourism here in Liverpool for the last ten years. I am sure you are aware of the changes taking place in Liverpool, and that one of the major growing industries is tourism, providing employment and also changing the public's negative views about the area and its people.

Liverpool has had a rough deal in the media, but despite this, had 20 million visitors to Merseyside last year, many from overseas who come especially because it was the birth place of the Beatles. Unfortunately, thousands leave thoroughly disappointed because we still haven't a permanent Exhibition here. The old Beatle City Exhibition failed for a number of reasons and is now owned by a London businessman with no knowledge of the subject and no love for Liverpool.

The newly formed Merseyside Tourism Board recognise the importance of catering for this growing sector of the tourist market, and last year commissioned me to do a feasibility study for a new permanent Exhibition. This I did, and as a result we are planning to open a new Exhibition in the newly restored Albert Dock complex. (You would be amazed at the thousands of young visitors who know more about the Beatles than any of us who were around at the time).

I have spent the past year researching, talking to designers, raising the finance and planning on how to tell the story in the simplest terms without sensationalising the events which are of a controversial nature.

I know that the Beatles are a part of the past, as far as you are concerned, and we respect that - therefore do not expect you to be involved in the project, but I hope that you may have some happy memories of the early days of Merseybeat; (the Cavern, Aintree Institute, Litherland Town Hall, The 'Blue', Bob, Allan, the other groups) and that you will give the project your blessing. I have also written to Paul, Ringo and Yoko, to let them know what is happening, plus I think you may be aware that I have spoken to Derek Taylor about my proposals.

I look forward to hearing from you.

Yours sincerely,

Directors M.A. Byrne R. Byrne P.S. Birtwistle

mpL

1 Soho Square · London W1V 6BQ

8 December 1988

Dear Mr Byrne

Thank you for your recent letter concerning your Exhibiion at the Albert Dock in Liverpool and requesting an interview with Paul McCartney.

I regret to inform you that owing to his extremely hectic schedule at present, Paul is not accepting any invitations for the foreseeable future. He is therefore unable to grant you an interview. Nevertheless, he would like to thank you for considering his involvement and wish you every success for the future.

Yours sincerely

Sarah Haddeley

PP RICHARD OGDEN

MPL Communications Limited · Registered in England No. 944968 · Registered Office 1 Soho Square London W1

BREAKING GROUND AND LAYING THE FOUNDATIONS

Bernie: It was a very exciting day when the builders moved in, but also very daunting. The first (and quite major) job was to create a new entrance into the basement from the Britannia Courtyard, a major structural job including cutting through the original three-foot-thick dock walls!

From the day we broke ground in December 1989, we had set ourselves the ambitious target opening date of Easter 1990. This gave us just five months to get everything done!

It was difficult to underestimate the mammoth task ahead of us. We were two novices, directing a team of architects and builders on how to transform an inhospitable, disused dock basement, which hadn't been touched for over 100 years, into a tourist attraction. It took blind ambition to get from what was a bare, dark, dusty basement to our Beatles Story dream.

CREATING THE ENTRANCE STAIRWELL

We knew the task ahead was not going to be easy, especially because the budget was tight. As work progressed, local interest grew through media coverage, and it became apparent to all involved that what had once been a pipe dream was now becoming a reality. Mike and I were constantly on the go and our kids became very independent. Even if we arrived back from the site before 9 or 10 pm, we were often on the phone or working late into the night.

From November 1989 to May 1990, we were working 'eight days a week'! Each morning at 8am, Mike would have a site meeting with the team of architects and builders to discuss the previous day's progress. We were hit by various challenges along the way, many of which had to do with the fact that we were working on a listed building, but our excellent architects rose to the challenge and overcame many of the problems. We were limited with space – just 7,000 square feet to fit everything into, but it was always our hope that at a later date we would be able to expand to allow us to do more.

PREPARING THE FOUNDATIONS

MIKE LENDS A HELPING HAND TO THE BUILDERS

Mike: The low, solid brick basement ceilings posed one of the main challenges as there was nowhere to install the required air conditioning pipework. We had to dig down into the floors to create vents for fresh air to come in. It was quite innovative but an extra expense. Fortunately, we had been advised to build a ten percent contingency into our costings.

Another unforeseen obstacle was in creating the signage for the entrance. I wanted the sign to stand out to attract passers-by and be clearly seen, but the people who looked after the heritage of the Albert Dock had a very different perspective on this! They wanted a subtle sign that blended with the traditional look of the docks, and they also didn't want us to attach it to the brick. They said we were defacing the walls of the listed building. After much negotiation about the size and colour of the letters we came to a compromise.

Being in the basement of a dockland warehouse that was nearly 150 years old presented its own set of issues. The fact that we were below the waterline of the River Mersey meant that we had a constant battle with salt and moisture. Walls and ceilings had to be painted with a special sealant to prevent salt from penetrating the fabric of the exhibition.

Pumping stations were in use to keep the river out, and we would have to give access to Albert Dock officials to inspect them when they felt it was necessary. This would later prove its importance as the exhibition was flooded on more than one occasion, forcing us to close until the pumps were back in action.

INSTALLING THE UNDERGROUND VENTILATION SYSTEM

They said we were defacing the walls of the listed building

THE EXTERNAL SIGN BEING INSTALLED – AN EXCITING DAY!

TELLING THE STORY

The heart of the exhibition would be the narrative, written by Bernie, and this would be woven into the exhibition's features in chronological order. The exhibition had nearly a hundred boards of text and images, which told the story in detail, and we needed a graphic designer to work with Bernie to plan the story out, on easy-to-read boards.

She originally wrote out every single board by hand, eventually moving it over to her word-processor. This was a huge and laborious task which saw Bernie writing night after night into the early hours to get it all done on time.

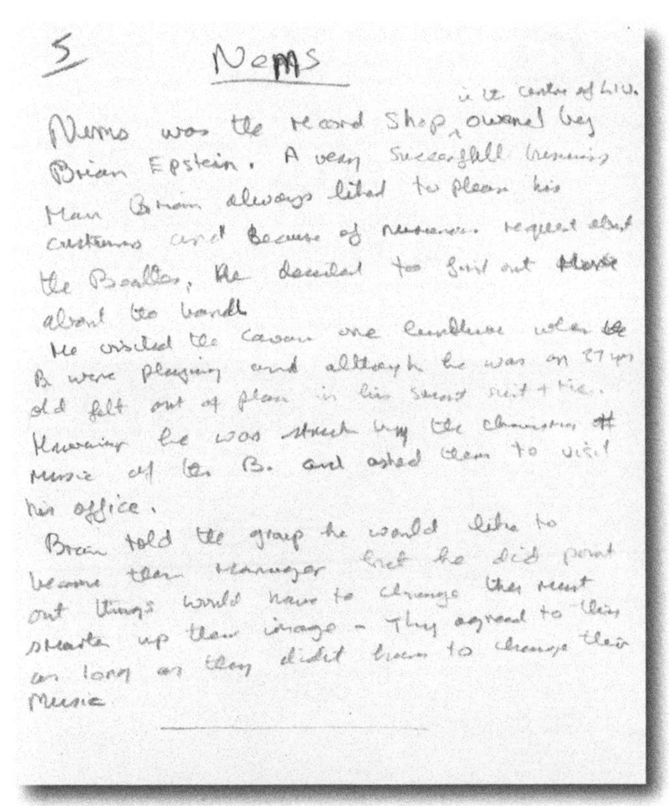

5 Nems

i.e. centre of Liv.

Nems was the record shop, owned by Brian Epstein. A very successful business. Man Brian always liked to please his customers and because of numerous request about the Beatles, he decided to find out about the band.
He visited the Cavern one lunchtime when the B were playing and although he was only 27 yrs old felt out of place in his smart suit + tie. Hearing he was struck by the charisma + music of the B. and asked them to visit his office.
Brian told the group he would like to become their manager but he did point out things would have to change they must smarten up their image - They agreed to this as long as they didn't have to change their music

BERNIE'S HANDWRITTEN NEMS PANEL

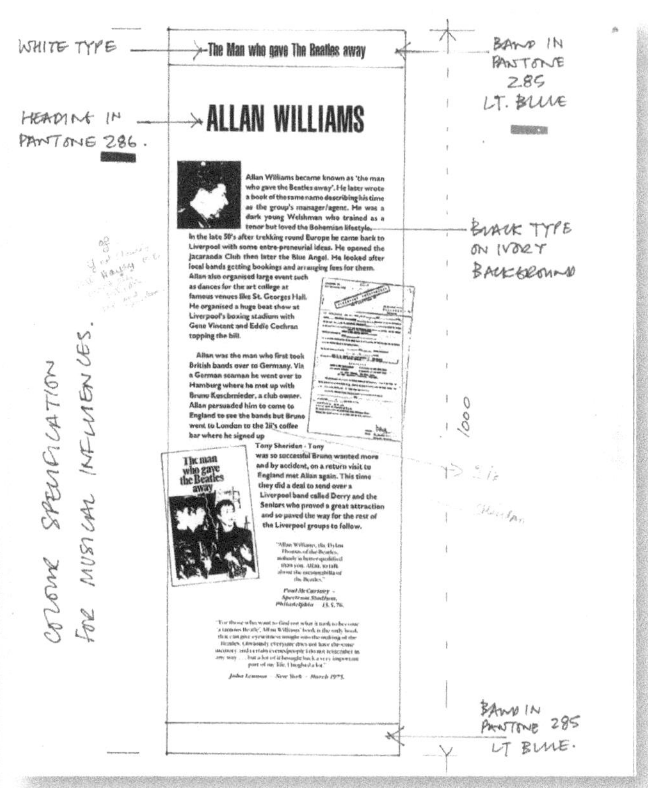

ALLAN WILLIAMS DRAFT BOARD

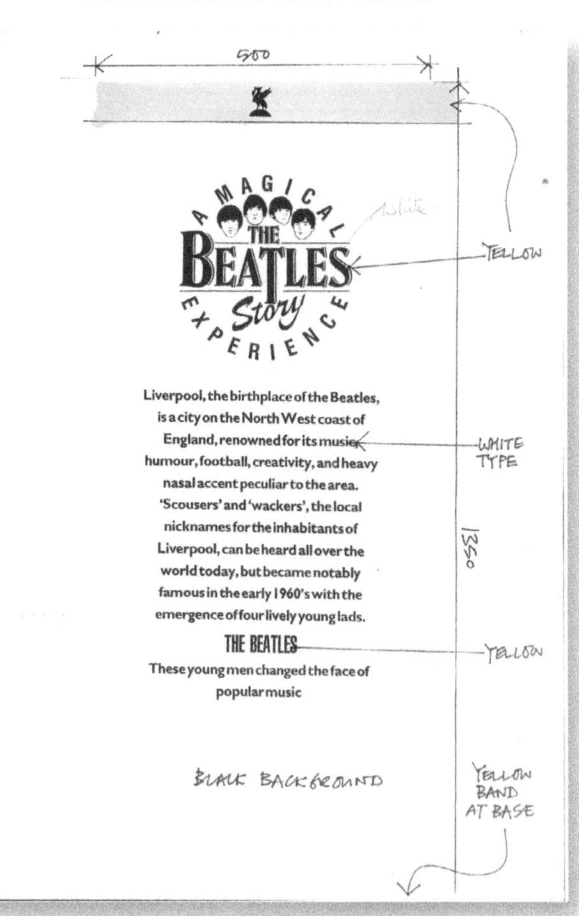

DRAFT DESIGN FOR THE WELCOME BOARD – BERNIE WROTE, DESIGNED AND COPY CHECKED EVERY SINGLE BOARD

We had decided early on that we wanted to work with people who, like ourselves, would have a feel and passion for the subject. We found a company based in Chester called Loines Furnival who fitted the bill. One of the partners, Mike Loines, had also grown up through the Beatles era and was excited to be involved.

Bernie worked day and night, drafting and amending over a hundred boards of text and images. This was all done by going back and forth over fax and post as well as weekly meetings as there was no email or internet at the time!

Loines Furnival also provided designs and sketches for the many signs that featured in the exhibition, such as The Star Club and Tabu signs in Hamburg, and Hessy's and NEMS.

THE LAYOUT

MIKE WITH THE PROJECT'S ARCHITECT, STEVE QUICKE (FAR LEFT) AND THE TEAM OF BUILDERS

Concepts were discussed, reviewed, and thrashed out until we were happy with the eighteen features that we had originally planned. Construction of The Beatles Story was well and truly underway by now and Mike was on site daily, even with a torn ligament in his ankle which meant he was on crutches for a large period (he fell off a stage!), overseeing the building work. Visiting the site was great fun. Not only was it good to see things progress, but the lads on site had a great sense of humour. They were excited about working on such an unusual project.

It was gratifying to be able to take family and friends down to the site, and show them that our dream was actually becoming a reality. They had been hearing Bernie and me talk about this ambitious and unlikely project for over a year and I'm not sure even they could believe it was really happening.

MIKE ON CRUTCHES IN THE EARLY DAYS OF THE BUILD - HE HAD FALLEN OFF A STAGE DURING A SHOW!

CREATING THE EXPERIENCE

Bernie: When sourcing content, it appeared that as soon as we mentioned the word "Beatles" the price would increase. Copyright as far as Beatles photographs were concerned has always been a money-making business so we were fortunate that we could call on our friends and some of The Beatles' relatives like Mike McCartney and Julia Baird.

Good friends from the 60s were keen to support us and see their memories being preserved; many of them had been in Merseybeat bands themselves such as Don Andrew (The Remo 4), Johnny 'Guitar' Byrne (Rory Storm and the Hurricanes) and Brian Johnson (Rory Storm/The Strangers). They loaned or gifted pictures, leaflets, tickets and posters from their personal collections to lend authenticity to several of the sets and trusted us to look after them as if they were our own.

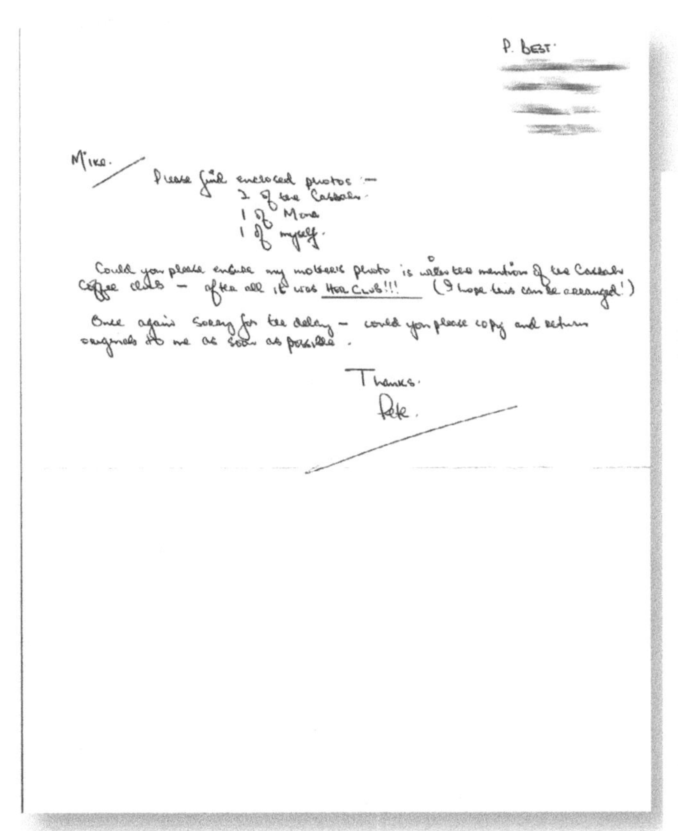

P. BEST.

Mike.

Please find enclosed photos :-
2 of the Casbah.
1 of Mona
1 of myself.

Could you please ensure my mother's photo is with the mention of the Casbah Coffee club – after all it was HER CLUB!!! (I hope this can be arranged!)

Once again sorry for the delay – could you please copy and return originals to me as soon as possible.

Thanks.
Pete.

LETTER FROM PETE BEST ABOUT LOANING PICTURES

With their help, we managed to keep down what could have been quite prohibitive costs. We also contributed many items of our own that we had accumulated over the years.

—∞—

"as soon as we mentioned the word 'Beatles' the price would increase"

—∞—

Don Andrew and his wife Lyn contributed a great deal, helping us to recreate the early days with their memories of the 60s. Don loaned us lots of photographs and reproduction show posters and was a reliable sounding board from the very beginning for us to add to the authenticity and fill in any details we were hazy on. When we were building the Cavern stage, he organised the painting of the famous Cavern backdrop.

He called on the help of former members of The Fourmost (one of Brian Epstein's signed acts), Joey Bower and Dave Lovelady, to paint it. They had set up a painting and decorating business, so were perfect for the job. Don brought in a projector and projected a life-size image of

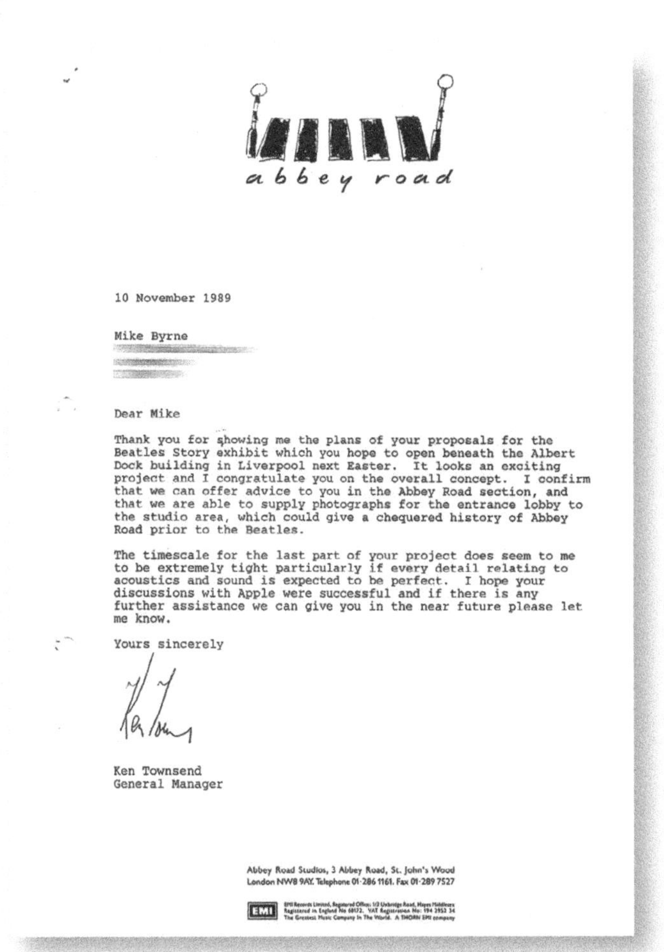

abbey road

10 November 1989

Mike Byrne

Dear Mike

Thank you for showing me the plans of your proposals for the Beatles Story exhibit which you hope to open beneath the Albert Dock building in Liverpool next Easter. It looks an exciting project and I congratulate you on the overall concept. I confirm that we can offer advice to you in the Abbey Road section, and that we are able to supply photographs for the entrance lobby to the studio area, which could give a chequered history of Abbey Road prior to the Beatles.

The timescale for the last part of your project does seem to me to be extremely tight particularly if every detail relating to acoustics and sound is expected to be perfect. I hope your discussions with Apple were successful and if there is any further assistance we can give you in the near future please let me know.

Yours sincerely

Ken Townsend
General Manager

Abbey Road Studios, 3 Abbey Road, St. John's Wood
London NW8 9AY. Telephone 01-286 1161. Fax 01-289 7527

EMI

SUPPORTIVE LETTER FROM ABBEY ROAD

PAINTING THE CAVERN BACKDROP

To: Mike Byrne

From: Bob Wooler

Reference: MB Era Photographs, etc

Message: Dear Mike: I'm afraid - once again - I'm going to have to defer matters for a few days. I was contacted earlier this week by some visiting Americans who wanted a 'horse's mouth' tour of Beatleland, complete with my personal reminiscences. This I agreed to do but it involved a couple of days. Consequently I have been interrupted in my big sorting out operation in my office at 20 Tithebarn Street. However, I should have everything done by next week-end, so stand-by for action the following week. I have been doing some sorting out, however, and I came across some items that may be of interest to you personally. These go back at least 10 years (about the time I've had the office, so there's a helluva lot of stuff there!). At least they should bring some memories back for you! I'll be in touch again in about a week's time.

Signed Bob

Date Sat. 9 July 1988

NOTE FROM BOB WOOLER

the original backdrop onto portable wall panels. They traced the design onto panels, then painted it and filled in the colours to get it as close to the original as possible. Another great support and provider of original memories was Bill Harry, and his wife Virginia. They advised us on the design of the Mersey Beat office, and he helped write the script for a recreation of a phone call between him and Bob Wooler. Their conversation about booking The Beatles was played through an old telephone handset situated in the office, which people could pick up and listen in to.

Bob Wooler was also a great help. We had approached him a while before we got funding to ask for his support and anything he could contribute.

"Thankfully, we decided to put a copy on display, as after a few days it was stolen"

Mike: Abbey Road Studios were very supportive and not only advised us on the layout of Studio Two, as it would have looked, but also provided photographs for permanent use in the exhibition.

Sometimes, if an original document or picture was too precious to display, we would make a copy. This was certainly the case when Charles Rosenay loaned us John Lennon's application form for permanent US residence, which included his fingerprints and personal details. Thankfully, we decided to put a copy on display, as after a few days it was stolen! We secured copies of posters and tickets to walls using a strong adhesive and would often find that they had been picked and peeled at the corners by over-zealous fans.

Bernie: Life was hectic as I was dividing my time between graphic designers, photo libraries, film studios, and prospective lenders, but it was all worthwhile to see our dream coming together. I spent hours in London visiting a variety of major libraries to hunt out specific photographs. One visit to a film library almost proved fruitless when some of the films we wanted to use had been stolen. This was only discovered when they went to get them for me!

FINISHING TOUCHES - THE FINAL BUILD

Bernie: Once the main walls, joinery and floorings were all in place, the features had to be brought to life with voiceovers, pictures and sound effects which had to be edited together to create the overall effect and sensory experience that we had envisaged from the very start. As we saw it coming together, Mike and I started to realise that our dream really was becoming a reality. We were still working eighteen-hour days, at a very fast pace, as the deadline for opening approached.

There were a number of specialist companies who we brought on board to achieve this, and again we found them to be very accommodating with their creativity and flexibility in trying to bring our vision to life. The Works were an audio-visual company who helped us to create automatic lighting sequences timed with music and audio. This was crucial to giving some of the sets a beginning and an end such as the timed lighting in The Cavern, Psychedelic/Sgt. Pepper area and the White Room. The aptly named Prop Art made life-size dummies of The Beatles to stand in our Abbey Road studio, a Bill Harry model for Mersey Beat and a 'lady of the night' who adorned a corner of Hamburg.

LADY OF THE NIGHT MODEL

When the numerous pieces of signage arrived courtesy of Chris Benson Signs, we couldn't wait to get them fitted. They provided the Star Club and Tabu signs in Hamburg, as well as signs for NEMS, The Grapes pub, EMI studio, the Abbey Road Belisha beacon and a huge juke box featuring the names of rock 'n' roll stars who had influenced The Beatles.

Last but not least, Art Attack created moulded doorframes and windows for Hamburg and Mathew Street, suitably treated to look aged and weather worn.

JUKEBOX FAÇADE IN THE EARLY INFLUENCES SECTION

The timed sequences, lighting, smells, sound effects, background music and voiceovers that were vital to creating the heart and soul of the experience required a substantial technical set up. The leading company in this field was Electrosonic, who provided us with all the technical equipment we needed in each set, as well as the main control room. Steve Roughley worked some very unsociable hours with us, into the night, to get everything done on time.

In conjunction with many others who made smaller but very significant contributions, these creative professionals glued The Beatles Story together and made it fit for public consumption at last.

PROMOTING A NEW ATTRACTION

Mike: Alongside the physical build, there was the brand image to create and a full marketing plan to be devised. I had quite a lot of experience in this area owing to years of publicising shows and events, in addition to my years working in newspapers. Bernie and I already had a good idea of how we wanted the logo to look, and it was gratifying to see the idea come to life in the hands of our designer.

MIKE'S EARLY HAND-DRAWN LOGO IDEA

Mike: As the building work progressed, from November 1989, we began to roll out the marketing plan to ensure the world would know we were opening in the summer of 1990. But our timing had to be right. Having such a high-profile subject as The Beatles meant we didn't want too much publicity too soon.

Bernie: Although the Merseyside Tourism Board was now looking forward to Liverpool having a permanent Beatle attraction, we still felt that some people in tourism didn't have much faith in us. I suppose this was understandable as we were unqualified and inexperienced in the exhibition and museum sector. There were also still reservations about the appeal of The Beatles as a tourist attraction, partly because previous Beatle-related projects had failed. There wasn't credible precedence for this type of exhibition to succeed.

Mike: The lack of faith in us was very tangible when we wanted to distribute our pre-launch flyer from Merseyside Tourism Board's stand at the World Travel Market, in Earl's Court - one of the biggest tourism events in the world and the place to exhibit. Unfortunately, we were not allowed to give them out as we hadn't yet become members of the Tourist Board.

We had always planned to join but simply hadn't had the time to do the paperwork. At times like that, we felt very much on our own, but fortunately, we made many new friends along the way who were very supportive.

Having such a high-profile subject as The Beatles meant we didn't want too much publicity too soon.

ALTERNATIVE IDEAS FOR THE LOGO

OPENING THE EXHIBITION

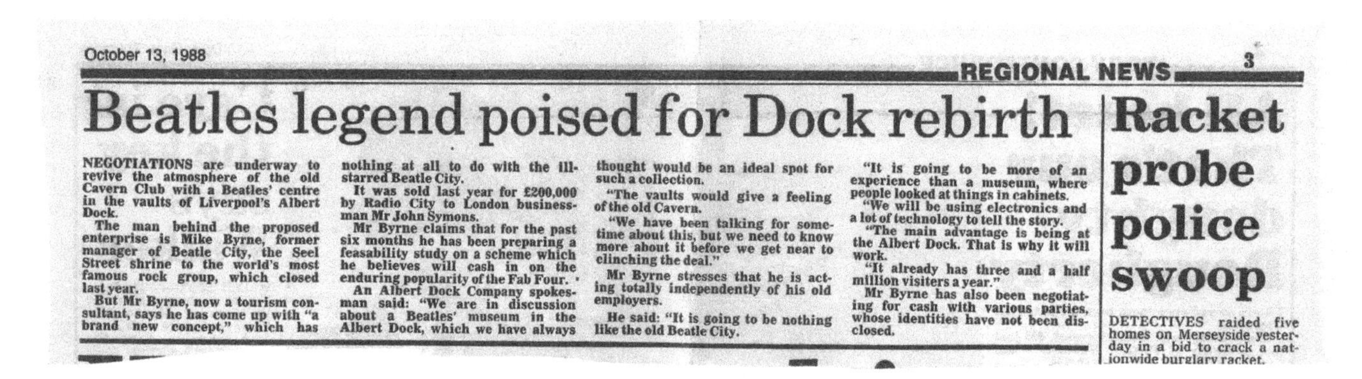

October 13, 1988

REGIONAL NEWS 3

Beatles legend poised for Dock rebirth

NEGOTIATIONS are underway to revive the atmosphere of the old Cavern Club with a Beatles' centre in the vaults of Liverpool's Albert Dock.

The man behind the proposed enterprise is Mike Byrne, former manager of Beatle City, the Seel Street shrine to the world's most famous rock group, which closed last year.

But Mr Byrne, now a tourism consultant, says he has come up with "a brand new concept," which has nothing at all to do with the ill-starred Beatle City.

It was sold last year for £200,000 by Radio City to London businessman Mr John Symons.

Mr Byrne claims that for the past six months he has been preparing a feasability study on a scheme which he believes will cash in on the enduring popularity of the Fab Four.

An Albert Dock Company spokesman said: "We are in discussion about a Beatles' museum in the Albert Dock, which we have always thought would be an ideal spot for such a collection.

"The vaults would give a feeling of the old Cavern.

"We have been talking for some-time about this, but we need to know more about it before we get near to clinching the deal."

Mr Byrne stresses that he is acting totally independently of his old employers.

He said: "It is going to be nothing like the old Beatle City.

"It is going to be more of an experience than a museum, where people looked at things in cabinets.

"We will be using electronics and a lot of technology to tell the story.

"The main advantage is being at the Albert Dock. That is why it will work.

"It already has three and a half million visiters a year."

Mr Byrne has also been negotiating for cash with various parties, whose identities have not been disclosed.

Racket probe police swoop

DETECTIVES raided five homes on Merseyside yesterday in a bid to crack a nationwide burglary racket.

Mike: The original target date set for the opening was Easter 1990, but we had to revise that date after modifications meant the project grew. Every contractor on the site was working long hours as they knew the pressure was on, but by March, everyone from the electricians and carpenters to the architect and designers was telling me the same thing – that we had to revise our opening date, so we moved it to the start of May. We had hoped to hit Easter to benefit from Easter holiday trade, but it just wasn't possible. By now the local press had become interested in our venture and were regularly reporting on our progress.

Alongside overseeing the final elements of the build, researching merchandise and stocking the shop, and promoting it, we also had to recruit staff – we advertised for security men and shop staff, and were inundated with applications. After a long process of elimination, we employed a group of people who we felt would make a good team. The opening day was now set in stone for May 3rd, 1990.

—~—

Bernie: The week before we were due to open Mike and I were on our last legs. Since January 1990 it was like being in the middle of a storm with no end in sight. We were exhausted, having worked 18-hour days for months, yet the adrenaline had kept us going and now at last we were nearly there. We couldn't really believe it. The dream had turned into a reality, although I think we were too tired to appreciate what we had achieved.

Press releases were sent to international press agencies, and on May 1st we had a press launch and preview day when national and international press and TV came down, including some Japanese and American journalists. Local press like Granada and Look North West came and we were relieved to receive very positive reviews.

We held another preview on May 2nd for hoteliers, tourism contacts and Albert Dock tenants, in the hope that they would tell their guests about it.

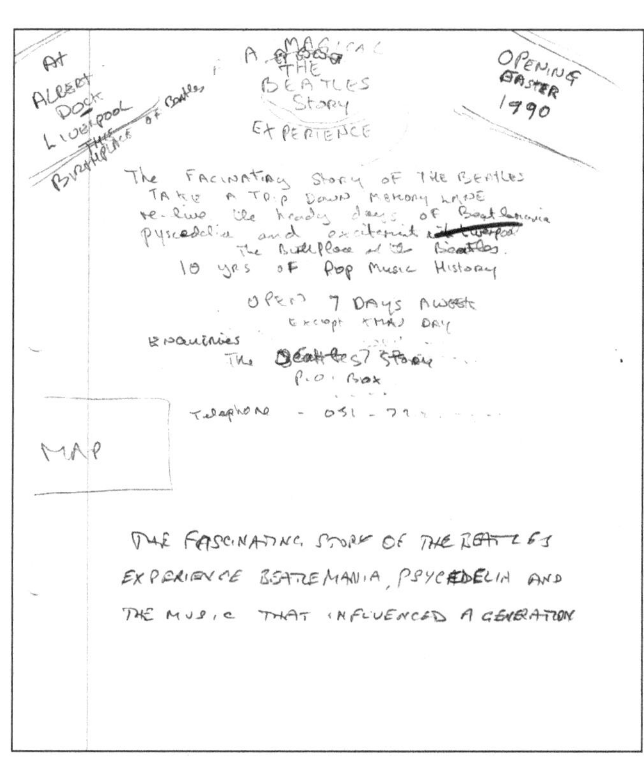

BERNIE'S HAND-DRAWN SKETCH FOR THE PRE-OPENING DAY FLYER

The public opening day was very successful. Richard and Judy featured us on their ITV 'This Morning' show which was broadcast from the Albert Dock every day. Gerry Marsden of Gerry and the Pacemakers, Bob Wooler, Allan Williams and Bill Harry were special guests. Gerry played and sang his hit records and told us that our replica Cavern was more authentic than the new one in Mathew Street!

Mike: Gerry and I had known each other from the Cavern days. He was always generous with his time, never asked for a fee, just a bottle of his favourite wine and a meal for his driver. It was a critical success from day one and congratulations and best wishes came from far and wide. We were elated that it was finally open. However, this was only the beginning, and the real hard work was about to begin, as we had to get people through the doors.

Yesterday!

Gerry and Mike among scenes from the hey-day of the Beatles

Fab Four story rockin' down at the dock

By Paul Byrne

THE latest chapter in The Beatles Story has been written at Liverpool's Albert Dock.

In the week that the city prepares to celebrate the life of John Lennon, Liverpool singing star Gerry Marsden has given the seal of approval to the exciting new £1m venture.

The atmosphere of the original Cavern Club has been recreated at the Albert Dock where former musician Mike Byrne is adding the final touches before today's big opening of The Beatles Story.

Concert

Gerry will be joining Echo readers on board the Royal Iris for a night to remember on the Mersey on Saturday.

While thousands of pop fans watch the massive Lennon concert at Liverpool's Pier Head, Echo readers will be

Gerry and the Pacemakers.

Before the big night Gerry popped into the new-look Cavern Club to get warmed up for the occasion.

Thousands of tourists are expected flock to the city for the Lennon concert, and hundreds of visitors are likely to take a Ticket to Ride through time, back to the hey-day of the Beatles.

recapture something of the unique atmosphere of the Cavern.

● A few tickets for the Royal Iris are still available. They cost £12 50, half the price of the Lennon concert, and that includes a Scouse meal. Applications should be made to the Echo in writing with cheques and postal orders made payable to "Merseycats" and sent to Lennon Cruise, Dept C, Liverpool Echo, PO Box 48, Old Hall Street, Liverpool L69

MIKE AND GERRY MARSDEN – 'FAB FOUR' STORY NEWSPAPER ARTICLE

y, February 1, 1990

Ticket to ride through time!

IMAGINE descending into the vaults of the Albert Dock — and finding yourself back in the Cavern in 1961.

Or plunged into the hysteria of a Hamburg nightclub on a night the Beatles were playing.

Whether like me you were a toddler and missed the lot, or you were lucky enough to experience the Merseybeat era, Mike Byrne's new venture is a ticket to ride through time.

And it is being hailed as a great new tourist boost for the city, with a quarter of a million visitors expected each year.

The sights, the sounds, the screams and, yes, the smells — all recreated in a £1 million hi-tech 'Beatles Experience' exhibition that is the brainchild of the enterprising former musician and has attracted the backing of Wembley Stadium Ltd.

Gearing up for an April opening in time for the massive influx of visitors for the Lennon memorial concert in May, Mike said today: "It's a totally up-to-the-minute experience.

"I don't want to just produce a museum. I want to allow people to experience what it was actually like. Go for a walk along Mathew Street, see what they would have seen, feel the atmosphere, go down into the Cavern or down a Hamburg street.

"The way it's laid out takes visitors from archive, to atmospheric stuff to graphics. Three of the Beatles are still alive, so it's not like a heritage thing where you do a dummy of Ann Boleyn being beheaded. It's a story that is continuing to this day.

"It's a complicated story because of all the lawsuits that went on, their political views, the musical barriers they broke and so on."

Ably assisting Mike during the years of painstaking research has been his wife Bernadette, a Beatles tour guide in Liverpool for the last eight years. And just recently she's been the leg woman as well as his right-hand man since he badly injured his leg during his stage cabaret act a few weeks ago!

"You might say it's getting better all the time," said Mike, "with a little help from my friends!

☐ Mike Byrne in the warehouse that will hold the Beatles Story exhibition.

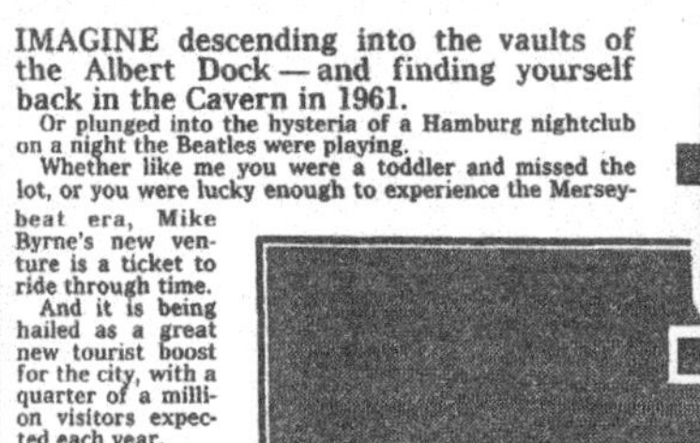

Linda McDermott reports on a new experience being created in the dock for Beatles fans

Detail

"Seriously, though, we have spent months going through books researching material and paying meticulous attention to detail. We knew most of the story anyway having grown up in the same era and known them from the Cavern days.

"I'm really pleased with the way the interior transformation is going. I'm indebted to Liverpool architects Franklin Stafford, who've gone along with me on a wing and a prayer for the first year of pulling together the concept.

"I have always believed Liverpool should have a proper tribute to the Beatles and I believe the Beatles Story will be just that."

The 9,000 square foot development taking shape in underground warehouses at the dock will use the very latest technological tricks to give time travellers a realistic taste of Liverpool in the '60s.

It will follow the Fab Four's progress from the Mersey to the Maharishna, through Beatlemania and psychedelia, to the group's split, Lennon's murder and up to the present day.

It will not, promises Mike Byrne, be simply a turgid collection of old relics and memorabilia. The place will pulsate to the Merseybeat sound, there will be archive film material culled from 300 hours of ITN footage, a walk-through yellow submarine and realistic street walks.

One of its major features will be a replica of the Cavern Club. The vaulted low ceilings of the Albert Dock warehouses give an authentic atmosphere.

Interior decorators Art Attack are even giving the old brickwork special treatment to look 30 years old, complete with scuffs on paintwork from all that twistin' and shoutin'!

"This isn't just going to be a collection of souvenirs," says Mike, "it's going to show people what it felt like to be in the Cavern, or in Hamburg when the Beatles were just starting out."

He should know. He played alongside the Beatles in the crazy Cavern days.

As an apprentice tailor in his father's business around the corner from Mathew Street, Mike spent lunchtimes in the Cavern and became friendly with members of other groups, including Paul McCartney.

He formed his first group, Mike and the Thunderbirds, and later won a talent contest backed by Rory Storm and the Hurricanes — with Ringo Starr on drums.

A spell on the cabaret circuit led to jobs as compere and entertainment manager at two of Liverpool's top nightclubs, followed by a two-year spell with the Ken Dodd Laughter Show.

In the '80s Mike left his job as a local newspaper promotions manager to join the company that ran Beatle City and went to America with the Beatles exhibition.

"That really opened my eyes to the enthusiasm there is for the Beatles in the States," he says.

"Since then I've spent the last two years raising the finance and getting everyone together to make this one of the best attractions in the world and something that Liverpool can be proud of.

"We are building a focal point for all those tourists and disappointed fans from around the world who want a proper tribute to the Beatles in their home city.

"Enthusiasm overseas is really phenomenal, particularly in the States and Japan. We've already had a lot of inquiries from foreign fan clubs."

Wembley Stadium Ltd. showed its confidence in Mike and in Merseyside's tourist pulling power by providing the biggest slab of cash backing.

Business development director Alan Murray said: "We are sure this is going to be a winner.

"Both the chairman, Brian Wolfson, and I come from Liverpool and there's certainly an emotional link for us with the place, the people and the Beatles.

"But we based our decision on sound commercial judgement. It is simply a cracking idea. We are sure this will be a major tourist attraction and it fits with Wembley's overall corporate strategy to enter into exciting new areas within the leisure industry."

The project is being welcomed by Albert Dock developers and the MDC as another jewel in the crown of the waterside complex.

Ray Guy-Jobson, managing director of the Albert Dock company, said: "The addition of the Beatles Experience to the existing retail and commercial attractions can only add to the dock's tourist appeal. There's a lot of hard work gone into the planning of this and we're sure it will be something else for Merseyside to be proud of."

'TICKET TO RIDE THROUGH TIME' PRE-OPENING NEWSPAPER ARTICLE – FEBRUARY 1ST, 1990

FROM RAVE REVIEWS TO THE REALITY OF A RECESSION

Mike: Despite the positive reviews and the satisfaction of having finally realised our dream, the first few years were tough, as they are in any new business. Britain was suffering the first effects of a recession, which lasted for three years. British households were feeling the pinch so visiting tourist attractions was way down on the list of many families' priorities. Another setback was the Lockerbie air disaster, which discouraged international visitors, especially from the lucrative American market, as did the Gulf War in 1991.

In addition to this, Beatles tourism still wasn't supported by the council or appreciated by the locals. It really felt like an uphill struggle. I was interviewed about it by The Liverpool Echo in 1993, three years after we had opened. I highlighted the fact that Liverpool still wasn't capitalising on its greatest export.

In it, I give Memphis as an example of how a city celebrates every aspect of its greatest product, Elvis Presley. He is EVERYWHERE! You can see him in shops, cafes, hairdressers and on every street corner. I state examples of how we could be doing this in Liverpool – for example renaming the airport as the John Lennon Memorial Airport (this eventually happened eight years later in 2001) and having signs at the end of the M62 motorway saying "Welcome to Liverpool – the Birthplace of The Beatles". Again, this eventually happened.

But the laid-back locals of the time felt it wasn't the done thing to enthuse about The Beatles; astonishingly, the general feeling seemed to be "What have The Beatles ever done for Liverpool?" Looking back now, this seems hard to believe, but we experienced this negativity to what we were trying to do every single day.

Bernie: We sent out an invitation to five hundred taxi drivers across Merseyside offering free admission to them and their families. We figured that if they knew the location and had experienced the exhibition for themselves, they could help promote it to tourists who came to the city on Beatles pilgrimages. Incredibly, only fourteen taxi drivers accepted out of five hundred, such was the apathy at that time.

We worked tirelessly to stimulate visitors to come to The Beatles Story with new initiatives, often in conjunction with the Merseyside Tourism Board, Cavern City Tours and the North West Tourist Board. One major example of this was a partnership we initiated with Regional Railways. Mike and I met them at The World Travel Market and asked if they had ever been to Liverpool. They looked slightly uncomfortable and bemused as to why they should visit, and we offered them a free weekend in Liverpool. We gave them the full VIP Beatle experience, tour of Liverpool and Mersey ferry ride, as well as the wealth of museums Liverpool had to offer.

This resulted in the hugely successful 'Live It Up in Liverpool' partnership, funded by Regional Railways, offering their passengers half-price entry to ten Merseyside attractions, including ours. By the mid-1990s, attitudes towards Liverpool as a tourist destination were slowly starting to change. This article explains how perceptions started to change for the better, as transport partners and external stakeholders started to see the potential of Liverpool as a destination.

"What have The Beatles ever done for Liverpool?"

Bernie's Boston broadcast

THE Mersey message will be broadcast to America today in a unique link-up with Boston.

Bernadette Byrne, a Merseyside Tourism Board guide, is spreading the word in a live radio interview on Boston's WVBF Radio from London.

The station is broadcasting for a week from the Hilton International hotel and decided its listeners should get the low-down on Liverpool.

Bernadette said: "I will be pushing Merseyside as much as possible.

Bernadette Byrne

"I think people need to be told that there is so much to see here that they really do need to spend more than a day-trip away from London."

She said that she hopes to open the eyes of Bostonians to the many attractions throughout the whole region.

"There is a lot more to Merseyside than Beatles Tours," said Bernadette, a Merseyguide since 1983.

While Bernadette is waxing lyrical on Liverpool, tourism boss Samir Rihani will also be doing his bit for the region across town.

The chief executive and [illegible] Caroline Griffiths are attending an exhibition near the Barbican to promote the North West.

They will be trying to attract tourism developments to Merseyside by highlighting sites available throughout the region for conference centres, hotels, theme and leisure parks and other tourism-related industries.

The North Meets South exhibition is in conjunction with other tourist agencies and public and private sector organisations throughout the North West.

● Caring image for tourism: Page 26.

BERNIE GIVES INTERVIEW TO BOSTON RADIO ABOUT VISITING LIVERPOOL

Liverpool Echo Beatles Special, Tuesday, August 24, 1993 PAGE NINETEEN

THE BEATLES FOREVER

On Sunday the massive convention flea market is held at the Adelphi Hotel with live music, speakers and films, followed by a big concert in the evening at the Royal Court.
After the all-day street festival on Monday the Bootleg Beatles are in concert at the Empire, the theatre where the Beatles once failed a talent contest in the very early days.
For those who still have the strength there is a lunchtime party back in the Cavern.

It's time to spread the gospel to the whole world

BUSINESSMAN Mike Byrne reckons Liverpool has still to wake up to its potential as "Beatle City."

"We should be doing more to promote the Beatles," thinks Mike, who runs the Beatles Story in the Albert Dock.

"I don't think we really do enough as a city to commemorate the Beatles as a pop phenomenon."

Beatles rock? Beatles chewing gum? Beatles haircuts? Maybe there's a mint to be made somewhere. After all, Memphis Tennessee makes big bucks out of a certain Elvis Aaron Presley.

Entrepreneur Mike reckons: "If this was Elvis's birthplace the airport would be called John Lennon Memorial airport, there would be signs at the end of the M62 saying 'Welcome to Liverpool — birthplace of the Beatles'.

"Instead, we have the biggest pop group the world has ever seen and no one mentions it."

Beatles business in Liverpool battles against a sense of "seen it all before." It is somehow "not done" for laid-back locals to enthuse about the Beatles — even if they are fans, he says.

"We take it for granted that the Beatles came from Liverpool.

"There are lots of opportunities presented by the Beatles which could benefit the city in terms of jobs, but we're slow to take it up."

By Diane Massey

Other people in business, who should make it their business to know the Beatles story, are misinformed or uninformed.

Take taxi drivers, for example, says Mike. "A woman ordered a taxi from the Beatles Story here the other day. She asked the cab to pick her up but he didn't know where it was.

"That's an example of how people who are in the tourist business to an extent are not aware of the tourism in their own city."

The Beatles Story is probably the only Beatles "museum" of any size in the area — although Mike prefers to call it "an experience."

But if you think about it, it's a bit like a London cabbie not knowing the way to Madame Tussauds.

The Beatles could be an export earner. There are 50,000 Japanese in the British fan club in Japan alone.

Of all the Beatles souvenirs — pens, T-shirts, key rings etc — on sale in the foyer of The Beatles Story, only the coffee mugs, to Mike's knowledge, are actually manufactured on Merseyside.

There is a growing academic side to the Beatles industry which local universities could explore. Beatles songs are now included in the national curriculum.

A Japanese student from Osaka University recently spent a month in Liverpool researching a Beatles thesis.

Beatles are fast becoming marketable history. Beatles memorabilia is big business. Mike Byrne is sure we are missing out — and maybe he is right.

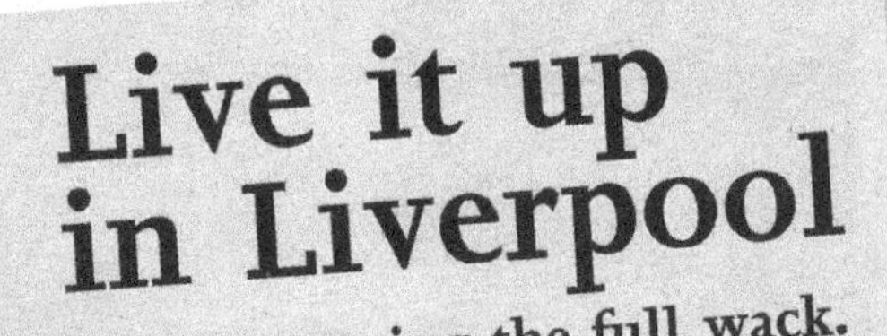

WE WERE RIGHT TO DREAM... AGAINST ALL THE ODDS

Despite the sleepless nights and stressful board meetings, we never doubted that our vision was sound, and that The Beatles Story would be a success for a long time to come. It eventually turned a profit after three years, which is standard for new ventures, and if it hadn't been for the recession, The Beatles Story would have been profitable much sooner.

The Beatles Story's continued success, going into its fourth decade, proves the enduring popularity of The Beatles. In 2015, it marked 25 years in business, and we were pleased to join in the celebrations with Martin King, the Managing Director, and his wonderful team. Seven years on, under the leadership of the new General Manager, Mary Chadwick, it's great to see the exhibition continue to evolve and expand on our original vision, paving the way for generations of Beatles fans for years to come.

To date, The Beatles Story has welcomed five million visitors.

A STORY OF SUCCESS — AT LAST

Sat 26/6/93 ECHO

Mike's big 'Beatles' gamble now a hit

BEATLES Story boss Mike Byrne's greatest gamble is finally paying dividends.

By Jules Stenson

Jubilant Mike expects his Fab Four extravaganza to make a profit this year — for the first time.

Mike sunk £40,000 of his own into the £750,000 venture at Liverpool's Albert Dock three years ago ... and now the venture has paid off.

Chance

Paul, Ringo and George have not visited the exhibition or donated memorabilia, but many people closely connected with the Beatles have visited — including Julian Lennon.

Mike, 50, said: "It was a madcap idea, but I took a chance. I wanted to recapture the feel of Liverpool during the sixties."

Former singer Mike admits launching the business in the recession has been a struggle.

But last year the Beatles Story broke even after 120,000 visitors poured in.

Mike took a big gamble when he packed in his job on a local paper, mortgaged the family home and started on the plan.

One look at the comments from comic Ben Elton and others in the celebrity visitors' book, shows the mix is working well.

"Whenever I get depressed I have a look at that," said Mike.

Mike Byrne ... "madcap"

NEWS RELEASE NEWS RELEASE NEWS RELEASE

THE BEATLES STORY

THE BEATLES STORY is Liverpool's newest tourist attraction. The spectacular walk through experience was built in the basement vaults of the Britannia Pavilion, Albert Dock at a cost of almost £1 million.
THE BEATLES STORY is the brainchild of Mike Byrne, a former Merseyside musician and his wife Bernadette a regular visitor to the Cavern Club who knew the Beatles personally in the early days.
It is the result of 2½ years of research and development. Mike says "A tribute of this kind has long been overdue for the City of Liverpool and for the thousands of fans who visit the city every year".
Already over 200,000 visitors of all ages have enjoyed reliving the heady days of Beatlemania.

The fascinating Beatles Story is told in 18 seperate features including a street in Hamburg, a full size replica of the Cavern Club with basement smells, a psychedelic scene and a walk through Yellow Submarine with real fish swimming past the port holes.Plus Beatles music and rare film footage.

THE BEATLES STORY has already featured on many T.V shows throughout Europe, America the Far East, even the U.S.S.R. and a host of celebrities have voiced their approval'

" It's brilliant, just like the old days" said Gerry Marsden of the Cavern.
Joyce Yates from Radio City " Incredible likeness of the Cavern".
" Magnificent" said Ray Coleman (John Lennon and Brian Epstein biographer).
"What a Magical History Tour " Ben Elton.

Mike hopes that THE BEATLES STORY will give people of all generations a taste of what the 60's was all about " This isn't a museum as such, it's a living, vibrant experience".

Open 7 days a week throughout the year.

CONTACT MIKE BYRNE FOR FURTHER INFORMATION

The Beatles Story, Britannia Vaults, Albert Dock, Liverpool L3 4AA. 051 709 1963

HOW WE TOLD THE STORY OF THE BEATLES IN 18 FEATURES

Mike: The Beatles Story that Bernie and I founded in 1990 had one clear vision - to tell the story of The Beatles' rise to fame in an experiential way – something that hadn't been done before. Instead of cases of memorabilia and static words and pictures, we wanted visitors to be immersed in the feelings, atmosphere and excitement that we experienced at the time, starting with 1950s Liverpool, then following their unprecedented and fantastic journey right through to the breakup and solo years. Some of the straplines we planned to use explain what we wanted to create: 'Take a Trip to Hamburg', 'Feel the Cavern Beat', 'Tune in to Flower Power' and 'Take a Trip Through the Yellow Submarine'.

The hardest part was deciding which highlights of their phenomenal career to include in the 6,000 square foot space we had to work with. We finally settled on eighteen distinct sets that were woven together to create the story. Each was chosen because of its importance and impact on The Beatles' lives.

Only when we decided to write this book, did we delve into the depths of our attic, and unearth box upon box of material in the form of handwritten notes, letters, sketches, photographs, set designs and correspondence (many on faded fax paper!), the sum of which went on to produce The Beatles Story. We had genuinely forgotten how much work, time and effort went into it! We found multiple different versions of the planned layout, including features that didn't make the final cut. For example, whole features such as The Casbah and a fan's Beatle-obsessed bedroom were dropped, even after the build began.

Bernie and I researched and designed details of the sets to the nth degree; from sounds, temperatures and smells to floor coverings and lighting. We used varied and distinctive materials to create separation between key stages of The Beatles' lives. Soundproofed tunnels and different floor textures such as cobblestones, carpet and wooden floorboards gave the effect of passing through different periods. We wanted to invade all the senses, hence our strapline: *'See It, Hear It, Feel It and Even Smell The 60s'*.

1. THE WAR YEARS

As the first feature of the exhibition, we were determined to transport visitors back in time from the present day to wartime Liverpool, and we knew the best way to do this was to flood their senses with sounds and images of the war years. Air-raid sirens and the sound of warplanes flying overhead greeted people as they

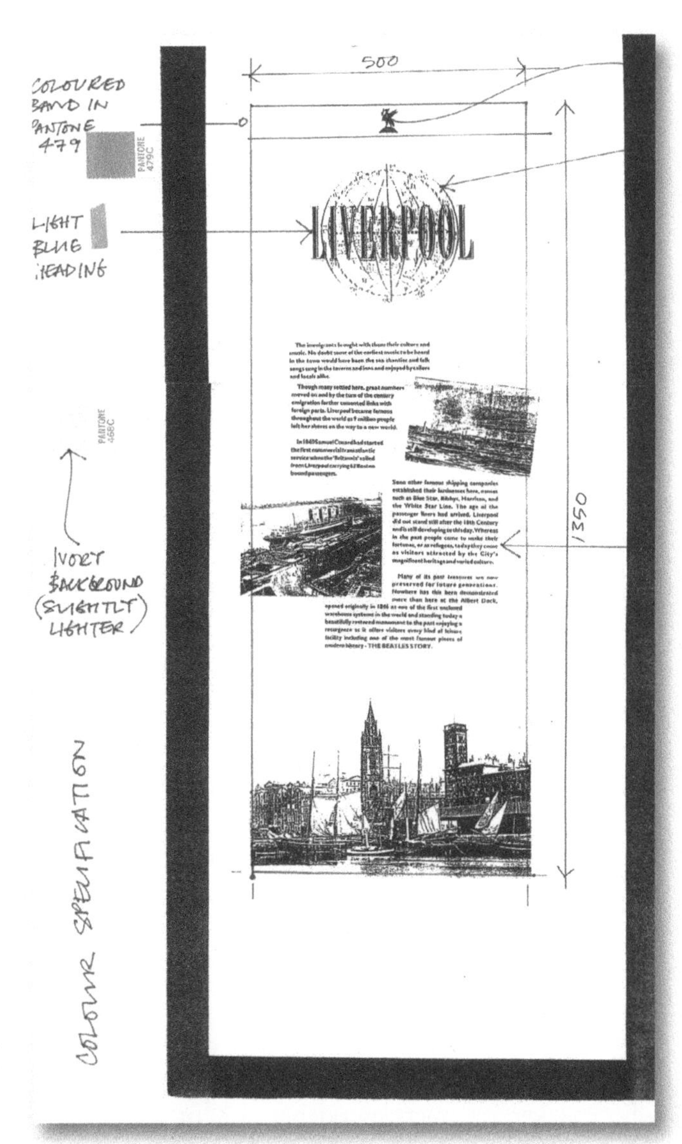

entered, closely followed by nostalgic music of the big-band era, accompanied by black and white film footage of wartime Liverpool. All four Beatles were born during the Second World War, so we featured images of the Liverpool that they grew up in, showing their early childhood homes and family photos.

We got special permission to exhibit The Beatles' birth certificates.

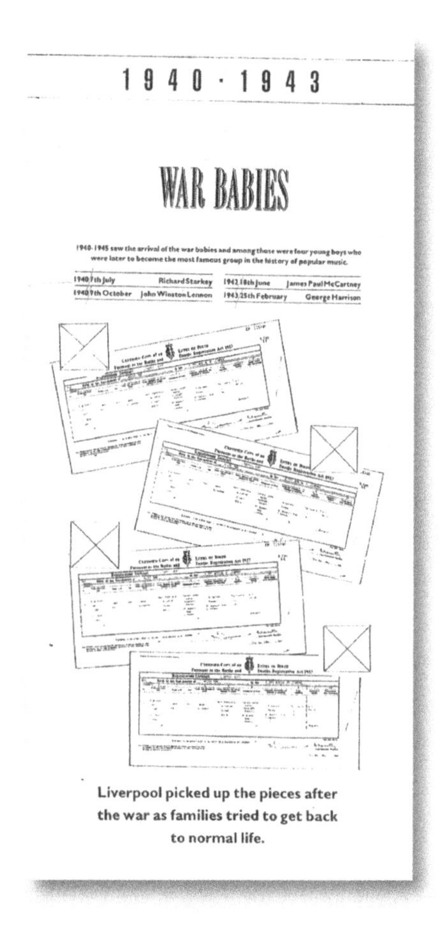

We talked about the booming shipping trade, and the strong 'scouse' (Liverpool) accent unique to its inhabitants – something The Beatles were renowned for, particularly John. (It was unusual for artists at the time not to disguise their accents or put on an American accent). Photographs of Liverpool slums showed the devastation after it had been bombed during the war and sounds of the time included the clatter of trams across cobbled streets, the rumbling of the ground beneath the Overhead Railway and the excitement of scrambling on board the Mersey Ferry to New Brighton.

There were storyboards dedicated to each Beatle, detailing personal insights into their home lives, schooling, families and holidays. We were fortunate to get help in this section from Julia Baird, John's half-sister, and Paul's brother Mike, who checked out facts and generously provided some private family photos for us to use.

A compilation black and white film included footage of Liverpool's war years, musicians of the time such as Glenn Miller and the airmen stationed at US Burtonwood air force base not far from Liverpool. We were lucky to make contact with a film historian named Clive Garner who used to have a show on Radio Merseyside called Music and Memories. He had a vast archive of pre-war Liverpool newsreels and was very helpful in sourcing and providing the footage that we needed.

Accompanying this was a scripted voiceover telling the story of The Beatles' early years. This played on a timed loop, giving groups of visitors a comprehensive introduction to the early background of their lives. The aim was to add interest for non-fans as well as fans.

We used pictures of our own families to portray what life was like at the time, including the clothes, social life and music. It's important to understand that in the early 50s, young people listened to the same music as their parents and dressed the same. When rock 'n' roll arrived courtesy of Radio Luxembourg and some of the American GIs, this all changed, and we felt it important to illustrate Liverpool life as it was when the war ended.

The plan was that by the time visitors had left this soundproofed room, they had been taken back to a very different time and given some understanding of the world that The Beatles inhabited during their formative years.

2. EARLY INFLUENCES

From wartime Liverpool, we forwarded to the next feature, which encapsulated the early influences that would shape The Beatles. Britain was experiencing a whole new type of music led by skiffle and the big acts at the time were Lonnie Donegan with 'Rock Island Line', and Chas McDevitt and Shirley Douglas who had a number one hit with 'Freight Train'. We showed film footage of Bill Haley arriving in England, when he was greeted by thousands of young fans, which caused much consternation from parents and older generations. Whole cities banned the showing of the 1955 social drama film Blackboard Jungle, which featured his big hit song, 'Rock Around the Clock'.

Every teenager in Britain was influenced by fashion, music or films in the late 50s and early 60s, and it was very different from what had gone before; that's why it was important to explain this as part of the group's background.

A seismic explosion of raucous rock 'n' roll music closely followed, thanks in the main to Elvis Presley, Little Richard,

DRAFT DESIGNS FOR EARLY INFLUENCES FEATURE

Chuck Berry, Buddy Holly and Jerry Lee Lewis. They appeared on the scene within months of each other, changing the face of popular music forever, and were blasted out of Radio Luxembourg to teenagers across Britain. This included the four young Beatles, who were compelled to pick up instruments and emulate this sound. We portrayed this influx of new music using a giant jukebox and showed how it influenced The Beatles' early foray into music.

All of The Beatles were still at school while American rock 'n' roll was unfolding, but John Lennon had formed The Quarrymen and George had formed a group called The Rebels with his brother Peter and friend Arthur. They were already performing at small local events and venues before Paul met either of them. Charles and Sandy Roberts kindly allowed us to reproduce their early picture of The Quarrymen performing on the back of a lorry in Roseberry Street.

We described the historic moment when John met Paul at St. Peter's Garden Fete in the Liverpool suburb of Woolton. We gave a timeline of key events that brought them together as a band, including George meeting Paul on the bus, John thinking George was too young to join, and how they met Pete Best at his mum's club The Casbah, eventually becoming the first line-up of The Beatles (via some interim line-ups including Johnny and The Moondogs!).

To further set the scene, we included detail about the popular Liverpool clubs and venues of the time, such as The Iron door, Samson and Barlows and The Black Cat. There was so much information that we wanted to include in this section that it could easily have taken up three times the amount of space that it did. We originally wanted to make a full feature out of The Casbah, as this had been such an important part of the formation of the band – not only did they perform there numerous times, but this was where they met Pete Best, who they auditioned in time to take him on their first Hamburg trip. We had to choose carefully and condense three key years of information into one feature.

3. HAMBURG

The Beatles made a total of five trips to Hamburg between 1960 and 1962, and their time there should not be underestimated in terms of the impact it had on them as a group. They initially went over as five individuals who were very unrehearsed, as Pete Best had only been asked to join them the week before. The trip was organised by Allan Williams, their first manager, who used to book them to play at The Jacaranda, one of his clubs. They had to quickly find a drummer to go with them on the trip. Having secured Pete as drummer, they all squeezed into one van that didn't even have seats. The passengers included Allan, his wife Beryl, her brother Barry, and Lord Woodbine, a local musician and artist booker who had been to Hamburg previously and had contacts there.

THE BEATLES VAN BEING LIFTED BY CRANE ONTO THE FERRY

Having to play for eight hours a night was exhausting, but it helped them hone their craft and develop their sound as a tight, energetic rock and roll band that would return to Liverpool and wow audiences with their sheer raw energy and togetherness. They came back a different band with a whole new look, sound and attitude.

When designing the 'Hamburg' set we thought about how we could best recreate a trip to the seedy and exciting streets of 1960s Hamburg. We imagined John, Paul, George, Pete and Stuart travelling for the first time in their crowded van to a foreign country. They arrive in Hamburg, drive onto the Reeperbahn, get out of the van and are greeted with a cacophony of brand-new

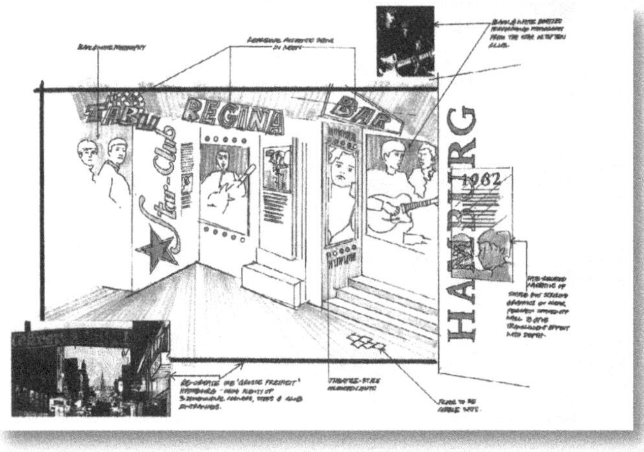

HAMBURG ARTIST IMPRESSION

sights, sounds and smells… walking on cobbles, they hear German voices, and are surrounded by the flashing neon lights of The Reeperbahn; nightclubs, pulsating live music, prostitutes and drunken sailors.

We played a 'live' recording of the Beatles New Year's Eve show, which had been recorded on a Grundig two-track tape machine. The poor, muffled sound quality playing out of the entrance to our mock Star Club added to the overall atmosphere, combined with the sound of German voices coming from hidden speakers. An eight by six foot black and white picture of the lads dominated the entrance to the Star Club.

BERNIE IN THE PART-BUILT HAMBURG SET – FEBRUARY 1990

On the opposite side of the set, we recreated a window next to a doorway, to give the impression you were looking into Astrid Kirchherr's flat. Astrid and her boyfriend Manfred first saw The Beatles play when they were a couple, and they became friends with the whole group. They had an immense influence on The Beatles' style, giving them their famous mop-top haircut and introducing them to leather trousers and black heeled boots. Astrid was an accomplished photographer, who took some iconic black and white pictures of them in Hamburg. Stuart and Astrid eventually fell in love and got

STAR CLUB ENTRANCE

ASTRID'S WINDOW FEATURING
SOME OF HER PHOTOGRAPHY

engaged, and at the end of their second residency in Hamburg, he decided to leave the group in order to stay with her and enrol at art college. Astrid played an important part in these early days, and we wanted to acknowledge this.

LIFE SIZE JOHN IN DOORWAY

Mike: Astrid and her good friend Ulf Krueger formed a company called K&K to promote and sell Astrid's photographic collection. I met Ulf at an earlier Beatles convention, told him that we wanted to create a tribute to Stuart and Astrid in our Hamburg section, and asked if he could provide us with any photographs. They provided us with a selection.

We were keen to be as authentic as possible and our architect Steve Quicke found some real German cobbles and architrave for the doorways, and our set designers even made a model of a prostitute to stand in the doorway. There were partly ripped posters advertising groups and clubs, and we also found a picture of John leaning on a doorway which loaned itself to being made life-size and put it in situ.

Allan Williams kindly loaned us copies of the group's visa applications and contracts between Allan and The Kaiserkeller for use in the exhibition. They were almost destroyed in a fire many years earlier, and we had to

OPPOSITE SIDE OF THE HAMBURG STREET
– WITH JOHN LENNON, 'LADY OF THE NIGHT'
AND ASTRID'S WINDOW

reproduce them in their charred state. We were also very fortunate that Brian Johnson, a friend of ours from a group called The Strangers, loaned us some great pictures from his days in Hamburg such as Kingsize Taylor and The Dominoes and Little Richard.

The Beatles played at various clubs during their five visits to Hamburg including the Indra, The Top 10 Club and The Kaiserkeller Club (where Rory Storm and the Hurricanes were billed above The Beatles), and their final residency was at The Star Club. Some of the biggest American rock 'n' roll stars played at The Star Club including Chuck Berry, Chubby Checker, Ray Charles, Bill Haley, Jerry Lee Lewis and Little Richard. We felt it was important to talk in detail about some of the venues and the calibre of artists who were playing there at the time, as this had such a huge impact on The Beatles that came back to Liverpool.

We dedicated a whole board to Tony Sheridan who The Beatles played with at The Star Club. He had a recording contract with Polydor, and they backed him on his version of 'My Bonnie'. On this recording, they were called The Beat Brothers because 'The Beatles' didn't translate well in German.

DOUBLE NOTICEBOARD WITH CONTRACTS AND GROUP PICTURES

4. THE MERSEY BEAT OFFICE

Leaving the bright lights and sounds of Hamburg, we took our visitors straight back to 1960s Liverpool and into the Mersey Beat office where Bill and Virginia Harry produced the fortnightly publication called Mersey Beat. Bill was one of John Lennon's best friends at art college and saw an opportunity to celebrate everything about the Liverpool music scene. He had tried to persuade the Liverpool Echo to cover the wealth of music coming out of Liverpool, but they weren't interested and continued to put everything under the jazz column! So he and his then girlfriend, Virginia, decided to do it themselves.

BILL AND VIRGINIA HARRY

It publicised news about rock 'n' roll, and the local music scene, which wasn't covered in the mainstream press. The first issue was published on 6th July 1961 costing just three pennies an issue, and within a couple of months the print run had expanded to 5,000, as avid fans used it as their local music bible.

There were more than 350 groups playing regularly, and Mersey Beat was a vital source of information for the hungry fans who wanted to read about their favourite groups. There were interviews and performance listings, and groups could advertise themselves in the hope of getting more bookings. It was at the centre of all things Merseybeat, and this is why it deserved its own set within The Beatles Story.

Thanks to his friendship with John Lennon, Bill featured The Beatles more than any other group. They topped a 1962 poll of the most popular groups, and the paper was a staunch supporter and promoter at this pivotal time in the development of popular music in Liverpool. Bill even gave John Lennon his own column using the pseudonym 'Beatcomber' after a column in a national newspaper called Beachcomber. One such column went like this:

Being a Short Diversion on the Dubious Origins of Beatles, by John Lennon

"Many people ask what are Beatles? Why Beatles? Ugh, Beatles? How did the name arrive? So, we will tell you. It came in a vision – a man appeared on a flaming pie and said unto them, 'From this day on you are Beatles with an "A". 'Thank you, Mister Man', they said, thanking him. And so, they were Beatles"

Future issues would also feature regular columns by Bob Wooler and Brian Epstein.

We were very fortunate to have known Bill Harry from way back, and he personally advised us on how to recreate his office with detail that only he could know. We wanted it to look busy and worked in, like a typical office day. There were copies of the Mersey Beat newspaper on the walls, pictures of the groups of the time, many of which were loaned to us personally by our friends, and a waxwork model of Bill sitting at his desk. We had an original Dansette Autochanger record player, which was capable of playing multiple records automatically without having to manually change them. This was Bernie's own personal player which she had kept from the 60s and it was perfect for the feature. Our brother-in-law, Norman, luckily had two solid wooden office desks which he was happy to donate.

BILL HARRY MODEL IN MERSEY BEAT OFFICE

DANSETTE RECORD PLAYER

NOTICE BOARDS IN THE CORNER OF THE MERSEY BEAT OFFICE

Bill told us that Bob Wooler used to visit quite often so we asked Bob and Bill to make an imaginary phone call about The Beatles. They did this and we had it playing through an old 60s style telephone for visitors to listen to. When Bill saw his waxwork, he said, "I never had a jacket like that!"

Despite only just leaving the noisy bustle of Hamburg, our architect created a soundproofed tunnel so that the only thing you heard as you entered the Mersey Beat office was Bill's Dansette record player playing the latest British hit records, and the sound of your own footsteps leaving the German cobbles and stepping onto the wooden floorboards of the office.

Bill went into partnership with Brian Epstein, who wanted to create a national music paper, and they merged Mersey Beat into it, calling it the Music Echo. Bill initially had editorial control, but after Brian introduced some London personnel without his knowledge, Bill decided to leave the paper and went into a career in music PR. He worked with many groups including The Kinks, Pink Floyd, David Bowie and The Hollies.

5. HESSY'S MUSIC SHOP

Leaving the stillness, warmth and bright light of the Mersey Beat office, visitors stepped through two doors, into semi-darkness and the sensation of chilled air that we pumped in through a vent. We wanted to create a distinction between the two features, and we did this using temperature as well as lighting, sounds and smells.

Visitors were greeted with the sight of Frank Hessy's music shop which, in real life, was just around the corner from Mathew Street and The Cavern. This was a cluttered window, packed full of musical instruments as it would have looked in the 60s, with a backdrop of black and white photographs of groups of the time.

There were three musical instrument shops in Liverpool in the 1960s: Cranes Music, which sold mainly grand pianos and violins for the classical community, Rushworth & Dreaper, which specialised in building church organs, and Hessy's, which catered for the young lads in groups who were springing up all over Merseyside.

Frank Hessy himself would often be at the door, greeting customers with his thick scouse accent, saying "Awright lad... warra you want?" This is where John bought his first guitar, and the down to earth, informal sales approach and hire purchase payment plan made it most groups' number one choice.

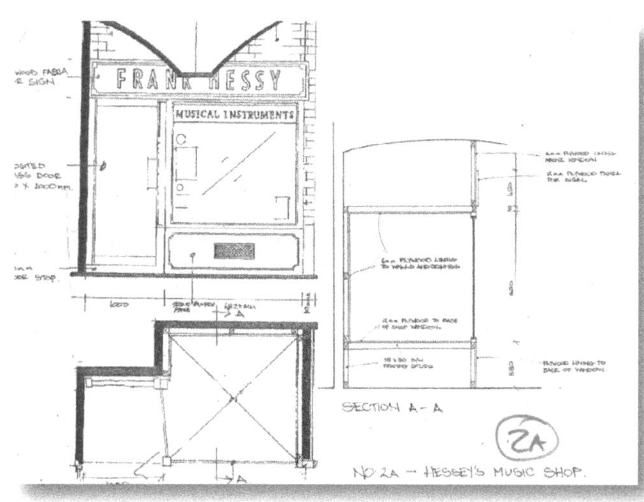

HESSY'S ELEVATION DESIGN – SHOWING HOW IT HAD TO BE BUILT INTO THE CURVED SHAPE OF THE CEILING

Mike: I had several friends at Hessy's including the managing director Bernard Michaelson, manager Pete Hepworth and Colin Ben who had once been our road manager. When we were building the Hessy's set, again we were so fortunate to be able to call on their first-hand knowledge of how to create the most authentic shop window possible. They sourced numerous guitars, drums and amplifiers from the 60s era, and Colin came down to personally dress the window. The backdrop was covered with pictures of Merseybeat groups and other 60s recording stars, many of whom were customers who had bought from there and given their pictures to the staff to put up. This is how the window would have looked at the time.

FRAMEWORK OF THE PART-BUILT HESSY'S WINDOW

HESSY'S COMPLETED SHOP FRONT

The Beatles Story had been open a year or so when one day I got a visit from David Rushworth, one of the partners from Rushworth & Dreaper's. He had seen our Hessy's feature and asked if we would include Rushworth's as well. I reminded him that I had approached him in the development stage for help, but he wasn't keen at the time.

The Hessy's feature is another example of how having friends in the right places not only helped us save money in the build, but assured accuracy in the detail of its recreation. If we hadn't had these relationships, it's highly likely we would have had to buy the instruments rather than have them on loan, and we were grateful for their generosity.

It became apparent that once our dream started coming to life, our old friends and contacts were pleased to see their own legacies being preserved in a permanent way. Hessy's sadly closed its doors for good in 1995, but its importance lives on in The Beatles Story.

6. MATHEW STREET

Bernie: Our main intention when designing Mathew Street was to capture and convey the excitement and anticipation of approaching The Cavern. This is something both Mike and I had done so many times first-hand, and we wanted our visitors to feel some of what we did all those years ago. Historically, Mathew Street was the centre of Liverpool's wholesale fruit and vegetable district, and as you walked towards The Cavern for the lunchtime sessions you could smell the fruit warehouses on either side of the road.

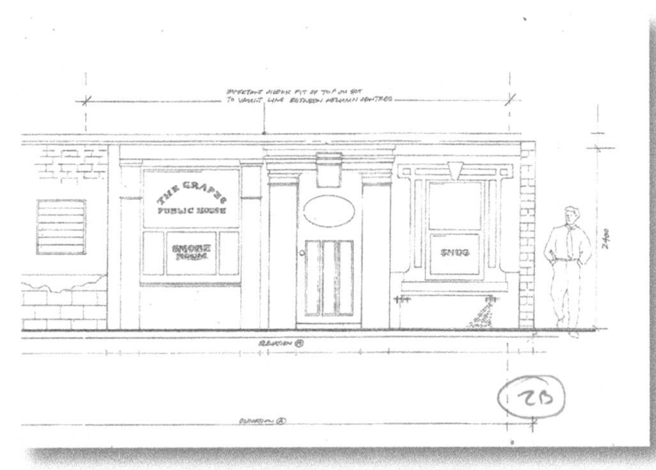

DESIGN FOR THE GRAPES

Mike: Going down Mathew Street from my dad's shop at lunchtime, I would be able to feel the vibrations of the bass drum and guitar beneath my feet from about ten metres away and would hear the muffled sounds of whatever was playing. As I neared the entrance, I would see and smell the pungent mist drifting out of the doorway, and this would add to the anticipation. I couldn't wait to get down to that 'cellar full of noise' and when you got inside, the raucous beat would hit you in the chest. All of your senses would be assaulted as you paid your one-shilling entrance and joined the other cave-dwellers for another electrifying session.

Mathew Street is where we introduced the first scent to give visitors not just the sight but also the smell that would have been encountered on a visit to The Cavern. There was a company which specialised in creating bespoke scented oils, which were poured into a kettle-like container and positioned discreetly in relevant areas. In Mathew Street we chose 'fresh apple' which would be intermittently released into the air to give a notion of how it was at the time, amongst the nearby fruit warehouses.

BERNIE INSPECTING THE WORKMEN'S HANDIWORK

CAVERN ENTRANCE AS SEEN FROM MATHEW STREET

Multiple sound effects came into play in this area. The jostling sound of drinkers came out of The Grapes pub, which was on the opposite side to The Cavern entrance. We hid a sub-woofer speaker in the recess of a mock warehouse which played the isolated bass line of 'Twist and Shout' into Mathew Street - this is how we experienced it as we approached the club. We added a fake rat running along a drainpipe, the sound of a cat meowing and a metal bin lid crashing to the floor for effect. We were mindful of appealing to families and knew that these fun details would appeal to children, making it easier for their adults to have time to read the story and enjoy the experience.

GRAPES PUB VIEW LOOKING TOWARDS HESSY'S

The bricks, metalwork and cobbled street leading to The Cavern were suitably distressed to look well-trodden as we tried our best to give as much detail as possible to create the overall feeling of 1960s Mathew Street. Our replica Grapes was so realistic, with silhouettes of drinkers in the windows and the sound of clinking glasses, that visitors often tried to go in through the fake door!

We were really happy with how Mathew Street turned out. It delivered the experience of sights, smells, sounds and even the feeling of being there outside, due to the chilled temperature change. It encapsulated everything we wanted to give to our visitors by way of a multi-dimensional experience.

7. THE CAVERN CLUB

According to records, The Beatles appeared at The Cavern Club 292 times. They built their early reputation here and this is where Brian Epstein first saw them play on 9th November 1961. Following this he asked the group to visit his office the next day and he made the momentous decision to manage them. Ringo was asked to join the Beatles just eight days before their last show there, on the 3rd of August 1963.

Mike: There was never any doubt in our minds that a replica Cavern would be featured, and it would form the centrepiece of the exhibition.

CAVERN MID-BUILD

Bernie: A replica Cavern was an essential feature. Mike and I had very clear memories of the club and were determined to make it as realistic as possible. The shape of the existing basement ceiling was a curved shape very similar to the original. We studied the designs in detail and the architects got as close to the real thing as possible, even getting the band room where we wanted it, to the left of the stage. We consulted with the original Cavern DJ, Bob Wooler, who was a friend of ours from the early days, and we also contacted musician and close friend Don Andrew, from the Remo 4, to make sure that our memories were serving us correctly. Their input was crucial in helping us to get important details right.

To replicate the square brick pillars of the original Cavern Club as much as possible, the builders had to build surrounds using old bricks around the circular iron

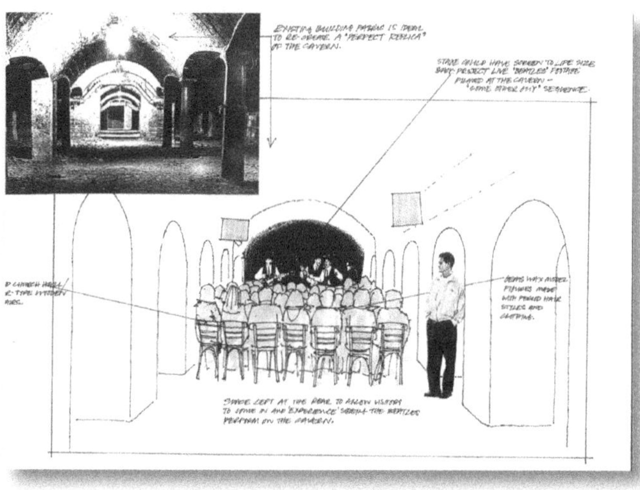

ARTIST'S IMPRESSION OF CAVERN FROM BUSINESS PLAN

basement pillars which had been supporting the Albert Dock warehouses above for over 150 years. The new pillars and any interconnecting brickwork were then distressed even further to make them look more authentic and then finished with a coating that gave the impression of condensation running down the walls. This was to emulate the humidity that used to get so bad it would sometimes even short the electric circuits and occasionally blow up the amplifiers on stage.

Using old photographs of The Cavern and the chairs helped us to work out the true width of The Cavern and build the dimensions of it from there. We wanted to get this right to show people just how small The Cavern really was.

As visitors entered, in contrast to the chilled air of Mathew Street, we blew warm air in over their heads to give the sensation we used to feel as we entered the hot, stuffy basement. The Cavern also had its own unique smell which clung to your hair and clothes; if you got there early, the prevailing stench was of disinfectant, so this was the second smell that we had made into an oil to be pumped into the atmosphere. We decided to spare tourists the truly obnoxious smell that was there at the time - a concoction of cigarette smoke, sweat, hotdogs and toilets!

MIKE ON STAGE WITH WOODEN INSTRUMENTS MADE BY THE JOINERS

As the Cavern build developed, we invited original members of Merseybeat groups down to the site to help reinforce the details, and some even helped paint the famous replica backdrop of the stage, which featured many of the original group names. Don Andrew from the Remo 4, Billy Hatton, Joey Bower and Dave Lovelady from the Fourmost and Johnny Guitar of Hurricanes fame all had input.

The real Cavern was very basic, with bare brick walls, three archways and simple furniture. Facing the stage, the left-hand arched space was completely empty of furniture and the cave dwellers would use that area for dancing in. The right-hand section would be the entrance and coffee bar and cloakroom, and the middle section which looked directly at the stage was filled with basic wooden chairs. We had to alter our design slightly and accommodate the coffee bar on the other side, but this couldn't be avoided owing to space limitations.

We scoured local auction rooms until we found chairs that were almost exact replicas, and we also sourced a dozen or so 60s style bar tables. To complete the stripped back look, we asked Billy Kinsley, the bass player with The Merseybeats, to make the replica speaker cabinets that hung from the ceiling. He was known for making bass cabinets for other Merseybeat groups and we knew he would be able to make them as close to the originals as possible. An old upright piano from Mike's Auntie Mary's house, along with Mike's old piano stool, were situated on the right-hand side of the stage to complete the look. The piano was originally there from the early Cavern days when jazz bands would play, but it became a useful addition for some of the beat groups who followed, such as Gerry and the Pacemakers, who would regularly use it.

We pasted up replica posters from the time, which would often prove too tempting to visitors, who would try to peel them off. We would regularly replace these, using stronger glue each time in an attempt to preserve them!

PADDY DELANEY WHEN HE CAME TO CHECK OUT OUR PART-BUILT CAVERN

Once the build was underway, we also called on the memories of some other old Cavern friends who had worked at The Cavern in the early days. These included the doorman, Paddy Delaney, and the man who started the original Cavern, Alan Sytner. Their memories helped reinforce that we were getting the finishing touches right.

Bob Wooler was not only involved in helping us to design 'our' Cavern, but we also asked him to do a voiceover for the introduction of the showreel that would be projected onto the back wall of the stage. Bob was only too happy to oblige, and it went like this:

"Hi there all you Cave-Dwellers, this is Bob Wooler, welcoming you to the best of cellars, we've got the hi-fi high and the lights down low, so here we go with the Beatles Show!"

Despite being from Liverpool, he didn't have a noticeable scouse accent, and we will always remember his dulcet tones, which could be heard throughout the beat sessions as he introduced the groups. He would play records from an old gramophone which was situated in the dressing room next to the stage. In addition to hosting the shows, he would also book the groups, design the Cavern adverts to go into Mersey Beat, and host and promote shows at

BEATLES STORY CAVERN WITH PROJECTION OF THE BEATLES TAKEN ON THE CAVERN STAGE

other Liverpool and Wirral venues. If anyone wanted to know about the Liverpool music scene they would go to Bob, and he went on to become a regular guest at Beatles Conventions.

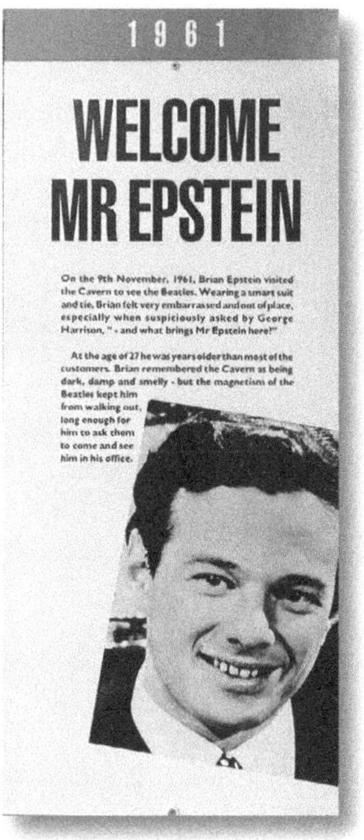

'WELCOME MR EPSTEIN'

BEATLES STORY CAVERN WITH BEATLES FIGURES

JULIAN LENNON VISITING THE BEATLES STORY

Bernie: We had a model created by a talented group of designers called Prop Art, which was intended to vaguely resemble Cilla Black. Our idea was to have the figure talk to the person who sat down next to her – triggered by a motion sensor. I voiced the recording saying "Hiya, The Beatles are coming on in a bit" and "I've saved you a seat, love" and these were saved on an EPROM – an Erasable Programmable Read Only Memory. However, we decided not to use the EPROM in the end as there was already a lot of background sound in The Cavern, and it would have been difficult to hear.

Our Cavern was also designed to be a live music venue and host functions, so it was set up with that in mind. A band room was situated at the side of the stage, as it was in the original, and we positioned a coffee bar at the back, which became a licensed bar when we had an event. When we held social events there with live music, it would get loud, hot and stuffy, and this is when it felt most like it did in the old days.

TV shows such as national daytime show 'This Morning' would regularly use The Beatles Story for interviews and there were live performances from stars including Julian Lennon, Status Quo, Chesney Hawkes and The Swinging Blue Jeans.

We could never have recreated an exact replica of The Cavern, but some of the key artists who had played at The Cavern commented on how close it was to the original. This included Gerry Marsden, Johnny Guitar and Billy Kinsley. We were very pleased with the end result, knowing we were giving visitors a flavour of our Cavern memories. Gerry Marsden performed on our opening day and said it was the closest he'd felt to playing back at the original Cavern.

OUR CAVERN - WITH THE STAGE SET UP FOR A PRIVATE FUNCTION

8. NEMS

NEMS - which was an abbreviation for North End Music Store - was Brian Epstein's record store, situated a mere two hundred yards from The Cavern. Brian's office was above the store, and it would be here that he first became aware of The Beatles.

There are a couple of different versions of how Brian Epstein first discovered The Beatles but the one we believe is the most reliable is from Bill Harry, who had persuaded Brian to sell his Mersey Beat newspaper in NEMS. Bill featured The Beatles in his newspaper more than any other group (prompting a rival group to comment, "You should call your paper Mersey Beatle!") so it's thought that Brian first noticed the group in the paper, and asked Bill Harry what he knew about them.

It was also around this time that a young fan went into NEMS and asked for a copy of 'My Bonnie' which was recorded by Tony Sheridan and The Beat Brothers. The Beat Brothers were actually The Beatles, and they had recorded it while they were in Germany. It was released on Polydor, a German record label, so many mistakenly presumed that The Beatles were a German group. Brian obliged the customer and ordered a copy for him, and as more and more requests for 'My Bonnie' followed, his interest in 'The Beat Brothers' grew. He discovered they were not German, and were actually a local Liverpool group called The Beatles.

After speaking to Bill, and reading Mersey Beat, he realised that they regularly performed just around the corner at The Cavern, and he wanted to see what all the excitement was about. Brian asked Bill to speak to Ray McFall, The Cavern's owner, and arrange for him to go to a lunchtime show. This historic visit took place on 9th November 1961, when he and his assistant, Alistair Taylor, went to watch The Beatles perform. Paddy Delaney let them jump the queue and they were greeted by Bob Wooler, the Cavern DJ, announcing, "We have someone rather famous in the audience today, Mr. Brian Epstein, the owner of NEMS!"

Bernie: I remember the day that Brian Epstein visited The Cavern. I was stood at the back, about to leave as I had to get back to work, when he and Alistair Taylor, his assistant, came down the stairs. We were a bit surprised to see them in The Cavern, so well dressed in suits. To most of us he seemed a lot older, and we wondered why he was there. Then Bob Wooler announced that we had a special visitor that day - Mr. Brian Epstein from NEMS! Not long after, it became clear that he was there on business, to find out what all the commotion was about. Not long after, he would become The Beatles' manager.

Mike: Despite being less than impressed by their gum chewing, swearing and scruffy demeanour, Brian could see their huge potential and was intrigued by their music, and so he asked Bob Wooler to bring them to his office above NEMS the next day. He offered to manage them, subject to them agreeing to smarten up their act. They agreed to his terms on the condition that he wouldn't try to change their music and just a few days later Brian became their manager.

BERNIE IN PART BUILT LISTENING BOOTHS

Bernie: Often, fans would leave The Cavern lunchtime sessions and head straight to NEMS to listen to the latest releases, and effectively this is what our visitors did, stepping out of our warm, lively Cavern and into the relative calm of NEMS. We were always mindful of our visitors' experience as they progressed through the exhibition and wanted them to relive the excitement of how we used to listen to new releases at the time. On one side of the NEMS set, we replicated the original NEMS

EPSTEIN'S SHOP ON WHITECHAPEL

store and installed soundproofed booths. By standing inside the booths, our visitors could listen to 'My Bonnie' – the record that was the catalyst for Brian's interest in The Beatles. This is what I used to do when I was an apprentice hairdresser working upstairs from NEMS, until eventually me and my colleagues were chased out by the staff who knew we weren't there to buy anything!

Working above NEMS meant I could pop in there quite regularly, at lunchtime or after work. Recreating the store interior was quite easy to do from memory. I have fond memories of George picking me up from outside of NEMS after work. He would wait on Great Charlotte Street in his Ford Anglia, though I used to get embarrassed when my colleagues would lean out of the window to try to see him.

On the other side of the room, we created a wall of vinyl 45s on shelves. The presence of the old vinyl gave the space a musty, papery smell, just as it had at the time. We had to think very carefully about how to secure the records in place to ensure we didn't end up with an empty wall at the end of each day! They were very firmly glued into place, but some have had to be replaced over the years after over-zealous fans have tried to look a bit too closely or take home a piece of memorabilia for themselves.

BRIAN
AND THE BEATLES

NEMS was one of the most popular record shops with the teenagers of Liverpool. On Saturday, 18th October, 1961, it is said that an 18 year old from Huyton walked into NEMS in Whitechapel and asked for a single called 'My Bonnie' by the Beatles. After further requests for the same record Brian's curiosity was aroused. He always liked to please customers if possible and was not aware of there being a Liverpool group on a record label.

It was Thursday, 9th November, that Brian, accompanied by his personal assistant Alistair Taylor, attended a lunchtime session at the Cavern to see the Beatles. He was fascinated by their music. A few days after a meeting at his Whitechapel office, (where Bob Wooler gave moral support posing as John's dad), he became their manager. Brian had been advised about the contract by a family friend and solicitor, Rex Makin. Ironically when the final document was drawn up Brian never actually signed it although this never made any difference to the promises he made to the boys.

However Brian did have strict rules and he insisted that if he became their manager they would have to change their image, dress more smartly, and stop eating, drinking and smoking on stage. In other words he wanted them to behave more professionally. The Beatles decided they could accept all that as long as Brian did not try to change their music.

Brian's task was only just beginning. He now had to persuade a record company to take an interest in the band, not an easy task when you lived in the north of England. In those days London had the complete monopoly of the music and record industry—making them listen in tin pan alley was not easy but Brian felt he could overcome the problem. Over the years he had given all the major companies, E.M.I., Decca, and Phillips, plenty of business and NEMS Limited was a well respected customer. He had no doubt they would be interested in his group.

The first attempt made by Brian to secure a contract was on the 15th December, 1961. In the audience at the Cavern was Mike Smith of Decca Records. He was there at Brian's invitation. He liked the group and said he would arrange an audition for them. The audition was booked for 1st January, 1962. The Beatles travelled down to London the night before and stayed at the Royal Hotel, Woburn Place.

New Years Day was spent at Decca's West Hampstead studios where the Beatles performed much of their repertoire from the Cavern, mostly cover versions of other people's songs plus a couple of their own early numbers but the Beatles were nervous and they were not happy with their own performance.

Dick Rowe was head of Decca's A & R Department and he told Mike Smith he could only sign up one group, the Beatles or the other band who had auditioned that day, Brian Poole and the Tremeloes-they chose the Tremeloes. Brian, shocked at the decision, travelled to London to put on some personal pressure but all to no avail. Brian walked out of Decca's office telling them one day his band would be bigger than Elvis.

Brian continued, unsuccessfully, to hawk the tapes round all the companies he could find. As a last resort he decided to take some advice he had been given and have a demo disc made. He took the tapes to a small shop in Oxford Street, London, where for £1 an acetate could be made. The engineer who did the job was impressed with what he heard and suggested that Brian should take the disc upstairs to E.M.I.'s publishing company, Ardmore and Beechwood. A meeting was arranged between Brian and Syd Coleman, who not only liked the acetate but offered to publish two of the songs. Syd then enquired if the Beatles had a record contract. When Brian said no Syd said he would put them in touch with a friend of his, George Martin, Head of A & R at Parlophone Records.

BRIAN AND THE BEATLES MOCK-UP

Next to this, we had a mock glass door with the silhouette of a life-size cut-out figure holding a phone to its ear, depicting Brian Epstein working in his office.

Brian Epstein's role in The Beatles' success cannot be underestimated. He would often be referred to as the 'fifth Beatle' and this is why we decided NEMS should be a key feature in The Beatles Story.

9. ABBEY ROAD

Next, we take a geographical leap from Liverpool to London's Abbey Road Studios. Abbey Road had already produced 33 number one hits before The Beatles recorded there, but it would become synonymous with The Beatles, who would eventually record 191 songs there, from 'Love Me Do' in 1962 until the recording of the 'Abbey Road' album in 1969.

The path to the studio was a recreation of the famous black and white zebra crossing, allowing visitors to tread our version of the crossing made famous on the cover of the 1969 album 'Abbey Road'.

After a number of record companies had turned The Beatles down for a record deal, an A&R man at Parlophone Records called George Martin recognised something special in this unusual looking and unique sounding quartet from Liverpool. He couldn't categorise them, but he was impressed that they could even write their own songs. George Martin, like Brian Epstein, was often dubbed the 'fifth Beatle', for his musical contribution to The Beatles' output.

APPROACH TO ABBEY ROAD ENTRANCE

Bernie: We approached Abbey Road to ask for their help and advice on how to design and dress the studio. They were very helpful and open to discussions and advised us on layout and materials to use. They also provided the wording for the narrative boards in this set. We had a very small space to work with, so had to minimise everything to represent Studio 2 as best as we could. We decided to drop the floor into the foundations by about four foot and covered the walls in soundproof pegboard to look like acoustic tiles, along with a parquet wooden floor.

We wanted the visitor to feel like they were in the control desk above, looking down onto the group as they were recording. The studio itself was quite bare and only had the guitars, drums and amplifiers they needed for the songs they were going to record that day. We asked Prop Art to make four life-size models to resemble the Beatles in recording mode. Ken Townsend, the then MD of Abbey Road, told us that one of the original tape units was being used at Leeds University in one of their sound engineering departments. We got in touch with them, and they were happy to sell it to us for use in the exhibition, for the princely sum of £75. This was a great, authentic addition to the Abbey Road set.

BERNIE INSPECTING THE STUDIO MID-BUILD

MODELS OF THE FAB FOUR IN SITU IN STUDIO 2

B.T.R. TAPE DECK FROM ABBEY ROAD

We bought a replica kit of Ringo's Ludwig drums and sourced authentic vintage guitars for John, Paul and George from Frailers Guitar Shop in Runcorn, which was a renowned music shop importing from America and Germany. We completed the overall look by again calling on the skills of Billy Kinsley to make us a 'coffin' bass cabinet - the type that Paul used. Finally, Hessy's provided us with two vintage Vox amplifiers.

We also featured an original 1960s Mellotron which had been kindly loaned to us by Chip Hawkes from The Tremeloes. The Beatles would later use one of these on 'Strawberry Fields Forever'.

The lighting in the studio went up as the music started and visitors could hear 'Please Please Me' being blasted out of the speakers as though it was being recorded in the studio at the time. This was followed by an imitation voiceover of George Martin saying, "Gentlemen, you have just made your first number one." Afterwards, the lights would dim as a cue for people to move on to the next set.

The album Abbey Road was released in September 1969. It brought George Martin and The Beatles together for one last time and George Martin stipulated that he would do it if they could go back to working in the way they had in the early days. The last track, 'The End', was the last time all four Beatles recorded together.

THE ARTIST'S IMPRESSION OF ABBEY ROAD

10. BEATLEMANIA

Leaving the relative calm of Studio 2, next we thrust our visitors into a very different atmosphere, bombarding their senses with the sights and sounds of 'Beatlemania'. We created a deliberately stark contrast between the two features to deliver a surprise element.

ARTIST"S IMPRESSION OF BEATLEMANIA SET

BEATLEMANIA – THE DEFINITION

The word 'Beatlemania' entered the English language on November 5th, 1963, as a way of describing the frenzied reaction they received when playing the Royal Command Performance at the Prince of Wales Theatre in London. From the relatively quiet appreciation of the fans in Liverpool, public reaction was now depicted by swarming teenagers and uncontrolled screaming that often meant the audience couldn't hear what the boys were playing.

At every concert and appearance, they were overwhelmed by the screaming of thousands of teenagers, to the point that they also couldn't hear themselves sing or play. This continued throughout their career, until their final appearance at Candlestick Park in 1966.

Bernie witnessed this first-hand in 1962 while she was dating George and going to their shows. She realised he was being noticed and stared at when they were out together, and saw Beatlemania unfold before her eyes at the Floral Hall when their car was mobbed and chased after the show. Although the term hadn't yet been coined, Beatlemania had certainly begun.

CORRIDOR OF SCREAMS

We wanted visitors to get a taste of what it must have been like for The Beatles, once their popularity grew. To make this happen, we created a 'corridor of screams' – a dark tunnel, only lit by seven large TV screens on one wall showing famous footage of hysterical fans taken from scenes at Heathrow Airport and the Liverpool Town Hall homecoming in 1964. The screams of thousands of adoring girls came from the speakers hidden in the walls and the volume was set as loud as possible to overwhelm the senses. Full size mirrors on the opposite wall reflected the TVs so that you were attacked by the noise and images, feeling completely surrounded by screamers as you walked through. This new phenomenon was something quite alien to the British public at large and caused some consternation with older generations. This wasn't an area that most people would stay in for long, and they would often make their way through with hands over ears as the footage was played on a loop, all day long. The importance of the soundproofing, particularly in this section, was obvious and came into its own.

To further reinforce The Beatles' popularity, a range of merchandise became available for their adoring fans. Suddenly, in addition to being able to buy Beatles records, fans could buy all kinds of items relating to their favourite group including figurines, tea towels, jewellery, trays, clocks, stockings and the iconic Beatle wig. Two collector friends of ours, Cherrille and John Sylvester, kindly loaned us a selection of superb items to put on display as people left the Beatlemania tunnel area.

11. THE AEROPLANE – GOING TO AMERICA

Leaving the dark and loud sensation of Beatlemania, the sounds of the screaming fans receded into the tunnel, only to be replaced with a new sound of jet engines from The Beatles' Pan Am jet plane, coming into land at Kennedy Airport, New York. This next scene represented The Beatles and Brian Epstein's next goal - to conquer America; and visitors walked straight into a replica of the inside of an aeroplane. We wanted visitors to comprehend just how momentous this time was.

We encouraged people to take a seat on the plane and put themselves in the shoes of The Beatles, heading over to the States for the first time. Pictures of the New York skyline were reflected in the porthole windows and visitors could sit in the seats, close their eyes and hear an American disc jockey from WMCA radio, counting down their progress live on air, as they made their historic journey over the Atlantic:

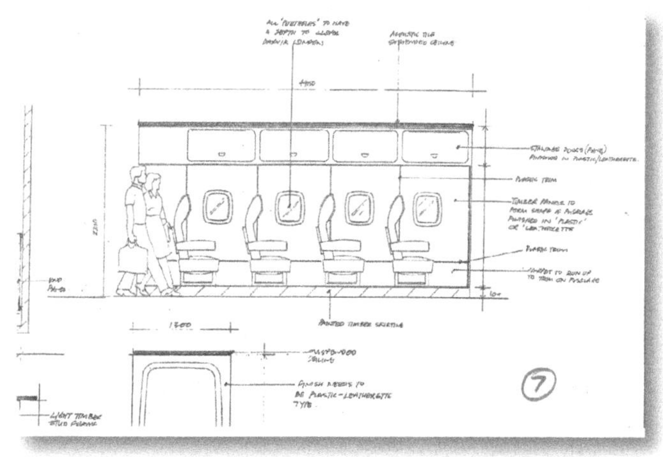

DESIGN SPECIFICATION - SECTION OF AEROPLANE

"It's now 6.30am Beatle time.
They left London 30 minutes ago.
They're out over the Atlantic Ocean,
headed for New York.
The temperature is 32 Beatle degrees."

On the plane, The Beatles were accompanied by the British press, who were invited along to watch and record the excitement as it unfolded. They didn't realise how popular they had become, but the pilot had called ahead and reported that there were thousands of fans waiting at the airport for them.

Mike: I had some contacts at Liverpool Airport who proved very useful in putting me in touch with some people who had a retired 'Dan Air' jet which was no longer in service (having crashed some years earlier!). They donated five rows of retro aircraft seats which were as close as we could get to Pan Am seats at the time.

American fans couldn't wait to have the mop-tops on American soil, and when they landed at Kennedy Airport,

HALF BUILT AEROPLANE SET

they were greeted by thousands of screaming teenagers. The screeching sound caused alarm among people on the plane who thought there was a problem with one of the engines, but it was actually the sound of 5,000 fans who had turned out to welcome them. The anticipation was unprecedented; they already had two singles in the Billboard charts and Capitol Records had saturated New York with posters and car stickers announcing, 'THE BEATLES ARE COMING!'

12. AMERICA AND THE TOURING YEARS

It was February 7th, 1964, when the Beatles touched down in America, and they were greeted by the kind of frenzied attention that only Elvis and Frank Sinatra had come close to experiencing before them.

As our visitors left the sound of jet engines behind, they turned a corner into a wall of flashing camera bulbs which went off in their faces. This simulated the barrage of press that greeted the Fab Four as they entered the airport terminal building for their first US press conference.

Our challenge in this section was to condense three unbelievably prolific and diverse years into one small room. This would include their US appearance on the Ed Sullivan Show and the first of two historic performances at Shea Stadium – a venue that held 65,000 people.

There followed two years of touring not just America, but also Europe, Australia and the Far East. Interspersed with this were dozens of TV appearances, interviews, the making of two films - A Hard Day's Night and Help - as well as constant writing and meeting the demands of the record label by delivering albums and singles to order.

AMERICA COLLAGE INCLUDING THE ED SULLIVAN SHOW AND MOHAMMED ALI

PHOTOGRAPHERS WITH FLASH BULBS WHICH WENT OFF AS VISITORS WALKED INTO 'AMERICA'

We could easily have trebled this section, but as we had to work within a limited space, we kept it very top line with a story board for each year dedicated to the key events that happened such as meeting Cassius Clay, having the top five spots in the Billboard charts, George receiving 30,000 birthday cards for his 21st and 500 American theatres showing the premiere of A Hard Day's Night simultaneously.

We showed a great piece of film footage of a press conference and the BBC interviewing an American disc jockey who had taken exception to John's comment about The Beatles being bigger than Jesus. He had decided to smash all Beatles records and encouraged his listeners to do the same.

Toward the end of this time, the group had a few controversial encounters, which would contribute to their eventual decision to stop touring. There was upset surrounding the album Yesterday and Today which became known as "The Butcher Album" owing to its distasteful, gory original cover image. In response to outrage from record retailers, the LP was withdrawn, and the cover was replaced with a less offensive image.

They also attracted protests when they appeared at the sacred Budokan Hall in Japan, a shrine to the country's war dead, and then found themselves inadvertently snubbing Imelda Marcos, the first lady of the Philippines, when they failed to turn up at a reception she was hosting. They didn't know about it and were exhausted from their travel. The country turned on them and they had to find their own way back to the airport without any police protection.

—ꟾꟾꟾ—

The America feature ended on a sombre note, when Brian Epstein sadly passed away, aged 32, on 27th August 1967. We got permission to show black and white news footage of a visibly shaken George and John being interviewed on the day he died. They were in Bangor at the time with the Maharishi and had just released Sgt. Pepper. They were relieved to be away from the strain of touring life and were riding high from the success of Revolver too. Brian's death came as a huge blow and rocked The Beatles' world in both a personal and professional way, and it altered the course of their career forever.

—ꟾꟾꟾ—

1963 1966

THE BEATLES TOURS

Here are just some of the many tours that The Beatles undertook between 1963- 1966.

HELEN SHAPIRO TOUR 1963

With Danny Williams, Kenny Lynch, The Beatles, The Red Price Band

FEBRUARY

2 Bradford Gaumont
3 Doncaster Gaumont
4 Bedford Granada
7 Wakefield Odeon
8 Carlisle ABC
9 Sunderland Odeon
10 Peterborough Embassy
23 Mansfield Granada
24 Coventry Theatre
26 Taunton Odeon
27 York Rialto
28 Shrewsbury Granada

MARCH

1 Southport Odeon
2 Sheffield City Hall
3 Hanley Gaumont

BEATLES TOUR 1963

With Gerry and the Pacemakers and Roy Orbison

MAY

18 Slough Granada
19 Hanley Gaumont
20 Southampton Gaumont
22 Ipswich Gaumont
23 Nottingham Odeon
24 Walthamstow Granada
25 Sheffield City Hall
26 Liverpool Empire
27 Cardiff Capitol
28 Worcester Gaumont
29 York Rialto
30 Manchester Odeon
31 Southend Odeon

JUNE

1 Tooting Granada
2 Brighton Hippodrome
3 Woolwich Granada
4 Birmingham Town Hall
5 Leeds Odeon
7 Glasgow Odeon
8 Newcastle City Hall
9 Blackburn King George Hall

BEATLES SHORT TOUR OF SWEDEN

October 24th to October 29th

BEATLES AUTUMN TOUR 1963

With Peter Jay and The Jaywalkers and The Brook Brothers

NOVEMBER

1 Cheltenham Gaumont
2 Sheffield City Hall
3 Leeds Odeon
5 Slough Adelphi
6 Northampton ABC
7 Dublin Adelphi
8 Belfast Ritz
9 East Ham Granada
10 Birmingham Hippodrome
12 Portsmouth Guild Hall
13 Plymouth ABC
14 Exeter ABC
15 Bristol Colston Hall
16 Bournemouth Winter Gardens
17 Coventry Theatre
19 Wolverhampton Gaumont
20 Manchester Ardwick Apollo
21 Carlisle ABC
22 Stockton Globe
23 Newcastle City Hall
24 Hull ABC
26 Cambridge ABC
27 York Rialto
28 Lincoln ABC
29 Huddersfield ABC
30 Sunderland Empire

DECEMBER

1 Leicester De Montfort Hall
8 Lewisham Odeon
9 Southend Odeon
10 Doncaster Gaumont
11 Scarborough Futurist
12 Nottingham Odeon
13 Southampton Gaumont
14 London Wimbledon Palais

BEATLES AT THE PARIS OLYMPIA 1964

Three week engagement in January with Trini Lopez and Sylvie Vartan

FIRST AMERICAN VISIT 1964

FEBRUARY

11 Washington Coliseum Washington DC
12 Carnegie Hall New York
(Plus two appearances on the Ed Sullivan Show)

BEATLES WORLD TOUR 1964

JUNE

4 KB Hallen Gardens, Copenhagen, Denmark
6 Blokker Exhibition Hall, Holland
10 Princess Theatre, Hong Kong
12/13 Centennial Hall, Adelaide, Australia
15 Festival Hall, Melbourne, Australia
18 Sydney Stadium, Syndney, Australia
22 Town Hall, Wellington, New Zealand
23 Town Hall, Wellington, New Zealand
24 Town Hall, Auckland, New Zealand
25 Town Hall, Auckland, New Zealand
26 Majestic Theatre, Christchurch, New Zealand
27 Majestic Theatre, Christchurch, New Zealand
29 Festival Hall, Brisbane, Australia
30 Festival Hall, Brisbane, Australia

FIVE WEEK TOUR OF THE USA & CANADA 1964

AUGUST

19 Cow Palace, San Francisco
20 Convention Center, Las Vegas
21 Seattle Center Coliseum, Seattle
22 Empire Stadium, Vancouver
23 Hollywood Bowl, Los Angeles
26 Red Rock Stadium, Denver
27 Cincinatti Gardens, Cincinatti
28 Forest Hills Stadium, New York
30 Convention Hall, Atlantic City

SEPTEMBER

2 Convention Hall, Philadelphia
3 Indiana State Fair, Indianapolis
4 Milwaukee Arena, Milwaukee
5 International Amphitheatre, Chicago
6 Olympia Stadium, Detroit
7 Maple Leaf Gardens, Toronto
8 Forum, Montreal
11 Gator Bowl, Jacksonville
12 Boston Gardens, Boston
13 Civic Center, Baltimore
14 Civic Arena, Pittsburg
15 Public Auditorium, Cleveland
16 City Park Stadium, New Orleans
18 Memorial Auditorium, Dallas
20 Paramount Theatre, New York

BRITISH TOUR 1964

With Mary Wells, Tommy Quickly, The Remo Four, Michael Haslam, The Rustiks and Bob Bain

OCTOBER

9 Bradford Gaumont
10 Leicester De Montfort Hall
11 Birmingham Odeon
13 Wigan ABC
14 Manchester ABC
15 Stockton-on-Tees Globe
16 Hull ABC
19 Edinburgh ABC
20 Dundee Caird Hall
21 Glasgow Odeon
22 Leeds Odeon
23 Kilburn Gaumont State
24 Walthamstow Granada
25 Brighton Hippodrome
28 Exeter ABC
29 Plymouth ABC
30 Bournemouth Gaumont
31 Ipswich Gaumont

NOVEMBER

1 Finsbury Park Astoria
2 Belfast King's Hall
4 Luton Ritz
5 Nottingham Odeon
6 Southampton Gaumont
7 Cardiff Capitol
8 Liverpool Empire
9 Sheffield City Hall
10 Bristol Colston Hall

BEATLES CHRISTMAS SHOWS 1964

With Freddie and The Dreamers, The Yardbirds, Elkie Brooks, Jimmy Saville, Mike Haslam and The Mike Cotton Band

December 24th to January 16th at the Hammersmith Odeon

EUROPEAN TOUR 1965

JUNE

20 Palais De Sports, Paris
22 Palais D'Hiver, Lyon
24 Velodromo Vigorelli, Milan
26 Palazzo dello Sport, Genoa
27 Teatro Adriano, Rome
30 Palais des Fetes, Nice

JULY

2 Plaza de Toros de Madrid, Madrid
3 Plaza de Toros de Madrid, Madrid

AMERICAN TOUR 1965

AUGUST

15 Shea Stadium, New York
16 Shea Stadium, New York
17 Maple Leaf Gardens, Toronto
18 Fulton County Stadium, Atlanta
19 Sam Houston Coliseum, Houston
20 Comiskey Park, Chicago
21 Metropolitan Stadium, Minneapolis
22 Memorial Coliseum, Portland
28 Balboa Stadium, San Diego
29 Hollywood Bowl, Los Angeles
30 Hollywood Bowl, Los Angeles
31 Cow Palace, San Francisco

BRITISH TOUR 1965

DECEMBER

3 Glasgow Odeon
4 Newcastle City Hall
5 Liverpool Empire
6 Rest Day
7 Manchester Ardwick Apollo
8 Sheffield City Hall
9 Birmingham Odeon
10 London Hammersmith Odeon
11 London Astoria
12 Cardiff Capitol

SUMMER TOUR OF GERMANY & JAPAN 1966

JUNE

24 Circus Krone, Munich
25 Grugahalle, Essen
26 Ernst Merck Halle, Hamburg
30 Budokan Hall, Tokyo

JULY

1 Budokan Hall, Tokyo
2 Budokan Hall, Tokyo
4 Araneta Coliseum, Manila

AMERICAN TOUR 1966

AUGUST

12 International Amphitheatre, Chicago
13 Olympia Stadium, Detroit
14 Municipal Stadium, Cleveland
15 Washington Stadium, Washington DC
16 Philadelphia Stadium, Philadelphia
17 Maple Leaf Gardens, Toronto
18 Suffolk Downs Racecourse, Boston
19 Memphis Coliseum, Memphis
21 Crosley Field, Cincinnati
21 Busch Stadium, St Louis
23 Shea Stadium, New York
25 Seattle Coliseum, Seattle
28 Dodger Stadium, Los Angeles
29 Candlestick Park, San Francisco

13. PSYCHEDELIA – SGT. PEPPER, MAGICAL MYSTERY TOUR & PEPPERLAND

FINAL PSYCHEDELIA AREA

Following the chaotic years of 1964-67, we transported people to a much more light-hearted and laid-back time of love, peace and psychedelia. This was the largest space in the exhibition, and it was dedicated to Sgt. Pepper, the Magical Mystery Tour, Pepperland and the Yellow Submarine. Gone were the black and white images of The Beatles' first five years, as this cacophony of sound and colour invaded the senses.

It was like stepping into a magical grotto made up of three very distinct and iconic Beatle creations – the side of the Magical Mystery Tour bus, a life-size tableau of the Sgt. Pepper album cover, and a wall dedicated to the Blue Meanies and Pepperland which led to a walk-through Yellow Submarine.

In 1967, fashions were changing and there was an explosion of colour as flower power and psychedelia took over. Mary Quant and Carnaby Street were famous, the Austin Motor Company launched the Mini Cooper and a young model called Twiggy showed off her own version of the 'mini' too – the mini-skirt. The Beatles had stopped touring in 1966, their hair got longer, they grew

SERGEANT PEPPER

A full colour, three-dimensional collage stage set recreating the detail of the album cover using full size wax models and cut-outs, complete with palm trees and flower beds. Music from the album will be played and animation will be used to move various pieces of the set. Spaces within the set present photographic opportunities for personalised momentos of the exhibition.

The original artist and photographer who created the album cover have been contacted in connection with their co-operation in the construction of the set.

Graphics and photographs will explain the concept of the Sergeant Pepper

THE MAGICAL MYSTERY TOUR

The Visitor enters the Mystery Tour drum to the accompanyment of a barage of disorientating sounds and images. The inside of the drum is lined with alternating, distorting mirrors and graphic panels, the roof revolves, the lighting rotates and we are transported into the unreal world of dreams and hallucinations.

PSYCHEDELIA RATIONALE FROM MIKE'S PRESENTATION TO INVESTORS

moustaches and they tried LSD, which contributed to the new, experimental sounds of Revolver and Sgt. Pepper.

Again, thinking of our younger guests, we knew we could have some fun here. We incorporated various distorted fun-house style mirrors into this area, and the Magical Mystery Tour Bus featured a handle that could be turned

MAGICAL MYSTERY TOUR BUS WITH OUR GRANDSON BILLY, TURNING THE HANDLE

1967

LONELY HEARTS CLUB BAND

Sgt. Pepper is the album which portrayed for many what 1967 and psychedelia was all about. Completely different from anything they had done earlier it showed the Beatles in their finest creative form. Released on 1st of June, it immediately entered the album charts at no. 1 and stayed there for 22 weeks. It also entered the top 30 singles chart and reached no. 21. It was in the album charts for 45 weeks and re-entered for a week in 1974. It had sold ½ million one month after release.

Sgt. Pepper was recorded at E.M.I. Abbey Road studios between 6th December, 1966 and 2nd April, 1967. It took 700 studio hours to record and cost £25,000.

Until 1971 Sgt. Pepper was the biggest selling British album of all time, a record later to be equalled by another Beatles' album, Abbey Road. By 1981 sales of these two albums had exceeded 10 million.

Sgt. Pepper was originally planned as a record of the Beatles' early lives but with the premature release of Penny Lane/ Strawberry Fields the theme discontinued and they began writing about current events of the time. The idea for the military band came from the style of clothes fashionable with their generation. The Group then felt it would be a novel idea to create their own mock band to present a non-stop show.

The Beatles had a great deal of fun producing this album. It was however to present their producer George Martin with one of the biggest challenges in his recording career. They wanted to include Victorian steam organs, farmyard noises and at one point a 41 piece orchestra, with no score to play! At the end of the record there was to be a note that was at a pitch only dogs could hear.

George's task was to turn these sounds into an album on a simple four track recording machine, but with his talent to interpret the Beatles' ideas, the innovative album was created.

SGT. PEPPER BOARD MOCK-UP

to reveal characters in the bus window such as the Walrus and The Blue Meanies.

Oil projector lamps created psychedelic patterns on the walls and ceilings. The projector bulbs used to blow on a weekly basis, and I'd climb on the back of John the security man to replace them! We added the scent of incense, which hung in the air as it would have in the late 60s.

The Sgt. Pepper cover was so important and iconic that we decided to make it life-size. The two-dimensional tableau dominated a whole wall, featuring life-size cut-outs of all the characters. The title song played every few minutes in the background, and the lights reacted with the music, getting brighter as the song progressed. We would have liked animatronics of The Beatles but at £100,000 a figure that was out of the question.

SGT. PEPPER LIFESIZE SET

Opposite this, an eight-foot-high mural of Pepperland was a riot of colour and images from the Yellow Submarine film, including Sgt. Pepper himself, The Blue Meanies, Apple Bonkers and The Fool on the Hill. We enlisted the help of talented local muralist and cartoonist George Nicholas, another friend of ours, who was perfect for the job as he was known for fantastic murals which brightened up the corridors of Alder Hey Children's Hospital. Ali, our daughter, was drafted in to help get it done on time. Oil lamps cast swirling, colourful patterns, adding a layer of atmosphere.

To highlight the launch and success of Yellow Submarine in multiple countries and languages, there were two posters from the Yellow Submarine cinema showing in Italy and Mexico.

Building and decorating this area was so much fun and we loved the end result, which we knew would give a

PEPPERLAND – A WORK IN PROGRESS

YELLOW SUBMARINE POSTERS IN PEPPERLAND

lot of pleasure to guests of all ages. When families entered, you would see children's eyes light up as they had the space to run about and see lots of eclectic characters from The Beatles' back catalogue. Seeing them full-size, when they had previously only seen them in books or on album covers, brought a lot of happiness and this seamlessly led to the next iconic Beatle symbol – The Yellow Submarine.

14. THE YELLOW SUBMARINE

Despite The Beatles' initial reservations about the Yellow Submarine film, it went on to be a worldwide success and became a much-loved Beatles production appealing to fans of all ages.

The whole score was written by George Martin, but The Beatles themselves were reluctant to be involved because it was made by the same people who had made an animated TV show that they didn't like. However, by agreeing to film a short scene at the end, it fulfilled a contractual commitment they had with United Artist pictures. This is why their characters were voiced by actors throughout the film. However, when they saw the end result, they were pleased, and were disappointed that they hadn't had more personal involvement. They attended the premiere, and the film was a smash hit all over the world.

Its bold and bright imagery is recognised the world over and we knew it would hold great appeal for visitors of all ages. The associated merchandise was a huge business producing many toys, books and artwork, which was aimed mostly at children.

1966

The Yellow Submarine

The song was first released as a double A-sided single record with Eleanor Rigby on 5th August, 1966, the same day as the album Revolver, on which it was also featured. It reached the top of the charts on 17th August and stayed there for 4 weeks.

It was written by Paul and John especially for Ringo. Some of the sound effects include John blowing bubbles through a straw, George swirling water in a bucket and a brass band. Paul and John can be heard talking as the submarine crew.

The song later appeared on many compilation albums after being released in January, 1969 as the soundtrack album to the film of the same name.

THE ALBUM - was released in January, 1969 and had sold 800,000 around the world within 3 months and over 1 million before the end of the year.

This was the first British Beatles album to contain non-Beatle material. On the B-side was the original music score of the film which was composed and orchestrated by George Martin.

THE FILM - was thought to be the first film based on a song. It was a full length cartoon telling the story of the Beatles' journey in a yellow submarine and their adventures on the way. The Beatles were all portrayed as cartoon characters who travelled to Pepperland, encountering Blue Meanies and other anti-music monsters. The Beatles themselves had nothing to do with the film, their voices were supplied by actors and although they were not very keen to be involved, they did agree to make a guest appearance at the end of the film. They also attended the premiere in London.

Yellow Submarine was produced by Al Brodax, head of the T.V. and Motion Pictures Division of King Features Syndicate.

It was written by Lee Minoff and Al Brodax, from an original Lee Minoff story.

The Yellow Submarine became popular all over the world. A great deal of memorabilia connected with the film was produced, one of the most popular items being a small cast copy of the submarine made by Corgi toys and enjoyed by children all over the world.

Trunks of treasure, a mock seabed, seashells, starfish, seaweed and wave patterns from hidden oil lamps helped create the underwater jungle of the Octopus's Garden, which led to a metal gangway to our very own Yellow Submarine. The Yellow Submarine was a moulded steel structure, which utilised the full 12-foot height of the basement ceiling. It was brought in section by section and assembled on site.

Children absolutely loved it as they could climb onto a raised platform to look out of the portholes where we had positioned fish tanks with real fish to give the impression of being underwater.

There were dials and instruments to play with, and a giant periscope revealed a cyclorama of Blue Meanies on the horizon. There were sound effects of water and instruments clanking, and as fish swam past the portholes, 'Yellow Submarine' played in the background. It was lovely to hear kids and adults alike singing along.

ARTIST'S IMPRESSION FOR MIKE'S BUSINESS PLAN

Mike: I remember walking through the exhibition one day and I got chatting to an American tourist who was with his 8-year-old son. The child knew a lot about The Beatles so I asked how he knew so much. His dad explained that it all started when he was a baby, and he was introduced to the Yellow Submarine film to keep him amused. He was immediately hooked and went on to learn the music and script from start to finish! As he got older, he started asking if he could see The Beatles. Sadly, he couldn't, but his parents brought him on a pilgrimage to Liverpool. It was lovely to see the joy on the boy's face as he could experience some of the fun and magic of the film brought to life, and millions of children the world over have been introduced to The Beatles in this way.

We displayed some of the merchandise that came from the film including an original Corgi metal toy Yellow Submarine as well as a jigsaw and playing cards.

YELLOW SUBMARINE – EARLY STAGES OF BUILDING

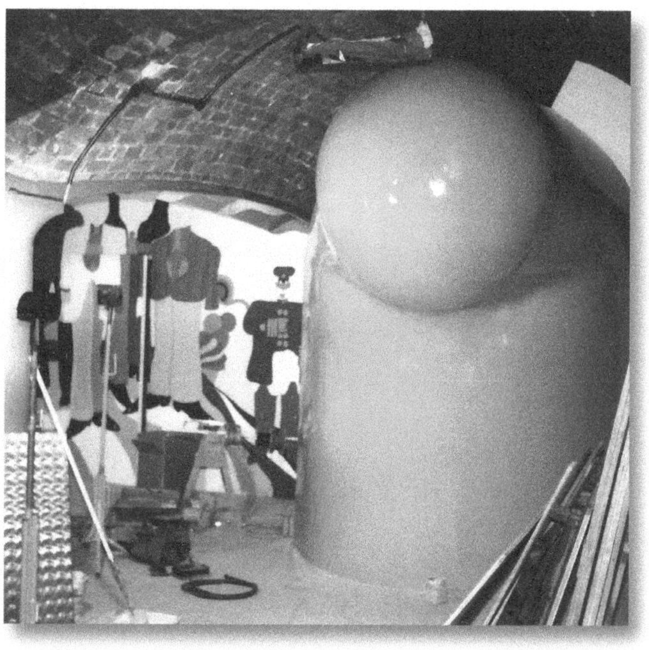

YELLOW SUBMARINE APRIL 1990 – MID BUILD

YELLOW SUBMARINE INTERIOR WITH PERISCOPE

15. LET IT BE

There was a deliberate and tangible change of atmosphere as the excitement and fun of psychedelia was left behind and the mood became much more sombre. This room captured the difficulties and disillusionment as the group drifted apart. The recording of 'Let It Be' and the film that accompanied it was difficult to say the least, as shown so graphically in Peter Jackson's Get Back documentary which was released in December 2021.

The Beatles had progressed from a comfortable and familiar musical and creative bubble, with a manager guiding them, to having to manage themselves. Individually they wanted to do their own thing. George felt his songs weren't being given the respect and attention they deserved, and tensions soon began to show.

Bernie: By now, space was at a premium and we still had to depict everything that happened between Yellow Submarine's film release in 1969 and the group's break up in 1970. Despite internal differences of opinion, they were still prolific during this period and produced some of their best work in the form of The Beatles (White Album) and Abbey Road. As well as their musical output, they had launched their own company, Apple Corps (pronounced Apple Core!). This comprised multiple departments including electronics, publishing, film and retail, and most notably their Apple Boutique which opened on Baker Street in London.

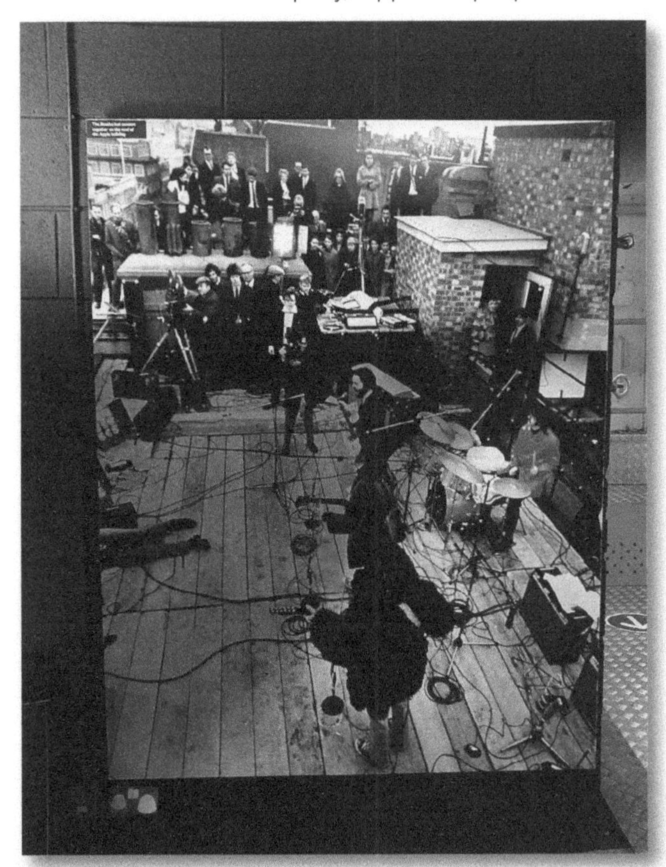

THE FAMOUS ROOFTOP PERFORMANCE ON SAVILE ROW

We featured a floor to ceiling replica of the outside wall of the building, originally designed by 'The Fool' – three Dutch designers, and again this was created by our muralist George Nicholas. On the right-hand side, there was a large picture of the famous roof-top concert that was to be their last ever public performance together.

We added an interactive game called 'Beatle Brain' - a computer game we had designed by a friend's son, to test the knowledge of our younger guests while their parents were reading about the impending break-up.

BEATLE BRAIN GAME

VISITORS WOULD WALK THROUGH A LARGE APPLE INTO THE BREAK UP PERIOD

At all stages of designing the exhibition, budget and space limitations were a daily factor, and by this point in the story, we were starting to run out of both. We had prioritised the years that The Beatles were together and had a lot of creative fun, designing some wonderful sets to bring it to life.

16. THE BREAKUP

Our vision for The Beatles Story was to give people a concise and in-depth history of John, Paul, George and Ringo's epic and unique journey. The story wouldn't be complete without including the break-up, which was a gradual demise that happened over a period of time.

Abbey Road was released in September 1969. It brought George Martin and The Beatles together for one last time and was reminiscent of how they used to work together as a group, with George Martin producing. Fittingly, the last track on the album was called 'The End'.

John 'left' the group before the album was released, but no public announcement was made until Paul announced the official break-up in April the following year, much to the shock and dismay of millions of fans around the world.

We had the idea of a circular room with a huge revolving 45 single of 'Hey Jude' on the ceiling. The designers had to find a motor that could make such a large wooden object turn, and the only one that they could find was a cement mixer motor. This was very difficult to install because of its weight and it soon transpired that we couldn't use it owing to the loud grinding noise it made as it rotated.

THE SOLO YEARS 'DRUM' FEATURE

In between separate images of each Beatle were full length mirrors and news footage was shown on a TV reporting the failure of the Apple Boutique and the news of Paul quitting the group.

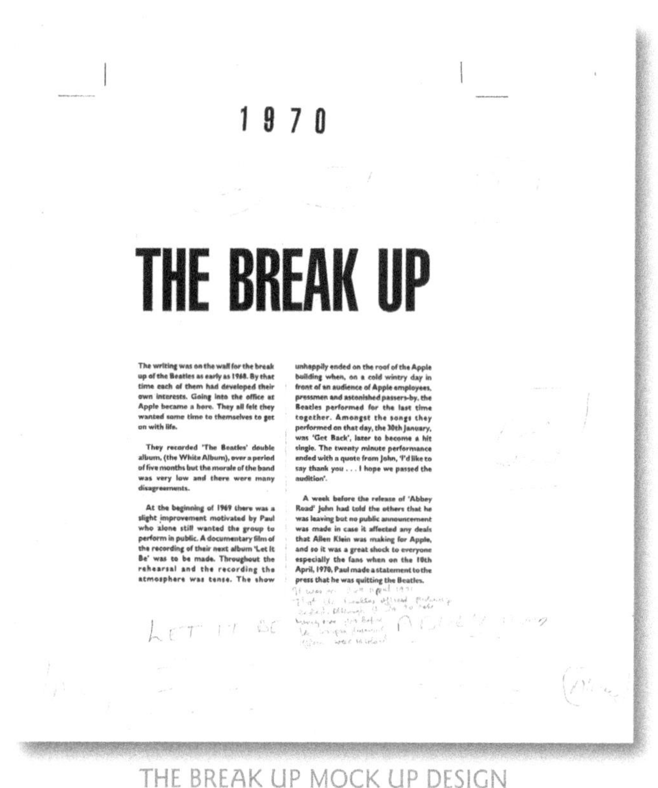

1970

THE BREAK UP

The writing was on the wall for the break up of the Beatles as early as 1968. By that time each of them had developed their own interests. Going into the office at Apple became a bore. They all felt they wanted some time to themselves to get on with life.

They recorded 'The Beatles' double album, (the White Album), over a period of five months but the morale of the band was very low and there were many disagreements.

At the beginning of 1969 there was a slight improvement motivated by Paul who alone still wanted the group to perform in public. A documentary film of the recording of their next album 'Let It Be' was to be made. Throughout the rehearsal and the recording the atmosphere was tense. The show unhappily ended on the roof of the Apple building when, on a cold wintry day in front of an audience of Apple employees, pressmen and astonished passers-by, the Beatles performed for the last time together. Amongst the songs they performed on that day, the 30th January, was 'Get Back', later to become a hit single. The twenty minute performance ended with a quote from John, 'I'd like to say thank you . . . I hope we passed the audition'.

A week before the release of 'Abbey Road' John had told the others that he was leaving but no public announcement was made in case it affected any deals that Allen Klein was making for Apple, and so it was a great shock to everyone especially the fans when on the 10th April, 1970, Paul made a statement to the press that he was quitting the Beatles.

THE BREAK UP MOCK UP DESIGN

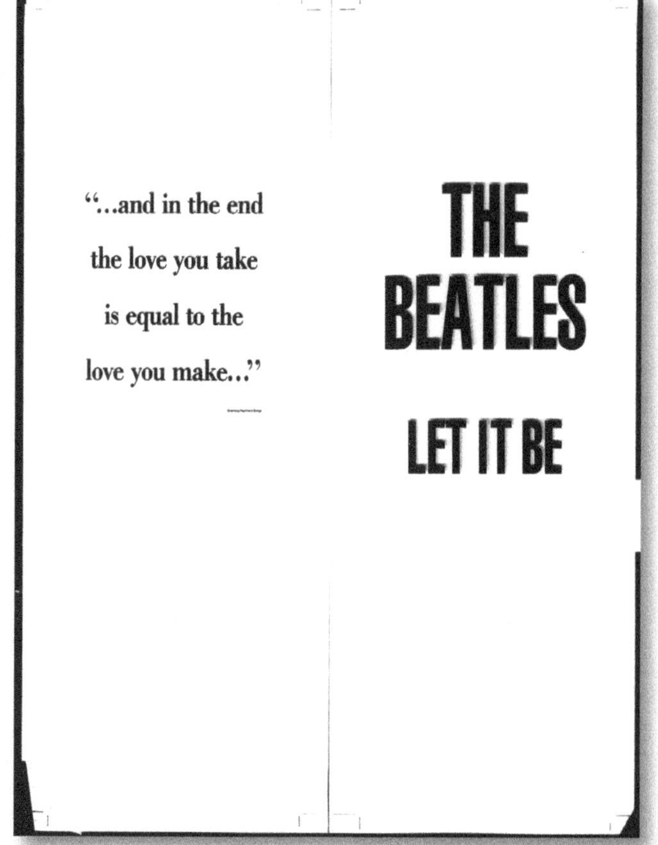

ACETATE FOR 'AND IN THE END/ LET IT BE' BOARD

17. THE SOLO YEARS

SOLO YEARS BOARDS DETAILING THEIR INDIVIDUAL ENDEAVOURS

Bernie: After the break-up, John, Paul, George and Ringo went their separate ways and worked on many interesting projects, which could have filled a whole new exhibition, but it was 'The Beatles Story' that we wanted to tell, and The Beatles' individual endeavours were not our priority.

However, John had died ten years earlier, and we wanted to briefly acknowledge what the three remaining Beatles were doing at that point in time. Naturally, this section would always need updating, but we did what we could with the limited time and space available. We summarised each of their solo career achievements on boards alongside a gallery of solo album covers.

SOLO ALBUMS GRID

18. THE WHITE ROOM

We wanted to commemorate John Lennon's death with respect and feeling. The year we opened was the 10th anniversary of his death and it was still relatively fresh in people's minds. The horror of the unnecessary murder of a pop star was still felt by fans and non-fans alike.

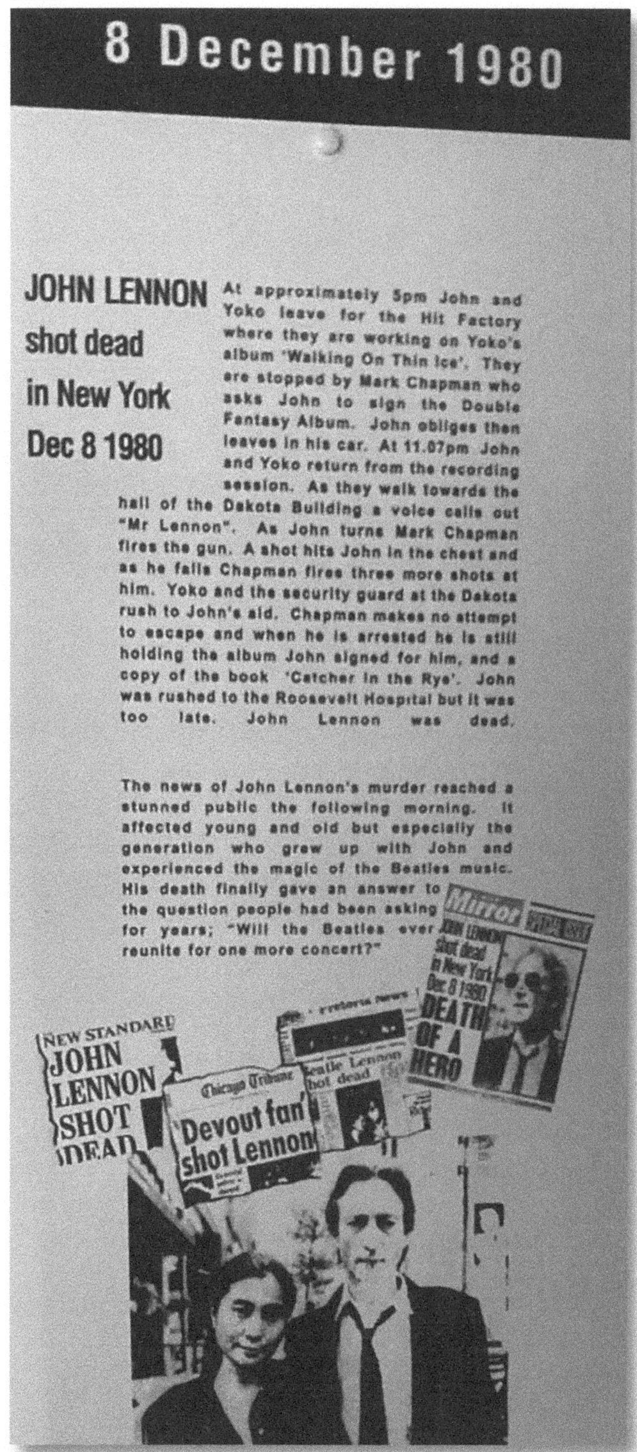

NEWS OF JOHN'S MURDER

We took inspiration from the 'Imagine' video and created a white, soundproofed space that felt totally isolated from everything else going on in the exhibition. This represented John and Yoko's white room at their home, Tittenhurst Park in Berkshire. We wanted to convey the feeling that John and Yoko had just left the room. There was a white grand piano in the centre, which was kindly loaned to us by our brother-in-law, Norman, and sprayed white by a friend in the motor trade. Floor to ceiling windows behind the piano evoked their garden view through white wooden shutters and a replica of John's Rickenbacker guitar stood in the corner.

THE WHITE ROOM'S BAY WINDOW MID-BUILD

As visitors entered the White Room, they became immersed in the tranquil calm of a very still, dimly lit, soundproofed room. The opening piano chords of 'Imagine' would start to play, and as John started singing the first verse, a single spotlight would illuminate a picture of John.

In the picture, he is seen sitting at the piano on which he composed 'Imagine'. This was a very special loan item, which Julia Baird, his half-sister, had kindly lent to us, amongst other items of personal memorabilia.

Again, Charles Rosenay remembers the strong, dramatic effect that the White Room had on the groups of American tourists that he used to take through: *"My groups would walk through, and they would be smiling and loving, and they would be on a different level, and then you would enter the White Room, catch your breath for a second and the room had just a different, wow factor. It changed and they were moved to a different level of emotion."*

Charles would eventually loan us a very unique and controversial item. He understood that our exhibition wasn't about memorabilia, but he felt this piece would be of interest and could have a special place in the White Room. He was right and we accepted his offer without hesitation.

The item on offer was John Lennon's immigration papers! He had fought for many years to get US citizenship, and it was this document, which had John's signature and fingerprints on the same page, that would allow this to happen. Charles was very excited and proud to own this unique item which meant so much to John.

THE WHITE ROOM WITH A FRAMED PICTURE OF JOHN COMPOSING 'IMAGINE'

He acquired it while he was publisher/editor of a fan club magazine called Good Day Sunshine. Along with putting out the publication, Charles was producing Beatles conventions and was closely associated with The Beatles on many levels in the US. When fans or collectors wanted to sell their records or paraphernalia, they would contact Charles and usually he would forward their enquiries to one of the national Beatle dealers who he knew. However, one day, a gentleman who had worked for the US government called about selling a document he had 'rescued'.

He told Charles that after a certain period of time, they were required to destroy obsolete legal documents, but it hurt him to see the John Lennon immigration sheet be burned with the other expired papers. So he tore it out of a legal book and wanted to share it with a Beatles fan club for the sum of eight thousand dollars. Charles didn't call any of his friends or collectors to buy it or even ask their opinion – he decided to find the funds to buy it for himself and took ownership of this historic document.

Charles was very familiar with The Beatles Story, having witnessed it being built from the ground up, and he said he had fallen in love with it! He felt that a one-of-a-kind document such as John's immigration papers should have a home in what he described as "that beautiful white room" – the room that had moved him and his groups so much when they visited. Mike happily agreed that this was the perfect place to exhibit the piece and it was soon in a frame for tourists to see and appreciate. Charles believed that this was a better home for it than anywhere else and said he felt very honoured too when he saw the plaque indicating that the piece was on loan from 'Charles F. Rosenay of Good Day Sunshine!'

Mike: It was on display for a while, but I realised that it was too valuable to keep the original on display, so we decided to replace it with an exact replica and keep the original in a bank vault until Charles could return to Liverpool to collect it. It was kismet, because the document was stolen not long after! We had CCTV but not on the White Room at that time, and we felt very lucky that the thieves only made off with a copy. The theft made the news, but we never did find out who stole the document.

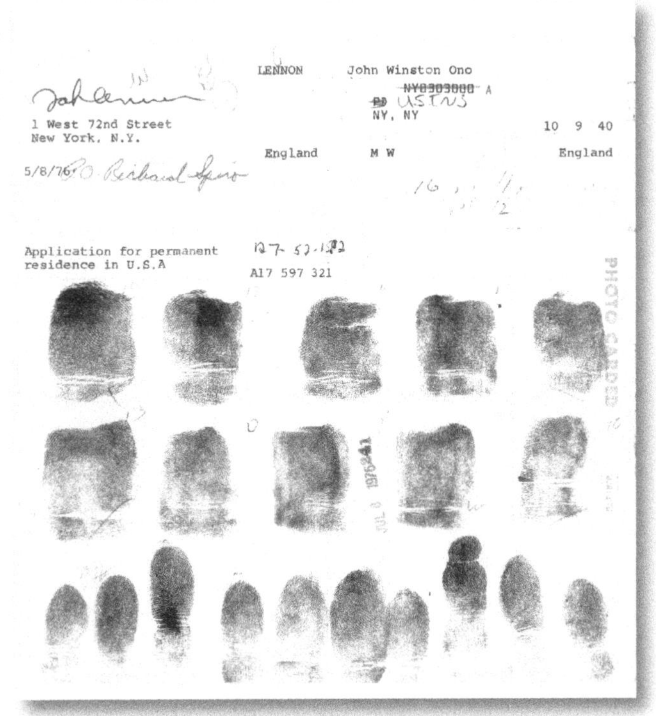

LENNON John Winston Ono
NY0303000 A
USINS
NY, NY
1 West 72nd Street
New York, N.Y.
10 9 40
England M W England
5/8/76
Application for permanent residence in U.S.A
A17 597 321
PHOTO CARDED

JOHN LENNON'S IMMIGRATION PAPERS

Mike: I always felt goosebumps when I passed through the White Room, and one night after hours, when the sound system was turned off, I heard children's voices and had no idea where they were coming from. The exhibition was closed, as was the Albert Dock outside. It was very spooky at the time!

The White Room feature was the perfect finale to the exhibition. It was an incredibly moving space which evoked strong emotions and left many visitors with tears in their eyes. This encapsulated our goal to give people more than just a museum of memorabilia – we wanted them to feel the same way about The Beatles, and their impact on the world, as we did. In our visitor book, many said this was their favourite part of the exhibition.

Lennon's prints have been lifted

JOHN Lennon's fingerprints have been taken — and police suspect they could be on their way to Japan.

By Will Rolston

The "marks", a framed exhibit at the Beatles Story, were stolen in a daylight robbery.

Security workers at the £3.50-a-time tour spotted the fingerprints were missing after the weekend.

The FBI paper, estimated value £50,000, was produced in 1971 over the murdered Beatle's suspected cannabis problem.

Gunman

Today acting Detective Superintendent Frank Thompson said: "We know that a number of Japanese coach parties toured the Beatles story at the weekend.

"They tend to be very fanatical, and we believe that one of them may have been carried away and taken the piece of paper from an exhibit."

The prints are understood to have been loaned to the popular Albert Dock centre by the American fan magazine Good Day Sunshine.

They were the main exhibit in a room dedicated to John Lennon who was shot dead by gunman Mark Chapman outside his New York apartment in 1980.

AND IN THE END...

Mike and Bernie's original mission was the tell The Beatles' story with feeling and emotion, focusing on the most significant moments from their lives, and they knew they didn't need millions of pounds' worth of memorabilia to do so.

They just needed their own memories, imagination and creativity, as well as valuable and authentic input from friends and supporters who were there.

EPILOGUE

Mike and Bernie continued to be involved in the Beatles Story as consultants, and were shareholders until it was sold in 2008 to Merseytravel.

They remained heavily involved in Merseyside Tourism for three decades and continue to promote Liverpool to this day.

They are proud of the legacy they have left to the City and Beatles fans Worldwide.

Long may The Beatles Story's success continue!

(P.S. Thanks to John, Paul, George, Ringo and Pete)

SPECIAL THANKS

'The Birth of the Beatles Story' started out as an illustrated book about how we built the exhibition. It soon became much bigger than this, thanks to the vision of **Tim Quinn**.
Tim interviewed us in 2018 when we were thinking about writing a book.
He recognised that there was a bigger story to be told and it is down to him that the book is in three parts and includes the backstory of our early lives.
Some of the original transcript is in this book and we are so grateful to him. Tim is a freelance broadcaster, TV presenter, cartoonist, show promoter and Head of Special Projects for Marvel Comics. A hugely talented and creative person who we are lucky to know!

We also want to thank our amazing daughter **Ali**, who, at the beginning of writing our story, unwittingly became the co-writer and editor. If she hadn't given us her time and expertise the book would not have become a reality, and certainly would not have been finished. She has now definitely earned the title of 'The 'Great' Great' - a nickname that was once held by Bernie's Mum.

THANK YOU.

ACKNOWLEDGEMENTS

We wanted to take this opportunity to not only thank the people who have helped us with this book, but also pay tribute to the people who supported us in our endeavour 'All Those Years Ago'!

First and foremost my good friend **Phil Birtwistle** who, in the early days, was the only person to invest and have faith in Bernie and I. Phil was an entrepreneur who launched **Merseymart** – the first free newspaper in Liverpool. Thanks also to Margaret, his wife for her support.

Don & Lin Andrew, friends from the days of Merseybeat who gave advice, memories and original posters for display. Don was the bass player with the Remo 4. He and members of the Fourmost, Joey Bower and Dave Lovelady designed and painted our 'Cavern' backdrop.

Bill Harry who, together with his wife Virginia, created the 'Mersey Beat' newspaper which became a must for every group member and their fans. He advised us on the original set design for Mersey Beat, and has been kind enough to let us reproduce various Mersey Beat articles in this book.

Bob Wooler the velvet voiced Cavern DJ and friend of the Beatles who became a great inspiration to many a young group member. It was Bob who gave the young Mike Byrne one of the best bookings of his life and assisted Mike & Bernie when they were building the Beatles Story.

Allan Williams the Beatles' first manager who together with his wife **Beryl**, and brother-in-law **Barry**, travelled by van to Hamburg on the Beatles first trip. Allan was kind enough to supply us with copies of the Beatles Kaiserkeller contracts as well as some great stories!

Pete Best – the 'backbeat' of the early Beatles. Thank you for the loan of the Casbah pictures and support over the years.

We acknowledge the friendship, time and generosity of **Margaret Roberts** who loaned us important early pictures of the Beatles and Bernie at the Cavern, from the Peter Kaye Collection. It is a Peter Kaye picture which adorns the cover of our book.

Billy Kinsley - the bass player with **The Merseybeats** who designed and built the replica speakers for the Beatles Story 'Cavern' and 'Abbey Road' features.

We are also grateful to **Mike McCartney** and **Julia Baird** for loaning us early photographs of John, Paul and George from their personal collections. Mike has also kindly allowed us to reproduce another of his pictures in this book.

Ron Jones and **Pam Wilsher** from Merseyside Tourism Board who persevered in creating the early Beatles tourism vision and developed Beatles Weekends.

We are indebted to **Steven Quicke** the architect who went above and beyond in his efforts to help us create and fulfil our dreams. He was with us at each step of the way and smoothed out many logistical problems. His efforts were complemented by **Mike Loines** and **John Furnival** the graphic designers.

Phillip and **Paul** from Lightworks for their ingenuity and skill in re-creating the 60's look throughout multiple features of the exhibition.

Special thanks to Liverpool Echo librarian **Colin Hunt** who helped us source many photographs from the early days of Liverpool and has been an invaluable advisor for this book. Also, Echo chief photographer, **Stephen Shakeshaft** who facilitated so many photo opportunities. We commissioned many pictures from our friend **Geoff Roberts**, a freelance photographer, who worked for everyone in the newspaper business. Sadly no longer with us.

Our **Hamburg** feature would not have been complete without the insight and cooperation of **Astrid Kirchherr** and **Ulf Krueger** from K&K.

Brian Johnson - drummer with The Strangers and Rory Storm, shared a unique collection of Star Club photographs with us, for use in our Hamburg set.

The Hessy's music shop feature was enthusiastically created by **Colin Benn**, with the support of **Peter Hepworth** and **Bernard Michaelson**. Bernard owned Hessy's and agreed to loan us the instruments in the window for free.

We are grateful for the loan of personal memorabilia from ardent Beatle fans and collectors, **Cherrille and John Silvester**.

Cavern Mecca - Sadly **Liz** and **Jim Hughes** have passed away but their memory lives on. Thanks to family members **Trisch Jones** and **Paul Sudbury** for photos and stories.

Charles Rosenay loaned us John Lennon's Immigration Card and shared the back-story in this book. He gave us his time and unending enthusiasm once again with memories of 80s Liverpool tourism.

Mark Naboshek - An American Beatles collector. He has been immensely helpful with the book in providing pictures and recalling his old memories of our time in Dallas.

Joan Griffiths - Bernie's childhood friend who was with her when they first discovered The Beatles. Her memories have helped to fill in some of the blanks from the early days.

Multi-talented muralist **George Nicholas**' artistic vision brought colour and vibrancy to our Psychedelia, Yellow Submarine and Apple features (with some assistance from Ali Byrne!)

Margaret Byrne (no relation), and **Johnny 'Guitar' Byrne** from Rory Storm & the Hurricanes filled in some of the gaps of our Merseybeat memories and contributed images to the book.

Charles and Sandy Roberts for loaning us copies of the first pictures of the Quarrymen which featured a young John Lennon. Charles booked them for the Roseberry Street concert in July 1957.

Many thanks to **Maureen and Norman Baker,** our sister and brother-in-law for the loan and gift of many items including the grand piano for the White Room, and also their support over the years.

Chip Hawkes from 60s group 'The Tremeloes' (and Chesney Hawkes dad) – kindly loaned us the Mellotron MK11 that was used on the Sgt. Pepper album.

Rod McDonald, **Mike Kontzle** and **Terry McCusker** - old bandmates who trawled their collections to find early photographs which were featured in the exhibition and the book. They also delved into their memory banks to recall some of our adventures while we were in groups together.

Clive Garner from the Wirral, provided us with early film footage from his impressive film archive.

Steve Phillips - a good friend and early supporter to Bernie and Mike.

Arthur Johnson facilitated bringing the 24 foot long 'Magic Eye' from John Lennon's swimming pool to The Beatles Story (it was too big to fit in the exhibition, but we displayed it in a shop unit!) He was a reliable advisor and willing promoter of the exhibition.

Neil Aspinall and **Derek Taylor** from Apple for eventually coming around to the idea that Liverpool should have this exhibition.

Dave Jones and **Bill Heckle** from **Cavern City Tours** for their support in the early days.

Martin King – former Director at The Beatles Story who continued our dream in later years and became a friend and supporter. **Mary Chadwick** and **Diane Glover** at The Beatles Story – thank you for your support with this book and for keeping our Beatles Story vision alive!

Matt Everitt – for your valuable advice, enthusiasm and ongoing support.

Teddie Dahlin – for taking our book and believing in it.

Lee Waymont – for finding and restoring your dad, Geoff's, beautiful Mathew Street pictures.

Roger Hull at the Liverpool Record Office.

Mike Jones for the information on Percy Phillip's studio and Mike's early groups.

Tony Hall - Liverpool Echo

Thanks to **Mike Brocken** for his help in attempting an earlier version of our story.

–

Thanks also to **Pete Cunliffe, Sarah Healey, Peter Wix, Hannah Baker, Austin Wilde.**

TO OUR FAMILY

Matthew Byrne – Your heartfelt contribution to this book, and your eagle-eyed copy-checking has been invaluable. Your support and love, and not forgetting your help in the early days (including late-night call outs to electrical emergencies at the exhibition!) always has been, and always will be, hugely appreciated.

Roddy – Thank you for the endless support, copy-checking, scanning, sense-checking and for loaning us your wife on and off for the past two years while she worked on this book.

Billy – The best grandson in the world. One day you will thank us for the Beatle brainwashing!

Our Mums and Dads – No longer with us, but always supportive and instrumental in allowing us to pursue our dreams.

Chris Byrne – my younger brother, sadly no longer with us, but always supportive of my sometimes seemingly mad-cap ideas!

In the 30 years that have passed, our memories have faded a little. Many others gave us time, help and advice, too many to mention – so we may have inadvertently left some names out.

So to everyone who contributed to bringing The Beatles Story to life... WE THANK YOU.

It Couldn't Be Done

By Edgar Albert Guest

Somebody said that it couldn't be done
But he with a chuckle replied
That "maybe it couldn't," but he would be one
Who wouldn't say so till he'd tried.
So he buckled right in with the trace of a grin
On his face. If he worried he hid it.
He started to sing as he tackled the thing
That couldn't be done, and he did it!

Somebody scoffed: "Oh, you'll never do that;
At least no one ever has done it;"
But he took off his coat and he took off his hat
And the first thing we knew he'd begun it.
With a lift of his chin and a bit of a grin,
Without any doubting or quiddit,
He started to sing as he tackled the thing
That couldn't be done, and he did it.

There are thousands to tell you it cannot be done,
There are thousands to prophesy failure,
There are thousands to point out to you one by one,
The dangers that wait to assail you.
But just buckle in with a bit of a grin,
Just take off your coat and go to it;
Just start in to sing as you tackle the thing
That "cannot be done," and you'll do it.

Lightning Source UK Ltd.
Milton Keynes UK
UKHW050342130422
401462UK00002B/70

9 781912 587667